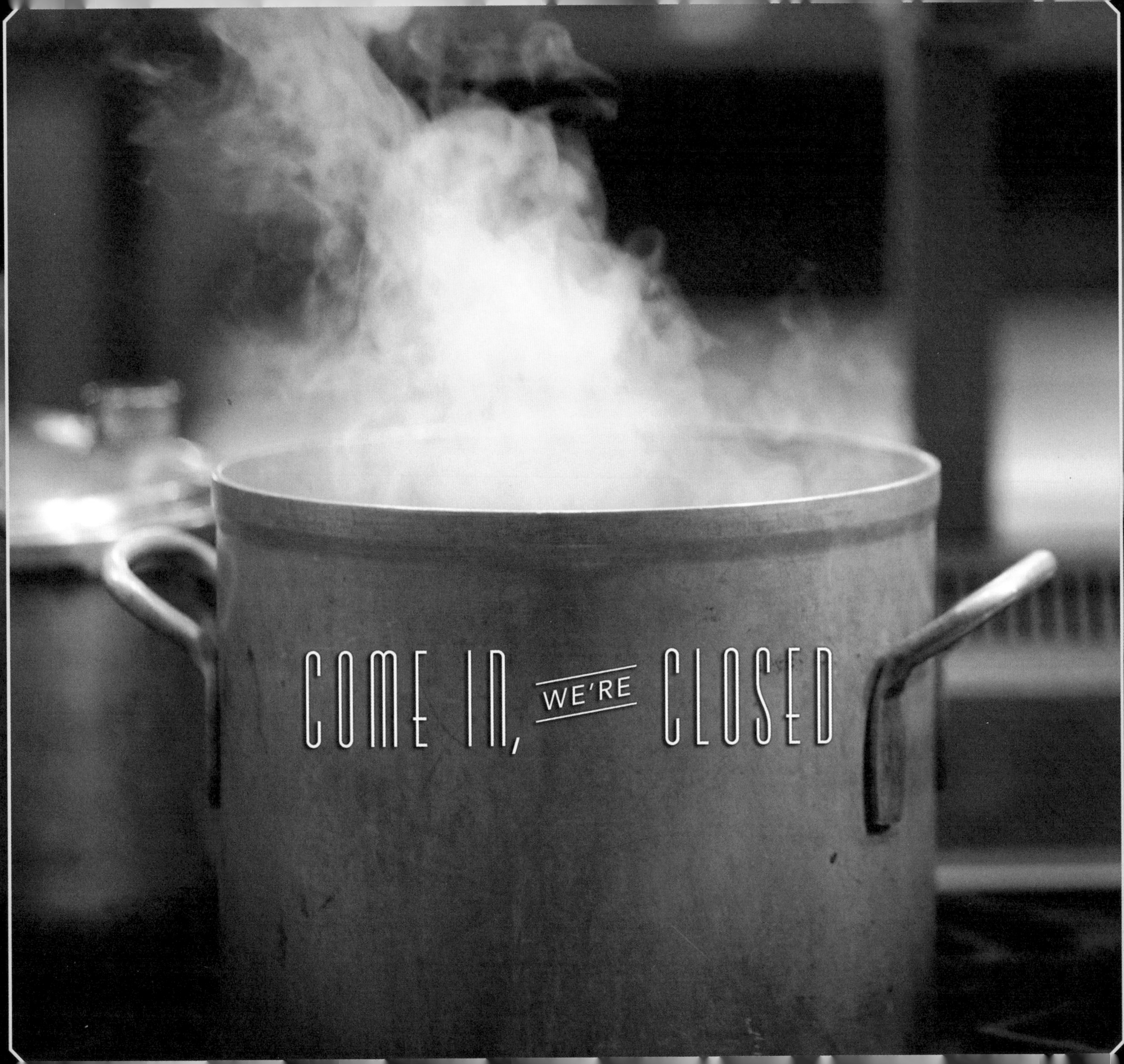
COME IN, WE'RE CLOSED

COME IN, WE'RE CLOSED

AN INVITATION TO STAFF MEALS AT THE WORLD'S BEST RESTAURANTS

By Christine Carroll and Jody Eddy

RUNNING PRESS
PHILADELPHIA · LONDON

• I'VE SPENT MOST OF MY TIME IN KITCHENS LOOKING DOWN. THAT IS NOT THE WAY TO LEARN. LOOK UP AND FIND KNOWLEDGE. STRENGTH. AND INSPIRATION IN THE PEOPLE WORKING AROUND YOU. EVERYONE HAS A STORY TO TELL AND SOMETHING TO TEACH.

ISBN 978-0-7624-4262-1
Library of Congress Control Number: 2011938582

E-book ISBN 978-0-7624-4707-7

9   8   7   6   5   4   3   2   1

Digit on the right indicates the number of this printing

Design by Joshua McDonnell

Edited by Kristen Green Wiewora

Typography: Avenir, Berkely, Lora,
and Valencia

Special thanks to Audrey Claire
Taichman and the staff at Cook

Running Press Book Publishers
2300 Chestnut Street
Philadelphia, PA 19103-4371

Visit us on the web!
www.runningpresscooks.com

PHOTO CREDITS:

Joshua McDonnell, Front Cover

Timothy Aguero, pages 162–171

Neil John Berger, back cover (top), pages 64–77

Kyle Delahunt, pages 230–241

Peter Frank Edwards, back cover (bottom), pages 10,
    13, 172–183, 274–287

Jenn Farrington, pages 254–263

Owen Franken, pages 184–195, 288–297

Ken Goodman, pages 2–3, 8, 52–63, 100–113

Chris Granger, pages 78–89

Robin Jolin, pages 264–273

Jason Lowe, pages 42–51, 128–135, 208–217, 242–253

Patrica Niven, page 254

Matthew Noel, pages 90, 95 (top), 99 (right)

Marc Piscotty, pages 136–147

Evan Sung, back cover (middle), pages 14–15, 30–41,
    196–207, 298–308

Kristin Teig, pages 1, 148–161, 218–229

Janis Turk, pages 91–92, 94, 95 (bottom), 96, 99 (left)

Eric Wolfinger, pages 16–29

Vigfús Birgisson, pages 114–127

TABLE OF CONTENTS

THIS BOOK IS DEDICATED TO
THE RESTAURANTS THAT FEED
THEIR STAFF LIKE FAMILY.

ACKNOWLEDGMENTS

Our sincerest appreciation extends to all who have joined us on this two-year adventure, helped us navigate its peaks and valleys, and pushed us to reach our destination. We have a beautiful cookbook because of each and every one of you.

A special thanks to our editor Kristen Green Wiewora, and designer, Joshua McDonnell, as well as our agent, Sally Ekus, for believing in our vision. Our heartfelt appreciation to our hardworking interns Elise Reinemann and Hannah Selinger as well as Anne Carroll, a recipe tester without equal. And most importantly, a toast to our families: Evelyn Bragelman, Mary Eddy, Eric Schatzman, Bill and Anne Carroll, and Andrew and Felix Trask. Thank you for keeping the home fires burning and the phone lines open while we were off eating, cooking, and writing. You are as much a part of this book as we are.

Our thanks goes out to the many people who offered their inspiration, talents, time, and resources: Mark Anderson, Jamie Bissonnette, Dante Boccuzzi, Monica Brown, Katie Button, Elizabeth Button, Floyd Cardoz, Elaine Caron, Allie Carroll, Wai Chu, Kyle Connaughton, Katy Corum, Janet Crandall, Kristin Cunningham, Michelle Demuth-Bibb, Katie Donnelly, Rachael Dufresne, Lucinda East, Jeffrey Elliott, Suzanne Fass, Tanui Franken, Pol Perello French, Mhairi Galloway, Kjartan Gíslason, Janice Goldsmith, Joseph Gruber, Einar Gustavsson, Phil Gutensohn, Lien Ho, Erica Johnson, Kristine Keefer, Michael Kress, Steve Legato, Melissa MacLeod, Caitlin Maguire, Anne McBride, Felix Meana, Sofia Piqueras Mir, Melany Mullens, Cristin Napier, Susana Nieto, Marta Mirasolain Oharriz, Ashley Primus, Kelly Puleio, Sean Rembold, Carissa Remitz, Jessica Rodriguez, Daniel Rosene, Peter Rosene, Sheila Rosene, John Ross, Nelly Sabdes, Fernando Salazar, Adam Sanderson, Ted Siegel, Randi Sirkin, Angie Tonnerre, Jasbir Uppal, Carrie Van Dyck, Diana Dogg Viglundsdottir, Erica Wides, and Josh Zoodsma.

Also, to David Waltuck, Thomas Keller, and Férran Adría for not only serving incredible staff meals but being among the first to write about them in books of their own. And finally, to the restaurants who allowed us to hover in their cramped kitchens only to then graciously share their meals with us. Your generosity made this book a reality. Thank you.

FOREWORD

The theme of this book is one that has occupied my mind the most in these last months. Staff meals seem to offer a different view of the professional kitchen. A way to go behind the scenes only to discover that the old adage is true: "To cook well, one must eat well." So when I visit restaurants, I am always wondering what dishes are being made for the kitchen and dining room staff? What menus are planned? For after all, how can people who serve food to others not eat fantastically?

A good family meal is important to me. I believe that to feed the staff of a restaurant is a valiant challenge. You have to carefully organize the daily logistics balancing the preparation time, the price per person, as well as the variety and quality of the food itself—two factors which hold as much importance as the others. In fact, the biggest disagreements that we had over the years at elBulli were about the family meal. So I took it upon myself to look for solutions. When we started to approach the staff meal in a more organized fashion—designing three-course menus in advance and shopping for specific ingredients for each meal—the food got better and better and people started leaving the table much happier. A good daily staff meal eliminated most of our problems . . . and it only cost three euros per person.

At elBulli we had such fun making our staff meals. We served simple things—roasted aubergine coated in miso, mussels with noodles, and Crema Catalana [the Spanish version of crème brûlée]—but always the best in terms of flavor as well as price. I am so passionate about this subject that I have dedicated a book to explain what we ate at elBulli each day. And now, from the hands of Jody and Christine, we are given the opportunity to enjoy staff meals around the globe. It is a passionate view on a subject that is still little known. Often, you'll find what is served to the staff does not necessarily correlate with the cuisine of the establishment. But I insist, where the cooks eat well, you will eat better.

FERRAN ADRIÀ
Director of the elBulli Foundation and
author of *The Family Meal*

INTRODUCTION

ven if you've never worked in a restaurant, you've probably seen a staff meal unfold. Perhaps you lingered over a late Saturday lunch, and noticed the hostess flipping the door's "closed" sign while cooks and servers slowly filled a corner table, their plates piled with braised hunks of meat or a fragrant curry—things you could have sworn weren't on the menu. You were right: they weren't. They are made for the staff only. In about an hour, the crush of their busy dinner service will begin. But right now? Now it's time for a breather: a few minutes off their feet to join the communal table's constellation, its lines connecting colleagues to good food and back again. It's a rare moment to laugh, to hydrate, to relax, and to eat—mightily—before the battle of service begins. It is the calm before the storm.

At its most elemental, a staff meal is the food a restaurant serves to its employees, from chefs to dishwashers, cooks to bussers, waiters, sommeliers, hosts, and managers—anyone whose steps perform the intricate choreography that gets food to your table. A longstanding custom in France as well as in Japan, staff meals are gaining popularity as an insider perk for restaurant workers around the globe. The finest examples are meals made daily by passionate cooks using

great (though often leftover) ingredients shared by everyone, free of charge, around one big table. At their most poetic, these meals highlight the raw beauty of people from all walks of life breaking bread together. In stark contrast, the not-so-great meals are chosen from an uninspired menu of bland, poorly executed, pre-processed options that are eaten in a hurry, or standing, or both. At worst, it is simply not served at all.

During stints in various restaurants over the years, we've sat down to our share of staff meals, some good, some not. We believe that a great staff meal is a perquisite of the highest order and is in fact, vital to a restaurant's success. With that in mind—and inspired by David Waltuck's cookbook *Staff Meals from Chanterelle*—this book began as a sort of edible thesis: to uncover and document the breadth and depth of the best staff-meal traditions in the restaurant industry. We started more than two years ago prodding our contacts in the restaurant business, then prodding our contacts' contacts, beseeching them all to share their best staff-meal stories. People spoke up! We tracked down countless leads across continents. In the final tally, we settled on twenty-five world-class restaurants in six countries across North America and Europe.

But honing our list of participating restaurants was only the start of our education in staff-meal schools of thought. As we spoke with chefs and owners and ate with their staff, we uncovered the common denominators in staff meal practices, but also some unexpected outliers. For starters, the meal can go by many names: such as "staff meal," "staff supper," and "family meal." But we also stumbled across more unusual variations during our travels, such as Morimoto's traditional Japanese term "makani," and The Slanted Door's tongue-in-cheek interpretation, "rice and bones." Although, in places where it was consistently made with care and affection, it is simply called "family."

Why "family"? For one thing, the dishes are usually served family-style, piled high onto mismatched platters or served straight from the beat-up roasting pan it was made in. More often than not, it's set out buffet-style to feed the staff quickly and casually—although several restaurants do take the time to set the table properly. And, just like at home, a family meal strives to be delicious and, for the most part, nutritious. As British Fergus Henderson, owner of the restaurant St. John warned us, "Never try and feed them slops." Because if the food isn't tasty, the staff may skip the calories altogether, leaving little fuel in the tank during the shift.

As for when the meal is served, we found many to unfold in that tiny slice of time bound by the end of the day's prep work and the arrival of the evening's first customer. It's the dead zone between what most consider normal mealtimes, taking place a little earlier than dinner but a little later than lunch, usually around the 4 o'clock mark. A few restaurants dismiss this norm and eat their meal in the wee hours after the customers depart, while some serve multiple meals throughout the day if their staff changes over. Thomas Keller's Ad Hoc, in Yountville, California, goes further, providing a once-weekly "mega family meal" for the entire staff to dine, stress-free, the night before the restaurant closes for two days on Tuesdays and Wednesdays.

As for the individual tasked with making the meal, in most restaurants virtually every cook on the line eventually shoulders the responsibility, whether solo or as part of a team effort. As Cochon co-owner and chef Stephen Stryjewski explained, even recent culinary school graduates are expected to cook a meal that is creative and delicious. While rare, a few restaurants, such as Arzak, employ one person specifically to prepare staff meals. Others, such as the Fat Duck, host stagiaires (short-term culinary interns) who, among many other duties, help to relieve the full-time staff of the responsibility. Still others, like Craigie on Main, use the staff

meal as a kind of final test for a potential new hire. If the meal doesn't make the cut, the cook doesn't get the job.

But while the person responsible for making the meal may vary, the ingredients are often pre-determined. Staff meal recipes normally involve the offcuts, leftovers, and excess from a day of kitchen prep. This leads to fantastic meals built around the trimmings from pricier proteins. Consequently, while the chicken breasts land on the customers' plates, the thighs are staff meal staples. Homemade smoked paprika sausages, Caesar pasta salad, and "sashimi-style" steamed thighs with ponzu sauce are just a few of the happy results. The day's vegetable scrap is usually transformed into sides and salads—such as the gnocchi-like mustard green malfatti at Ubuntu—and economical carbohydrates like potatoes, rice, and pasta round out the plate. Desserts, while rare, tend to be sweets that can be scaled up easily and dished out quickly, like Uchi's peanut butter and curry cookies, but truthfully, there often isn't time for the extra course. In most places the entire meal lasts only about thirty minutes, or a luxurious forty-five if the meal entails a pre-service pep talk or educational wine-tasting.

Then there's the fact that a cook needs to get the meal made fast, usually in just under an hour, something we all can relate to as we juggle our own busy lives. (Keep in mind, however, that many of the time-consuming tasks like homemade stocks, doughs, marinades, and

braises have already been completed as part of the restaurant's menu prep.) Though, unlike at home, it's a meal made to feed the masses—upwards of twenty-five in some places we visited—who all happen to be opinionated culinary professionals. It's a weighty task for even the most confident cook; however, all those we spoke with insisted that the opportunity to cook for their peers is a pleasure, not a chore. The time-tested game plan is to serve simple, stick-to-your-ribs dishes that have a personal viewpoint, the kind of food that cooks would choose to eat after a shift, such as McCrady's Double-Stack Bacon Burgers, Oleana's Chicken Shwarma, or The Bristol's Steak and Kidney Pie. Naturally, this leads many to poach favorite dishes from their childhoods, like the mom-inspired Iowa-Style Fried Chicken at The Herbfarm. Yet some cooks go in the opposite direction, using the communal table as a laboratory, refining a new recipe for the menu—or, in the case of Stéphane Reynaud of Villa9Trois, a new cookbook—and then testing it out on the staff. Still others use the free time to sate a nagging food memory like the slow-cooked pulled pork at Piccolo, a childhood favorite of chef and owner Doug Flicker. This kind of creative freedom for a cook is anomalous since daily tasks are typically dictated by a tangle of superiors. So with total control of the menu, staff meal is a chance for cooks to prove their salt to each other, and get valuable feedback—

even a promotion—in the process.

To our delight, the staff meals we experienced were ripe with inexplicable quirks, and unanticipated contradictions. We journeyed to Grace, in the northern reaches of New England, only to enjoy an authentic Southern gumbo made with tiny local Maine shrimp prepared by Executive Chef Eric Simeon under the acknowledged influence of his Creole grandmother. And yet, deep in the heart of Creole country, we joined the staff at Cochon in an Asian-themed feast of Gulf Coast blue crabs with sriracha and cilantro-scented herb butter, a nod to New Orleans's large Vietnamese population. At Ubuntu, Napa's vegetarian mecca, the meal for its very carnivorous staff was squarely centered on a succulent, sous vide pork shoulder cooked in whey and fermented olive brine. On the flip side, at St. John, Fergus Henderson's nose-to-tail temple of meat and offal worship in London, we enjoyed a vegetarian staff meal of creamy cabbage salad and curried rice with chickpeas. And, quite unexpectedly, considering its perch atop the world of modernist cuisine, the staff meal at wd~50 in Manhattan emphasized traditional, "old-school food," such as grilled hanger steak with classic béarnaise sauce—which, as Chef de Cuisine Jon Bignelli was quick to point out, "is still loaded with technique."

Their distinctions aside, these restaurants' family meals are serving just that: a family. Working in close quarters for

long hours under intense pressure has the potential to draw a restaurant brigade close, or shatter it to pieces. Gathering around the table before the rush of service is a preventative medicine of sorts. It's a restaurant's best and cheapest pill to avert a total kitchen collapse. Analogous to our own dinner tables, there is laughter, ribbing, drama, and dysfunction. Ultimately, however, there is camaraderie of the kind that can only be forged through food. Just like brothers and sisters, spouses, or lifelong friends, wait staff and cooks don't always see eye-to-eye. By creating a welcoming space around a good meal, honest communication has a fighting chance to

flourish—which means the restaurant can, too.

In the end, in researching the subject of this book, we logged countless frequent flyer miles, tested and retested more than a hundred recipes, and interviewed the owners, chefs, cooks, servers, dishwashers, even gardeners, who make the daily staff meal a reality. Their backgrounds, ethnicities, points of view, and experience vary widely, but they all realize the profound importance of feeding each other as best they can. These recipes are the meals that they serve every day, every week, all year. They were not staged for our benefit, nor polished to perfection for our visit, and the resulting authenticity

has led us on a journey of endless inspiration. We consider it an honor to have sat at each and every table.

Ultimately, despite any divergent views on the role of a staff meal or its daily practices, each chef and restaurant owner we spoke with shared the same underlying sentiment, neatly summarized by Annisa's chef and owner, Anita Lo: "I don't see how you can make your staff care about food if you're not feeding them well." We now believe, more than ever, that how a restaurant feeds its own says a great deal about its values. Those who make family meal a priority, despite the added cost or time, believe it not only benefits their staff but is also an indirect way of taking care of customers.

So whether served in a cramped basement or in a garden ringed by ancient chestnut trees, the staff meals within these pages are more than the sum of their parts. They are a daily reminder of why cooks and servers, chefs and owners, dishwashers and bussers, put up with their hot kitchen lives and set the table each evening: to nourish bodies and feed spirits. It's this pure distillation of hospitality that got us cooking in the first place, and somehow, some way, got us eating the best staff meals out there. It's our hope that these stories and recipes will encourage others to follow suit. That everyone with a family they care about— whether at work or at home—will pause for a few precious moments and eat well . . . together.

NOTES ON THE RECIPES

The recipes throughout this book originated in the restaurants we visited, and were made to serve a staff of twelve or larger. So that they can be made in a home kitchen, we have scaled them down to serve between four and eight diners. Please note that this conversion may yield results that appear slightly different than the photography since photos of the food were captured on site. But rest assured, they will taste just as good.

Conversely, there are instances in which ingredient additions or substitutions were made to the original recipe. All additions have been marked as "optional" in the ingredient list, and any substitutions made are listed in the recipe header or Notes. The photography will not reflect these additions or substitutions. However, don't be afraid to get creative and add or substitute with whatever you have on hand. As any staff meal cook will tell you, family meal is all about using what you've got.

To feed a crowd, measurements have been given in both imperial and metric so you can scale up by weight. Please note that salt, spices, and chilies do not scale up in the same proportion as the rest of the recipe. Often you will need much less. Use the scaled measurement as a starting point and begin by using half the amount, adding more to taste.

Shallots are a restaurant's workhorse, and appear in a majority of the recipes here. But when quantifying the amount for a recipe, there is often debate as to exactly what is one shallot. An average-sized shallot should yield about 3 minced tablespoons, and is about the size of half a small hard-boiled egg. As a rule, a small onion is equivalent to three regular-sized shallots, a handy ratio when you are in the produce aisle.

A good restaurant prides itself on its from-scratch stock. Therefore, many recipes in this book rely upon the flavor-enhancing properties of chicken, beef, fish, and vegetable stocks. If you cannot find the time to make your own, try to buy the highest quality stock available, avoiding any that contain artificial flavors or colors. We prefer to use low-sodium or unsalted stocks as this allows for better control of the salt content in the finished dish.

Several restaurants in this book used techniques for their staff meals that required restaurant-specific equipment including sous vide circulators, deep fryers, indoor grills, and liquid nitrogen. Where applicable, we have given the home equivalent.

While the method and ingredients listed for each recipe are what we could handily accomplish on our electric stove and a minimalist's approach to cookware, please regard them more as a general roadmap rather than dogged directions. As we witnessed time and again at the staff meals we visited, trusting your gut instincts while cooking makes all the difference in the world.

AD HOC

YOUNTVILLE, CALIFORNIA

GRILLED LITTLE GEMS WITH TORN GARLIC
CROUTONS AND CITRUS VINAIGRETTE

SKIRT STEAK STUFFED WITH
CHARRED SCALLIONS

RED FRESNO CHILE–GARLIC SAUCE

SKILLET-GLAZED KING TRUMPET MUSHROOMS

CHOCOLATE–PEANUT BUTTER CRUNCH BARS

ollowing a fine meal shared between sworn enemies, Samuel Pepys—a seventeenth-century English Parliament member who was also a fanatical diarist—sat down to record a simple observation: "Strange to see how a good dinner and feasting reconciles everyone." This lesson is not lost on Dave Cruz, the articulate chef de cuisine at Thomas Keller's family-style comfort food destination, Ad Hoc, located in the manicured Napa Valley neighborhood of Yountville, California. Every Monday night after service, Dave makes it a point to host a mega family meal. It is a rare specimen in the genre. Because everyone works the same shifts—the restaurant is only open for dinner and closes on Tuesdays and Wednesdays—the entire staff eats together, and they do so in peace with neither the pressure of a dinner service ahead nor the responsibility of reporting for duty the next morning. Dave best describes the meal as a water-in-carafes event, a time to trot out the fine-dining frills bypassed at their more utilitarian midafternoon buffets. As was probably done for Pepys and his parliamentary guests, this does in fact mean Monday night's table is set with linens as well as with roses. Although for the staff of Ad Hoc, the flowers are purely figurative.

"I've always thought that you don't need to wait for someone to leave to tell them all the good stuff about them," says Dave, explaining the Monday night "Thorns and Roses" ritual as roundtable discussion for lavishing compliments on your peers. The ceremony works like this: someone starts by giving someone else a compliment or "rose," the recipient accepts, and then hands out a rose of their own. Everyone has a chance to give a rose, and most everyone gets one on any given Monday night. The name itself is a piece of Ad Hoc history that stuck. For a short time "thorns" as well as their "rose" counterpoints were doled out. The somewhat controversial thorn critiques were quickly dropped, however, when things got prickly. Now it is an altogether utopian practice with a hint of Northern California commune, but its origins are squarely Greek—Dave picked up the habit during his college fraternity days, bringing it with him to Ad Hoc when owner Thomas Keller put him in charge. Now head chef for the first time in his career, Dave wisely saw an opportunity to orchestrate the restaurant's vibe: "It was like, maybe we could get something more out of staff meal than just getting full or getting drunk."

But before the roses, the meal must be served. A little before midnight an iPod shuffles through a mix of obscure indie tunes as five dark wooden tables are strung together in back of the dining room, a kind of comfortable rustic farmhouse as interpreted by city dwellers. The table is dotted with linen-lined baskets of Bouchon bread and half-full bottles of wine. Collected throughout the week from Ad Hoc's by-the-glass menu, they are tucked behind the lime green bar until Monday's family meal. The staff trickles in, pours a drink, and takes a seat; almost everyone has found the time to change out of their kitchen uniforms, making it feel more like a gathering of friends than colleagues. The meal commences. A mountain of skirt steak pinwheels with scallions poking out of their pink swirls slowly diminishes as the platter is passed from hand to hand. And just when bottoms of wineglasses appear, the music is turned off, Dave clears his throat, and the first rose is given.

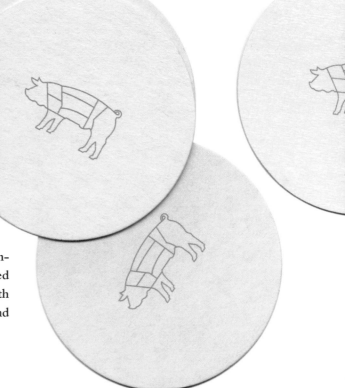

Some roses are funny, others serious, and while they may sound a bit manufactured in a corporate-conference sort of way, they are all completely heartfelt. Someone thanks the busboy for "bringing the thunder," another is appreciative of how a particular female server always comes to work with a smile, and yet another gives a rose to the entire kitchen staff: "You're killing it. It's just awesome." He points to his nearly empty plate: "This is family meal and it's the bomb. I hate to drop f-bombs, but . . . it's the *family* bomb." A departing cook gets showered in roses and gives out the final bloom of his Ad Hoc tenure: "This rose goes to everyone. You guys are like my family, and it's been probably the best restaurant I've ever worked in." Dave ends the Thorns and Roses ceremony by giving out a rose of his own. He speaks with hushed authority: "I have only one rose and it's for David Thomas. He's been the sous chef here for two years." Dave announces that David will be leaving the restaurant in just three weeks. "He's been phenomenal for us and for our kitchen and our restaurant. The work that he does is way beyond what you see. And to fill his shoes and have trust in someone is the hardest thing. So, for tonight, this is where we'll stop. David, this rose is for you." Glasses clink, the feasting continues, and any tension built up over the week evaporates. All is reconciled, at least for this week.

When you acknowledge, as you must,
there is no such thing as perfect food,
only the idea of it, then the real purpose of
striving toward perfection becomes clear:
TO MAKE PEOPLE HAPPY.
That is what cooking is all about.

A Conversation with Chef de Cuisine DAVE CRUZ

Can you walk us through how a typical week of staff meals is made?

We're only open five days a week—Thursday through Monday—so every day we have one person, Philip [Sales], our receiver/prep person, who will make a staff meal that goes up every day at 4 p.m. We even built picnic tables out back, and at four we try to all sit out there and have family meal. But things have evolved here. It's busier and it's hard to sit down every day, so we decided to have a big staff meal on Mondays.

What's different about the Monday meals?

We sort of gather up what won't last over the "weekend" and we cook it up together. We gather up the wine bottles too. It's family-style, sit-down, pass-around. The idea is that we all enjoy what we do so the interaction is a binder. We have an exchange of things that don't have to do with the restaurant. You don't get that if people are staggered throughout the day; if you don't have the time to sit down and bond.

Do you feel a different vibe on Monday during prep and service in the lead-up to the meal?

Oh, absolutely. Because everyone knows it's coming, they're pretty happy.

Are the staff meals planned in advance?

Not really. Another facet of the actual restaurant is that we design a set menu every day for our customers. In a way our staff meal is our menu's leftovers. If we use asparagus today, we probably won't use it again until next week, so it goes to us. We want to use up what we've got.

Do you ever invite guests for staff meal?

Yes. People from other restaurants. A manager or chef from other restaurants. The gardener, Tucker. And our dogs.

What are some publications that you like to tap into as a resource?

I love the style of *Donna Hay Magazine*. Before it went under, I loved *Gourmet*, mostly how much they related about the world.

Any food scraps that will always find their way into the staff meal?

There's a few. Fish cheeks. Why would you ever throw those away? And then it seems like on every steak there's the end piece that's a little charred. That's my favorite piece.

So what is your best advice for a new cook who is going to make staff meal for the first time?

Cook what you know.

If you had to sum it up, why is staff meal important?

Nourishment: feeding your body and feeding each other.

GRILLED LITTLE GEMS with GARLIC CROUTONS and CITRUS VINAIGRETTE

"This salad is very simple, using leftovers from service," explains Chef de Cuisine Dave Cruz. Except that at Ad Hoc "leftovers" means all sorts of fun things to play with: meaty Cerignola olives, leftover country bread, a radish or two pulled from the garden behind the restaurant, and lots of perky Little Gems, the toy poodle of the romaine cultivar. Quickly grilling the quartered heads kisses them with char but still allows them to maintain their crunch. "It's this combination of smoky and sweet, briny and peppery, crunchy and bacony that we really like," says Dave, "especially the bacon."

Little Gem lettuces (also called sucrine) look like miniature versions of their lankier relatives, romaine, but have the almost silky-tasting mildness of a butter lettuce. They are sweet, crisp, and hold up well to heat (as opposed to, say, spinach, which would melt to nothingness). If you cannot find Little Gems at a store or farmers' market, any hearty headed lettuce will work. Romaine, trimmed to the heart and quartered, is the best bet, but endive and radicchio would also grill well. The croutons are another treat hidden within this recipe. As Dave explains it, the idea is to brown the bread slowly on the stovetop, allowing the garlic oil and butter to be absorbed into the flesh of the bread. This leaves behind a crouton with a crunchy outside and, as Dave describes, a "soft, gushy, buttery, garlicky inside." And who can resist that?

Serves 6

TORN GARLIC CROUTONS

1 CUP (237 MILLILITERS) OLIVE OIL

CLOVES FROM 3 SMALL HEADS OF GARLIC (ABOUT 1 CUP)

HALF OF A 10-INCH (25 CENTIMETERS) ROUND LOAF OF COUNTRY BREAD

KOSHER SALT TO TASTE

4 TABLESPOONS (56 GRAMS) UNSALTED BUTTER

CITRUS VINAIGRETTE

1 CUP (237 MILLILITERS) FRESHLY SQUEEZED ORANGE JUICE

¼ CUP (59 MILLILITERS) CHAMPAGNE VINEGAR

2 TABLESPOONS (25 GRAMS) GRANULATED SUGAR

1 CUP (237 MILLILITERS) CANOLA OIL

KOSHER SALT AND FRESHLY GROUND BLACK PEPPER TO TASTE

LITTLE GEMS

6 HEADS LITTLE GEM LETTUCE (SEE RECIPE HEADER)

¼ CUP (59 MILLILITERS) OLIVE OIL

KOSHER SALT AND FRESHLY GROUND BLACK PEPPER TO TASTE

6 SLICES (167 GRAMS) THICK-CUT SMOKED BACON, FRIED AND CRUMBLED

2 LARGE RED RADISHES, VERY THINLY SLICED

½ CUP (91 GRAMS) GREEN CERIGNOLA OLIVES, SLICED OFF THE PIT

For the croutons: Place the oil and garlic in a small pot. Heat over high heat until bubbles begin to appear, about 2 minutes. Lower the heat and gently simmer for 15 minutes, or until the garlic cloves are tender. Remove the pot from the heat; set aside to cool to room temperature.

Strain the oil from the cloves, reserving both separately. In a food processor, purée the cloves until they form a thick paste. Reserve for the Skirt Steak on page 24, or refrigerate in a lidded jar for up to 1 week. Yields about ½ cup (118 milliliters) purée.

Since Ad Hoc uses day-old bread, they remove the crust and discard but if using fresh, this step is optional. Tear the bread into irregular bite-sized pieces.

Heat a sauté pan large enough to hold all the bread in a single layer over medium heat. When warm but not hot, add half of the reserved garlic oil (storing the remainder in the refrigerator for another use) and the bread. As the oil begins to bubble, flip the bread pieces in the oil and season liberally with salt. Continue cooking and turning the croutons until lightly golden and slightly crisp, about 12 minutes. (Should the contents begin to sizzle, turn the heat down—you are going too fast.)

Add the butter and swirl the skillet to coat the bread evenly. The butter will begin to brown at the same pace as the bread. Continue to turn the bread until it is deep golden brown and very crisp, about 10 minutes more. Remove with a slotted spoon, drain on paper towels, season again with salt, and keep warm. (These will keep well in a sealed plastic bag at room temperature for several days, if you can resist snacking on them.)

For the citrus vinaigrette: In a small pot bring the orange juice to a gentle simmer over medium heat and reduce by half, about 12 minutes. Remove from the heat and add the vinegar and sugar, stirring to dissolve; cool to room temperature.

Using an immersion blender or a whisk, incorporate the canola oil into the juice-vinegar mixture in a slow, steady stream. Season with salt and pepper. Check the flavor balance, adding more oil, vinegar, or sugar. Set aside.

For the Little Gems: Trim each head of any limp or discolored leaves leaving the stem end intact. Cut each head lengthwise in quarters. On a sheet tray arrange the lettuces cut-side up, brush with the olive oil, and season with salt and pepper.

Meanwhile, heat a grill pan or cast-iron skillet over high heat until smoking. (Ad Hoc uses a gas grill with a high flame.) Place the quarters on the grill pan, cut-side down, in a single layer. Grill for about 1 minute, until a light brown char appears. Turn each wedge with tongs (Ad Hoc uses oversized surgical tweezers for precision) to the other cut side and grill about 1 minute more. The lettuce should be branded by the grill pan and lightly wilted, but not completely limp. Repeat with the remaining lettuce, wiping the grill pan thoroughly with a folded, damp cloth between batches.

In a large serving dish arrange the Little Gems, croutons, bacon, radishes, and olives. Whisk together the dressing if it has separated, then drizzle lightly onto the salad. Finish with a sprinkling of salt and serve while just this side of warm with extra dressing on the side.

SKIRT STEAK STUFFED with CHARRED SCALLIONS

Philip Sales—a thirty-year Thomas Keller veteran harking back to Keller's late-Eighties restaurant, Rakel, in New York City—knows a thing or two about making a staff meal. As the full-time family meal cook for Ad Hoc (as well as the pantry supervisor), he prepares a multicourse spread for the thirty or so staff members for the midday meal. Consequently, the staff adores him. So what is his best advice for those making family meal for discerning peers? Careful preparation. But also being mindful of the restaurant's bottom line: "I keep a good eye on what's left over from the night before," says Philip in his quiet Jamaican lilt. "Instead of having it sit longer, we utilize it for family meal." Though for Monday's meal, Philip gets a well-deserved night off. Today, the preparation of leftover skirt steaks

gets passed along to Dave and his team.

The skirt steak, while thin compared to other cuts, does have a variation in thickness from end to end. The thicker section is trimmed off and reserved for the Ad Hoc customer; it's easier to cook to medium-rare. "The part where it's really skinny," says Dave, "we eat that." Dave decided to put an Asian twist on this dish, slathering the long, thin pieces of meat with garlic confit paste (page 23) and rolling them up daintily with charred scallions tucked inside. He served them sliced into pinwheels for easier portioning alongside a homemade Red Fresno Chile–Garlic Sauce (page 26) for a hit of heat and sweetness.

Serves 6

2 LARGE BUNCHES SCALLIONS, TRIMMED

2 TABLESPOONS (30 MILLILITERS) OLIVE OIL

KOSHER SALT AND FRESHLY GROUND BLACK PEPPER TO TASTE

4 (10-INCH/25 CENTIMETER) SKIRT STEAKS (ABOUT 8 OUNCES/227 GRAMS EACH)

½ CUP (118 MILLILITERS) GARLIC CONFIT PURÉE (FROM THE GRILLED LITTLE GEMS ON PAGE 22)

2 TABLESPOONS (30 MILLILITERS) CANOLA OIL

Heat a grill pan or cast-iron pan over high heat until smoking. (Ad Hoc uses a gas grill with a high flame.) Toss the scallions with the olive oil and season with salt and pepper, then place in the pan in a single layer. Cook until charred black on one side, about 2 minutes. Flip and cook for 1 to 2 minutes more, or until tender. Remove from the pan and allow to cool slightly, then cut into 3-inch (7.5 centimeter) lengths (slightly shorter than the width of the skirt steaks).

Lay out the steaks in a single layer. Trim off any excess fat or sinew. Cover the steaks with plastic wrap or waxed paper and, using a meat mallet, lightly pound the steaks to achieve a uniform thickness of about ¼ inch (65 millimeters). (Each steak should be about 12 to 14 inches/30.5 to 35 centimeters in length after pounding.)

Season both sides of each steak liberally with salt and pepper, then rub one side of every steak with a thin layer of the garlic purée. Lay out the steaks so that they are perpendicular to you. Divide the scallions evenly among the steaks, arranging them in a single layer from bottom to top, like a meat ladder with green rungs.

Roll the steaks tightly into individual bundles. Tie the finished rolls at 1½-inch intervals with kitchen twine. (If you want to make these ahead, place in a container in a single layer, cover, and store in the refrigerator overnight.)

Heat the oven to 375°F (191°C) and place a wire cooling rack over a sheet pan. In a large sauté pan, heat a generous film of canola oil until almost smoking. Season the outside of the skirt steak rolls with salt. Sear until a brown crust develops, about 2 minutes per side, and then transfer from pan to rack.

Roast the rolls in the oven until medium rare, about 35 minutes. Check one roll by making a small slit with a sharp knife into its center. If the middle of the roll looks very pink (almost raw), continue roasting in increments of 5 minutes. It is better to err on the side of overcooking than under; this helps the rolls hold their shape when sliced. Remove the rolls from the oven; rest for 15 minutes. Snip the twine, slice the rolls into large pinwheels, and serve with Red Fresno Chile–Garlic Sauce (page 26) on the side.

RED FRESNO CHILE–GARLIC SAUCE

The red Fresno chile is easily mistaken for a red jalapeño. Upon closer inspection you'll find it is a bit stockier at the stem end, like a jalapeño wearing shoulder pads. It is widely used in Latin cooking for its medium heat and mild sweetness, and can be found in most Latin supermarkets. Jalapeños (red or green), fresh cayenne peppers, or serranos can all be substituted. Extra sauce can stand in as a sweet and spicy vinegar-based dip for any Asian fried snack, including the crispy octopus suckers (page 201), fried onigiri (page 281), and scallion jeon (page 36).

Yields 1½ cups (355 milliliters)

16 RED FRESNO CHILES (ABOUT 8 OUNCES/227 GRAMS), STEMMED, SEEDED, AND QUARTERED

8 GARLIC CLOVES

½ CUP (118 MILLILITERS) CHAMPAGNE VINEGAR

½ CUP (100 GRAMS) GRANULATED SUGAR

1 TEASPOON (6 GRAMS) KOSHER SALT, PLUS ADDITIONAL TO TASTE

For the sweet chile-garlic sauce: Place the chiles and garlic cloves in a small nonreactive container. Cover with the vinegar and sugar. Cover and refrigerate overnight or up to 12 hours.

Strain the liquid from the solids, reserving both separately. Blend the chiles, garlic, and salt along with ¾ cup (178 milliliters) of the liquid until puréed, about 1 minute. You want the blender to spin freely and the finished sauce to be pourable but not watery. Adjust the liquid and salt if necessary. Dave strains the finished sauce through a fine-mesh sieve, resulting in a much thinner, more refined end product. (We prefer to keep ours chunky so we skip the straining.) Store covered in the refrigerator for up to a week.

SKILLET-GLAZED KING TRUMPET MUSHROOMS

Whether slightly shriveled, bruised, or torn, any king trumpets that do not make the cut for the customers' plates get turned into this simple side dish. In other words, it is an ugly mushroom makeover. It also makes great use of mushroom stems, a by-product for restaurants that only have eyes for the more fetching cap. Small baby portabella mushrooms (look for ones about the size of a marble) can be substituted, and white button mushrooms will also work if other, more flavorful, mushrooms are not available.

Serves 6

2 TABLESPOONS (30 MILLILITERS) OLIVE OIL

1½ POUNDS (680 GRAMS) KING TRUMPET MUSHROOMS, LEFT WHOLE

1 SHALLOT, FINELY CHOPPED

2 TABLESPOONS (28 GRAMS) UNSALTED BUTTER

1 SPRIG THYME

½ CUP (118 MILLILITERS) CHICKEN STOCK

KOSHER SALT AND FRESHLY GROUND BLACK PEPPER TO TASTE

In a sauté pan heat the olive oil over medium-high heat until just shy of smoking. Add the mushrooms and sauté until lightly brown on all sides, about 6 minutes. Add the shallot, butter, and thyme and sauté until the shallot is slightly golden, about 1 minute. Add the chicken stock and cook to reduce the liquid down to almost nothing, about 3 minutes. Begin to swirl the pan, to coat the mushrooms with a shiny glaze. Season with salt and pepper. Remove the pan from the heat, pluck out the thyme, and serve the mushrooms immediately.

CHOCOLATE–PEANUT BUTTER CRUNCH BARS

Sous chef Sarah Zozaya's transformation of the Ad Hoc pastry program has not gone unnoticed, especially at the Monday staff meal's Thorns and Roses ceremony. After a year of tweaking recipes and adding new ones of her own, she received a rose one night from a server. He noticed that several regular customers went from skipping dessert to asking for extras in their doggie bags. "That was really cool," says Sarah with a generous smile. These peanut butter bars helped earn the compliment.

Sarah picked up the recipe as a young cook in Sacramento and has been fine-tuning it ever since. Her most recent epiphany was to mix the peanut butter with ground feuilletine (airy French flakes similar in texture to dried crêpes) to add a soft crunch to an otherwise heavy layer. The dessert's end result—nutty and lightly sweet with a dark chocolate tang—is the uptown version of the pedestrian peanut butter cup, and the single most-requested staff meal dessert. On the nights the bars appear solely on the customer menu, the staff gets to enjoy the trim left behind after portioning. "Usually that's what staff meal is . . . the borders," says Sarah. The staff knows, as she does, that they taste just as good.

Yields 24 bars

CRUST

5 CUPS (540 GRAMS) CHOCOLATE COOKIE CRUMBS (SEE NOTES)

8 OUNCES (2 STICKS/220 GRAMS) UNSALTED BUTTER, MELTED

FILLING

4½ CUPS (1.1 KILOGRAMS) SMOOTH NATURAL PEANUT BUTTER

2½ CUPS (200 GRAMS) GRAHAM CRACKER CRUMBS

2½ CUPS (170 GRAMS) GROUND FEUILLETINE (SEE NOTES)

1 CUP (220 GRAMS) PACKED DARK BROWN SUGAR

2 TEASPOONS (12 GRAMS) KOSHER SALT

8 OUNCES (2 STICKS/220 GRAMS) UNSALTED BUTTER, AT ROOM TEMPERATURE

TOPPING

12 OUNCES (340 GRAMS) 70% DARK CHOCOLATE, CHOPPED

1 TABLESPOON (15 MILLILITERS) CANOLA OIL

NOTES

Ad Hoc makes their chocolate cookie crumbs from their signature TKO cookies. If you live nearby a Bouchon Bakery—Thomas Keller's expanding pastry chain—TKO cookies are available for purchase. Otherwise, substitute Nabisco Chocolate Wafer Cookies, chocolate animal crackers, or in a pinch, Oreo cookie halves with the white filling scraped off. Grind any one of them to fine black sand in the food processor, then fish out any large chunks; regrinding again if necessary. (This is the same way they make their graham cracker crumbs.)

Ground feuilletine is used to give the bars their light crunch. For a small fortune, the crêpe-like flakes can be found online at specialty bakery sites like micheldefrance.com. For a less-expensive substitute, try unfilled and unflavored Pirouette cookies, gaufrette wafers, or do what we did and use crispy rice cereal (cornflakes would work too). They can all be ground as instructed for the chocolate crumbs to achieve the coarse-sand consistency of crushed feuilletine.

For the crust: Line a half-sheet tray (18 x 13 inches/45 x 33 centimeters) with aluminum foil. Mix the crumbs and butter to a wet-sand consistency. Press the mixture onto the sheet tray with the palms of your hands to form a uniformly thick crust, about ¼ inch (6 millimeters). Chill in the refrigerator, uncovered, for 30 minutes.

For the filling: Combine the peanut butter, cracker crumbs, feuilletine, sugar, and salt in the bowl of a mixer fitted with a paddle. Mix on high speed until combined and aerated, about 5 minutes. Add the butter and mix on high for 1 minute more, until just incorporated. Be careful not to overmix, as the mixture could separate. Remove the crust from the refrigerator and spread with the peanut butter mixture using a small offset spatula in an even 1-inch (2.5 centimeter) layer. Refrigerate for at least 1 hour, uncovered.

For the topping: Melt the chocolate with the oil in a double boiler set over simmering water, about 6 minutes, whisking occasionally to combine. While the chocolate is warm but not hot, pour it over the peanut butter. Smooth into a thin layer with a small offset spatula. (The chocolate coating must be applied and spread quickly or it will seize and become unspreadable.) Place the sheet tray in the freezer, covered in plastic wrap, for a minimum of 6 hours to set completely.

Using a knife dipped in very hot water, portion the bars while still frozen into 24 rectangles. (At Ad Hoc they cut them in the walk-in freezer on very hot days.) Serve immediately or store in the freezer until the dessert hour.

The bars can be kept in the freezer, wrapped tightly, for several weeks. They go from solid to squishy very quickly; serve them straight from the freezer and skip them altogether for a summer picnic.

ANNISA

NEW YORK, NEW YORK

FRIED SCALLION JEON
SPICY KIMCHI, TOFU, AND SQUID
HOT POT (KIMCHICHIGAE)

WAGYU BEEF BIBIMBAP

Anita Lo steps into her restaurant, Annisa, like the petite head honcho of a convoy of Harley riders. A neon-green bandana tied around her shiny black bob, she is half smiling, half scowling as she brushes by the restaurant's pumpkin-colored booths, curved like autumn half-moons and still looking brand new. (While the West Village restaurant first opened in 2000, a fire destroyed the interior in July of 2009. It reopened nine months later, just a few months before our visit.) Already dressed in her executive chef uniform—plain white chef's jacket, black pants tapering to blunt hems, black shoes with a sturdy toe box—she strides to Annisa's tiny kitchen with an intense authority, one that borders on intimidating. Then we look down. Two fluffy balls of white and gray bounce behind her: Adzuki and Mochi, Anita's shih tzus. They are adorably disheveled with small bunches of hair pulled back in spiky pigtails. According to Anita, Mochi is an aloof princess, and Adzuki, a social butterfly. The dogs instantly soften Anita's hard edges. A little.

Today Anita is making the staff meal herself. She does not always have the time to do this personally—she is often called out of the kitchen and into the media spotlight especially after her fierce run on the first season of Bravo's *Top Chef Masters*—but Anita makes it clear that a daily staff meal is nonnegotiable. It is a habit she picked up as a young cook

while working downtown at David Waltuck's Chanterelle, the now-shuttered restaurant known for its stellar staff meals and the cookbook chronicling them. So after shopping at the nearby farmers' market, Anita works by herself in the fluorescent-lit basement kitchen, creating a flavor-packed Korean trio of dishes: whole fried scallions with the most delicate crispness, salty and sweet beef bibimbap, and kimchi and seafood stew full of spice and fresh squid. It seems that for Anita, making staff meal is a stoic,

highly organized, and mainly solitary process: a time that she can shrug off her celebrity chef status and simply be Anita, the no-frills, tough-as-nails cook.

So it is to our great surprise that right before we leave, Anita hands us hand-drawn, illustrated notes she jotted down prior to our visit, a colorful journey of her top five staff meals at Annisa. It starts with an unapologetically flashy title in bold red with sun rays flying off of it: "Anita's Top 5 Most Memorable Staff Meals!" And right then, we know we are

neath is of a Picasso-esque face, its mouth a taco shell, the eyes shedding three tears. Then she continues the tale in all caps: "But he and that same woman are now married and have two little kids!" A drawing of the taco-shell face turned upside down, smiling, is underneath with the words "all true" beside it.

Further down the page there's a drawing of a green bird in mid-flight with the body of a goose but the head of a fish. "One day, a cook brought in a whole flock of ducks and geese that she shot on Thanksgiving night near her home in South Carolina," writes Anita. "They tasted like fish. We ate it with *beurre rouge*. It was strange, like a livery-tasting *matelote* [a French fish stew] with hints of gun shot."

On the final page there is a pastel-colored parade of cartoonish chickens, pigs, vegetables, and razor clams. "We once had an intern, an older woman from Korea, who talked nonstop," writes Anita, making it clear that she was animated and maybe a touch crazy. "For her first staff meal she made about a dozen dishes! Enough for five times the number of people working that day. She almost couldn't fit it all on the table. Everyone went silent and she kept bringing it out . . . we were flummoxed!" Anita swaps her black pen for a bold red marker. She signs off: "I thought . . . this is why they call it family meal. Bon Appétit! XO Anita." And just like that, her hard edges dissolve, completely.

getting a rare glimpse into her other, more Adzuki, self. First we see a picture of a goofy purple octopus and a bowl of soup with a big pink heart drawn around it. Inside she writes "Justin Borah's Tako head New England–style chowder *in the* head." She sums it up as the winner for the best use of octopus parts.

She starts the second page off more seriously: "Perhaps one of the saddest staff meals was when David Marlone made fish tacos. The love of his life had just dumped him." The drawing under-

A Conversation with Chef and Owner ANITA LO

Why is a daily staff meal important?

I don't see how you can make your staff care about food if you're not feeding them well.

Have you always served a staff meal here at Annisa?

Yeah. And I love making it myself; I just haven't had time lately. In France we had a really good staff meal. And it was a daily, sit-down thing. I've worked in a lot of restaurants in the United States that just put up chicken every day, or old fish, and everyone just eats on the line, standing. And then I worked at *Chanterelle* . . .

Our heroes! The epitome of staff meals in America . . .

And I just realized that it's really important. They're like my restaurant parents. We had great staff meals. I learned so much from it. This was in the early nineties, and you couldn't get better food if you went out and spent money in a bistro. We would have, like, blood sausage for family meals. It was so awesome.

The kimchi fish stew looks incredible. Do you make your own kimchi here?

No, I buy it. I used to make my own. I worked in a restaurant called Mirezi, back in the nineties, that was a Korean-owned, pan-Asian restaurant, and they sent me to Korea where I learned the technique. Today I am using kimchi from a festival I did last week, I had a lot left over. I really can't stand wasting food. It drives me crazy. And it's not just economic; it's environmental. It's about respecting food and nature. Family meal is built around that.

What are five ingredients you always have on hand to make the staff meal?

Soy sauce, fish sauce, rice vinegar, kombu, and bonito.

Do you remember your first staff meal when the restaurant reopened after the 2009 fire?

Annisa was closed for nine months, but my entire staff came back after the fire, except for three people. So it was kind of awesome. I made the first staff meal. Whatever I made—I don't remember, exactly—I don't remember it being that great. But I do remember wanting to make that first one.

Do you use any cookbooks for staff meal inspiration?

Absolutely. I always say that my favorite cookbook is *Joy of Cooking*. You learn from staff meal and sometimes it's really delicious and it ends up on the menu.

For somebody who's new to staff meal, what's your best advice?

You have to make something that you've made many times before, that you make at home. If it's spaghetti and meatballs, whatever. Keep it simple.

If you could invite anyone to your staff meal, who would it be?

To my staff meal? Family.

FRIED SCALLION JEON

A dish once served in the Korean royal court, *jeon* refers to a host of pan-fried pancakes filled with various combinations of meat, fish, or vegetables, all bound together by a simple flour batter. They are typically served as an appetizer or part of the banchan offerings, a Korean meal's collection of small side dishes that blanket the table. This recipe is Anita Lo's simplified version of the dish. Skipping the pan-frying altogether, she treats it more like a Korean tempura, dipping the scallions in the batter, then quickly deep-frying them. The end result is a grown-up version of onion rings; they do, in fact, go great with burgers.

To keep the jeon from becoming greasy, Anita's best piece of advice is to use very cold seltzer water; chilling it for at least a few hours in the refrigerator is recommended.

Serves 6

DIPPING SAUCE

½ CUP (118 MILLILITERS) SOY SAUCE
½ CUP (118 MILLILITERS) RICE VINEGAR
1 LARGE GARLIC CLOVE, MINCED
1 TABLESPOON (5 GRAMS) GOCHUGARU (KOREAN GROUND CHILES; SEE NOTE)
1 TABLESPOON (5 GRAMS) FINELY CHOPPED SCALLION GREENS
1 TEASPOON (3 GRAMS) TOASTED SESAME SEEDS

SCALLIONS

6 BUNCHES SCALLIONS
2 QUARTS (1.9 LITERS) SAFFLOWER OIL
1 CUP (125 GRAMS) ALL-PURPOSE FLOUR
¼ CUP (32 GRAMS) CORNSTARCH
1 TEASPOON (5 GRAMS) BAKING SODA
1 TEASPOON (6 GRAMS) KOSHER SALT, PLUS MORE FOR SEASONING
1¼ CUPS (300 MILLILITERS) SELTZER WATER, WELL-CHILLED

NOTE

Gochugaru is Korean red chile pepper powder that is both coarser and slightly less spicy than other ground chiles. Crushing dried red chile flakes in a mortar with a pestle will yield an approximate, but spicier, substitute.

For the dipping sauce: Combine all the ingredients in a small bowl. Set aside.

For the scallions: Wash and thoroughly dry the scallions. Trim each scallion of its root and the top inch (2.5 centimeters) of its dark green top; you should be left with approximately 6-inch (15 centimeters) scallions. Pull off any brown or limp outer leaves, check for any lingering sand (rinse and dry again if necessary), and set aside.

When ready to serve, heat the oil in a heavy-bottomed stockpot to 375°F (191°C). Mix together the flour, cornstarch, baking soda, and salt in a large bowl. Whisk in 1 cup (237 milliliters) of the seltzer to make a batter that is thick enough to coat the whisk but still very pourable; add more water if necessary.

Dip a handful of scallions in the batter, turn to coat well, and using long-handled tongs, carefully place them in the hot oil in small batches. Rotate and dunk the scallions occasionally in the hot oil to ensure even cooking. Fry until puffed, crispy, and lightly brown on the edges, 1 to 2 minutes. Remove from the oil, drain on paper towels, and sprinkle with salt while still hot.

Serve immediately with the dipping sauce, or keep in a low oven (in a single layer) while frying the remaining batches.

SPICY KIMCHI, TOFU, and SQUID HOT POT (KIMCHICHIGAE)

While Anita Lo calls this slightly spicy dish a stew, it is more soup-like, cooking up very quickly, with no long simmering required. The foundation flavor here is baechu kimchi, the most commonly available made with spicy fermented Napa cabbage. Anita also decided to make use of squid and small pieces of sea bass left over after filleting, but any combination of fish or shellfish will work.

Serves 6 to 8 generously

2 POUNDS (907 GRAMS) SKIN-ON SEA BASS FILLETS

1 POUND (454 GRAMS) BABY SQUID

2 TABLESPOONS (30 MILLILITERS) CANOLA OIL

1 TABLESPOON (15 MILLILITERS) SESAME OIL

1 LARGE YELLOW ONION, FINELY CHOPPED

6 LARGE GARLIC CLOVES, MINCED

1 QUART (907 GRAMS) CABBAGE KIMCHI, DRAINED, LIQUID RESERVED

ONE 7-INCH PIECE (6 GRAMS) DRIED KOMBU (SEE NOTES)

2 TABLESPOONS (10 GRAMS) IRIKO (DRIED ANCHOVIES; SEE NOTES)

2½ QUARTS (2.4 LITERS) WATER

1 CUP (120 GRAMS) PEELED DAIKON, DICED INTO ½-INCH (1.25 CENTIMETER) CUBES

2 CUPS (260 GRAMS) UNPEELED LONG SQUASH, SLICED INTO ¼-INCH (65 MILLIMETER) HALF-MOONS (OR 1 LARGE GREEN OR YELLOW SQUASH)

1 CUP (170 GRAMS) FIRM TOFU, DICED INTO ½-INCH (1.3 CENTIMETER) CUBES

1 TABLESPOON (15 MILLILITERS) FISH SAUCE

1 TEASPOON (4 GRAMS) GRANULATED SUGAR

KOSHER SALT AND FRESHLY GROUND BLACK PEPPER TO TASTE

HANDFUL OF CHOPPED SCALLION GREENS

Remove the pin bones from the sea bass fillets. Cut into large (about 4-inch-long/10 centimeter) oblong pieces; larger chunks are less inclined to break apart in the stew. Separate the squid heads from their bodies, reserving both separately. Clean the heads of their innards, beak, cuttlebone (the thin, clear cartilage running down the center), and ink sac (reserve and refrigerate the ink; it can be added to pasta dough). Slice the bodies into ¼-inch (6 millimeter) rings; leave the tentacle-fringed heads whole. Set the sea bass and squid aside in the refrigerator.

Heat the canola and sesame oils in a large, heavy-bottomed pot over high heat. When hot, add the onions and garlic, sautéing until the onions are translucent but have not picked up color, about 4 minutes. Add the kimchi and half its liquid, the kombu, iriko, and water (there should be enough to cover everything amply; if not, add more). Bring to a boil, then reduce the heat and simmer for 15 minutes.

Fish out the kombu. Slice it in thin strips when cool enough to handle and return to the pot.

Add the daikon and bring the liquid back to a boil over high heat. Add the squash, lower the heat, and simmer until just tender, about 4 minutes.

Add the sea bass, squid, and tofu. Simmer until the sea bass and squid are just cooked through, about 5 minutes. If too much liquid has evaporated, leaving behind more "stuff" than "stew," now is the time to add more of the remaining kimchi liquid or a cupful or two of water (237 to 500 milliliters). Finally, season the soup with the fish sauce, sugar, salt, and pepper, adding more or less to your taste. For extra color, garnish the soup with the chopped scallions.

Set the entire pot, piping hot, on the table with a ladle, and serve generously to waiting guests.

Notes

Kombu (dried edible kelp) and iriko (small dried anchovies) are both Asian specialty items that help add depth of flavor to the stew. Iriko are sold by the pound in the refrigerated section of Asian markets and come in varying sizes. Try to find relatively small ones. While some prefer to use the larger ones for stock making, they have more "guts," which can impart a muddy off-flavor to your finished dish. For a less-pronounced fish flavor but still plenty of umami, substitute dried shiitake mushrooms for either ingredient.

WAGYU BEEF BIBIMBAP

Bibimbap literally translates to "mixed dish" in Korean. "It's like Korean fried rice," says Anita Lo, "but with lots of vegetables and beef." In this case, a handful of incredibly rich and meltingly tender scraps of pricey wagyu steaks were used; but the cheaper skirt or flank cuts can be substituted, as we've done here. Typically, all the components of a traditional bibimbap—sautéed spinach, stir-fried beef, and fried egg—are arranged colorfully on top of a big bowl of white rice, which the diner then gets to happily mix together, hence the name. At Annisa, Anita prefers adding and mixing everything herself in one big bowl so she can adjust the seasoning before serving. "It will just taste better." So feel free to do the same.

The components of this dish are stitched together with a sweet and spicy sauce made simply of water, sugar, and gochujang, the Korean fermented chili-soybean paste. Says Anita of the dark maroon condiment, "It's one of the basics of Korean cooking. In the old days every Korean house had three pots in their backyard. One for the gochujang, one for the doenjang [fermented bean paste], and one for the soy sauce." Used widely in Korean cooking to marinate meats and flavor stews, gochujang can be purchased in Asian specialty stores, including the national Korean chain, H Mart.

Serves 6 to 8

1½ POUNDS (680 GRAMS) FLANK OR SKIRT STEAK

1¼ CUPS (225 GRAMS) GRANULATED SUGAR, DIVIDED

1 CUP (237 MILLILITERS) SOY SAUCE

6 GARLIC CLOVES, LIGHTLY CRUSHED

2½ TEASPOONS (15 GRAMS) KOSHER SALT, DIVIDED PLUS MORE TO TASTE

3 CUPS (585 GRAMS) WHITE SHORT-GRAIN RICE

1 CUP (120 GRAMS) JULIENNED CARROTS (ABOUT 4 MEDIUM CARROTS)

1 CUP (130 GRAMS) JULIENNED LONG SQUASH (OR 1 SMALL YELLOW OR GREEN SQUASH)

½ CUP (118 MILLILITERS) GOCHUJANG (SEE RECIPE HEADER)

6 TABLESPOONS (75 MILLILITERS) SESAME OIL, DIVIDED

7 TABLESPOONS (103 MILLILITERS) CANOLA OIL, DIVIDED

1 MEDIUM YELLOW ONION, THINLY SLICED

3 LARGE EGGS

1 QUART (120 GRAMS) PACKED FRESH SPINACH

FRESHLY GROUND BLACK PEPPER TO TASTE

Slice the beef against the grain in thin 3-inch-long (7.5 centimeter) strips. (You should have about 3 cups/725 milliliters of beef strips total.) Mix the beef with 1 cup (200 grams) of the sugar, soy sauce, garlic, and ½ teaspoon (3 grams) of the salt. Marinate in the refrigerator, covered, for 4 hours or up to overnight.

Cook the rice according to package instructions. Fluff and keep warm in the pot it was cooked in.

Season the carrots liberally with salt; set aside at room temperature for 10 minutes, then squeeze dry in a clean kitchen towel. Repeat this salting procedure with the squash. (The step can be omitted, but it helps with the overall seasoning of the dish and leaches out excess liquid.)

Mix the gochujang with the remaining sugar and thin with a tablespoon or two (15 to 30 milliliters) of water until a just-pourable paste is formed; set aside.

Drain the marinated beef, removing the garlic cloves, and discard the marinade. In a large sauté pan, heat 1 tablespoon (15 milliliters) each of the sesame and canola oils over high heat. When nearly smoking, sauté half the beef for 2 to 3 minutes, or until just cooked through. Remove from the pan, set aside, and repeat with 1 tablespoon (15 milliliters) of each of the oils and the remaining beef. Keep warm.

In a nonstick pan over medium heat, fry the eggs in 1 tablespoon of canola oil until the yolks have set completely, about 6 minutes. Remove from pan and set aside.

Increase heat to medium-high, sauté the carrot, squash, onions, and spinach individually over high heat using 1 tablespoon (15 milliliters) of each oil until tender, 1 to 3 minutes each. After cooking, squeeze the spinach dry using a clean kitchen towel.

Warm the rice, add the beef, eggs, and vegetables to the pot, and pour in half of the gochujang sauce; mix thoroughly. Taste and adjust with additional sauce, salt, and pepper if desired. Transfer to a serving dish and serve immediately, with extra gochujang sauce on the side for drizzling over top.

ARZAK

SAN SEBASTIÁN, SPAIN

DUCK AND SHRIMP PAELLA

PIQUILLO PEPPER CONFIT

BEAUTIFUL LACE FRIED EGGS

[n route to San Sebastián, our Spanish-speaking GPS mutinied. Somehow, the famously gorgeous six-hour drive to the Basque region from Barcelona turned into a full-day misadventure thanks to the endless rerouting of our indiscernible guide. Luckily, there was a steady supply of thinly sliced jamon along the way. But as we set out to find Arzak the following day, we depart as Luddites with just a hand-drawn map and a hope that the game-changing dining destination will flag us. Arzak is, after all, the fountain-head of Spain's avant-garde cuisine. The restaurant that in the 1970s under the direction of visionary chef Juan Mari Arzak captured the attention of the entire world by transforming traditional Basque cuisine into a highly conceptualized, meticulously plated, and utterly transporting phenomenon. Or to state it more simply: the restaurant that launched the Spanish culinary revolution.

Yet we drive up and down the same Vespa-clogged suburban street twice looking for a storefront whose exterior reflects the modern food being served inside. Finally we find Arzak sweetly wheezing "old school." With its scalloped awnings, vintage cursive script, nineteenth century brick façade, and pensioners' apartments above, this is not the temple to contemporary gastronomy we were expecting. In fact—and to our delight—it turns out to be the very opposite: a citadel of tradition, especially at the staff meal table.

"Basques are powerful people. We need powerful food," says the silver-haired Juan Mari, a chef in his late sixties who radiates such sincere kindness, you can't help feeling like you are the most valued diner in his care. The third generation in his family to run the restaurant, Juan Mari explains that the 4 p.m. family meal always features traditional Basque dishes: "To remind us where we come from." His daughter and co-chef, Elena Arzak, agrees. Sitting at the marble table tucked into a cranny of the main kitchen—the same one she has been eating at since she could hold a fork—Elena tells us in her precise, matter-of-fact English about the rich history of Basque cuisine. It is a tale of how the simplest foods—like slow-roasted peppers, paella of shrimp and rabbit, fish stew with potatoes, or a pot of simmered lentils—fueled them over the centuries, first in their quest to win sovereignty, and now for their fight to preserve their distinct culture.

As we rise to start our kitchen tour, we wonder aloud what Juan Mari's favorite staff meal may be, and in a habit acquired through the years, Elena answers for him: "fried eggs and roasted peppers." The very dish that Esperanza Carrasco Perez, a cherubic cook with long jet-black hair, is making for the meal today. Later we will watch as she expertly bastes the sputtering eggs in a deep bath of Spanish olive oil, coaxing the borders of the whites to lacy crispness, and the yolks, molten and oozing. Agolfo Golfo,

the soft-spoken maître d' from southern Spain, explains that Esperanza's grace at the stove is no fluke. She has been cooking the staff meal here for more than twenty-seven years.

We eventually learn that Elena's staff meal favorite is paella, a dish also on the menu today. Nodding in the direction of Mikel Inda, the restaurant's second head chef, she tells us that this is the first time he has made the dish for family meal. Which may explain his unparalleled intensity at the stove. About an hour later, as the finished paella steams to tender under a kitchen towel, Juan Mari carefully carries the massive pot to a side table. He arranges a festive bowl of fresh fruit—whole oranges, bananas, and a pineapple—as the front of the house gathers around the table to enjoy their meal.

After plates are cleared, the second wave of diners, this time the cooks, takes their seats along with Juan Mari and Elena. They settle in around the marble slab beside a sea of caricatures—all of guests or employees past—scrawled onto the white tile walls surrounding them. Everyone pours long pulls of local red wine into squat glasses. Then Juan Mari lifts a forkful of paella, chews slowly, and looks over at Mikel. A wide grin raises the rims of his red Lucite glasses as he shoots him a thumbs-up and shouts, "It's good! It's good!" Mikel exhales in relief. He's passed the Arzak test: going back into history and honoring a classic, so he can move forward and create the future.

A Conversation with Chef ELENA ARZAK

...sophy?

...hing homemade.

...staff meal?

...nnot work well. ...eople here that ...em to learn to ...well. To us, it's

From the meal served today it's obvious that the staff meal is a showcase of regional Basque dishes. What are some staff favorites?

Fish soup with potato in the summer. Steaks with breadcrumbs and eggs. And lentils; I like lentils very much.

Anything that would not be served at the family meal lest it offend local Basque preferences?

It's true that Basques don't like coriander. Why? I have no idea. We like ginger, but not raw, just the powder. We also don't like coconut very much, we always mix it with something else, normally something white.

Growing up near the restaurant, with so many family members working here, did you always know you wanted to become a chef?

Not really. When I was eleven or twelve years old, I worked here over my summer break. We live very close so my sister, Marta, and I used to come for two hours and leave. We were taught one thing every visit. It was then that I noticed how much I liked it.

And why did you decide to stay?

I was lucky because since I was a child, my father introduced me to new ideas and let me make a lot of things. I remember when I was fourteen, I was allowed to help make the dishes for the dining room. For me that was the best! I credit my becoming a chef with his generosity of heart. I wouldn't be here without it.

Your family has owned and operated Arzak since the nineteenth century, and you now head the kitchen alongside your father. We know you have young children of your own— do you hope they follow in your footsteps?

The only thing I want is that they really learn to cook for themselves. In fifteen years I want them to know how to roast a chicken, cook a fish, simmer a broth, and make a soup.

What's your best advice to a young cook?

Sometimes you need to risk. If you don't always risk a little bit, you will always go on the same route. Also, listen to the people. For us this is very important. The people help you to find really what you want.

DUCK and SHRIMP PAELLA

Like the roiling gray waters of the nearby Bay of Biscay, the contents of Arzak's paella ebb and flow: some days with leftover proteins and seasonal vegetables, others, with the moods of the cooks. "This dish has as many variations as there are houses in this country," says Juan Mari. So when discussing the ingredient list, the Arzaks gave us plenty of substitutions: No duck? Use chicken or rabbit instead. No shrimp? Swap monkfish or snails in their place. Although when it comes to paella's VIP ingredient, the rice, it has to be Bomba, Spain's indigenous short-grain variety that absorbs up to three times its weight in liquid without turning to mush. Fortunately, Bomba rice is readily available online, but Arborio rice, normally used for risotto, is an apt substitute.

Serves 6

¼ CUP (59 MILLILITERS) SPANISH OLIVE OIL

1 POUND (454 GRAMS) SKIN-ON DUCK BREASTS, CUT INTO ½-INCH (1.25 CENTIMETER) CUBES

4 OUNCES (113 GRAMS) GREEN BEANS, TRIMMED AND DICED

4 LARGE ARTICHOKE HEARTS IN WATER, DRAINED AND COARSELY CHOPPED

1 MEDIUM TOMATO, COARSELY CHOPPED

1 LARGE GARLIC CLOVE, THINLY SLICED

¼ CUP (60 GRAMS) COARSELY CHOPPED ROASTED RED PEPPERS, PLUS SEVERAL THICK SLICES FOR SERVING (OPTIONAL)

2 QUARTS (1.9 LITERS) CHICKEN STOCK, PLUS MORE AS NEEDED

2½ CUPS (540 GRAMS) BOMBA RICE (SEE RECIPE HEADER)

PINCH SAFFRON THREADS

2 TEASPOONS (12 GRAMS) KOSHER SALT

1 POUND (454 GRAMS) LARGE SHRIMP, PEELED

½ CUP (72 GRAMS) FROZEN PEAS

LEMON WEDGES, FOR SERVING (OPTIONAL)

In a 12-inch (31 centimeter) paella pan or high-sided skillet (see Note), heat the oil over medium-high until smoking. Add the duck and fry until the pieces are browned, about 6 minutes.

Add the beans, artichokes, tomato, garlic, and the chopped roasted pepper—this is considered the sofrito—and cook until the vegetables are tender, about 3 minutes. Add the water (it should fill the pan with 2 inches/5 centimeters liquid) and allow to boil for 30 minutes, creating a flavorful stock. There should be at least 1 inch (2.5 centimeters) of liquid left in the skillet after boiling; if it has over-reduced, add enough liquid to accommodate the loss.

Stir in the rice, saffron, and salt. Bring to a boil, then reduce the heat to maintain a brisk simmer. Do not stir the rice again! This is important for the development of the socarrat, the caramelized crust at the bottom of the pan. Simmer the rice uncovered for 20 minutes, or until the liquid is absorbed and the rice is tender but not mushy. If it is still undercooked after 20 minutes, add more water (but do not stir!) and continue to cook until tender. Scatter the shrimp and peas on top of the rice and cover the entire skillet with a lid. Steam the shrimp for 5 minutes. During this time, monitor the heat; it should be high enough to develop the socarrat but not so high as to allow it to burn. When you can smell a pervasive toastiness, your socarrat is forming. Use a fork to poke into the rice at the bottom of the pan; if it meets with slight nubby resistance, your flavorful crust has been formed. After 5 minutes flip the shrimp over, cover the skillet with a kitchen towel, and remove the paella from the heat. Allow the paella to rest for 5 to 10 minutes; this allows for any excess liquid to be absorbed, and for the shrimp to cook completely.

Arzak serves their paella as is, without garnish, but tableside presentation is improved with artfully placed strips of roasted red pepper and lemon wedges. Serve immediately. Traditionally paella is eaten by guests directly out of the pan, from the periphery to the center. If guests do serve themselves, make sure they scrape up plenty of crusty-sweet socarrat at the bottom.

Note

Perhaps our greatest discovery in Spain was that owning a paella pan was not entirely necessary to make paella. Yes, the wide, shallow, thin-walled vessel helps develop more of the prized socarrat (SOH-kah-raht), the caramelized crust that forms on the bottom of the pan, but the Arzaks used a high-sided skillet (sometimes referred to as a rondeau) to make a massive batch of paella for the staff. The final product was no less paella, and no less flavorful, despite not being cooked in its namesake pan. Plus, there is no need to jockey the extra-wide paella pan awkwardly between burners. If you do need to serve more than six people, use two 12-inch skillets and two burners, not a higher, larger pot, as this will maintain the proper guests-to-socarrat ratio.

PIQUILLO PEPPER CONFIT

"When people come to San Sebastián," says Elena Arzak, "they come not only for the many great restaurants but for the pinxtos." The Basque equivalent of tapas, pinxtos (pronounced PIN-thos) are small, savory bites of food typically skewered by a wooden toothpick (also known as a pinxto) and served alongside glasses of wine in the local bars. Piquillos, the bright red peppers native to northern Spain, are incorporated into many of these exceptional bar snacks, adding a pop of color and mild spiciness. At Arzak they are topped with a Beautiful Lace Fried Egg (page 50) and eaten with a toasted wedge of housemade baguette: a near-perfect example of the profound simplicity central to Basque cuisine.

Serves 6

18 ROASTED RED PIQUILLO PEPPERS (ABOUT 1½ POUNDS/680 GRAMS), PRESERVED IN WATER, WHOLE AND UNDRAINED (SEE NOTE)

1½ CUPS (355 MILLILITERS) SPANISH OLIVE OIL, PLUS MORE AS NEEDED

5 GARLIC CLOVES, PEELED

KOSHER SALT AND FRESHLY GROUND BLACK PEPPER TO TASTE

Preheat the oven to 325°F (163°C).

Drain the peppers, reserving the liquid. Cut each pepper in half lengthwise, discarding seeds. Layer the peppers in a medium skillet and cover with the oil. The peppers should be immersed; if not, add just enough oil to cover. Add the garlic and bring the oil to a boil over high heat. Lower the heat and maintain a gentle simmer for 40 minutes, turning the peppers midway through the cooking process.

Remove the peppers and garlic from the oil and place in an ovenproof dish. (The oil can either be discarded or reused in the Beautiful Lace Fried Eggs, page 50.) Pour ¼ cup (59 milliliters) of the reserved pepper liquid over the peppers and roast, uncovered, for 20 minutes, or until very little liquid remains. Remove from the oven and season with salt and pepper. Serve immediately, directly from the baking dish.

These peppers taste equally good cold or at room temperature. Extra peppers (stored in the refrigerator for up to a week) play well with just about any sandwich.

Note

You can source Spanish piquillos from Spanish specialty stores or online, but they are expensive; we successfully substituted store-bought roasted red peppers. They held their shape nicely, although they lacked any smoke or heat.

BEAUTIFUL LACE FRIED EGGS

There is perhaps no easier way than this shallow-fry method to perfectly cook an oozy egg in about half the time. Plus, there is none of the worry of the eggs sticking to the pan. Enough oil is used here to keep glue unstuck! The eggs emerge from the oil molten in the center yet browned and crispy on the edges, and taste amazing even at room temperature. Using very fresh eggs here is important. Older eggs with their more viscous whites have a tendency to make the oil spit. Use caution.

Serves 6

1½ CUPS (355 MILLILITERS) SPANISH OLIVE OIL, PLUS MORE AS NEEDED (SEE NOTE)

1 GARLIC CLOVE, PEELED

6 LARGE EGGS

KOSHER SALT AND FRESHLY GROUND BLACK PEPPER TO TASTE

PIQUILLO PEPPER CONFIT (PAGE 48), FOR SERVING

TOASTED BREAD SLICES FOR SERVING

In a medium skillet heat the oil and garlic over medium heat. There should be at least ½ inch (1.3 centimeters) oil in the bottom of the pan; if there is less, add more oil. When the oil is rippling in the bottom of the pan but not smoking, remove the garlic and very carefully crack 2 eggs directly into the oil. Immediately season the eggs with salt and pepper. Fry for about 90 seconds, basting the eggs with oil until the whites on the outside set and become laced with light brown. Use caution (and wear an apron) as the oil does splatter. Using a flat metal spatula, carefully flip the eggs in the oil. Fry for 1 minute more or until the yolks are set to your liking. Remove from the oil with a slotted spoon, and transfer to paper towels to drain. Repeat the frying process with the remaining eggs, adding more oil as necessary.

Transfer the cooked eggs to a platter, season with salt and pepper, and serve with piquillo peppers and bread; guests can make their own open-faced sandwiches at the table.

Note

If you're making the piquillo pepper recipe (page 48), the olive oil used to confit the peppers can be repurposed for these eggs. It will, however, impart a hint of the pepper's smokiness and mineral tang.

51

Arzak

ONCE UPON A TIME THERE WAS A MAN, A MAN WHO WAS BORN IN A KITCHEN. SINCE HIS FATHER HAD SERVED ONCE VINEGARY WINE AT HIS TAVERN... HE GOT NICKNAMED AS "THE SQUADREL OF "ALTO DE VINAGRES" (Vinegar's Hights).

HE ALWAYS HAD HIS WAY, HE ALWAYS DID AS HE PLEASED, AND THAT'S WHY THIS PLACE IS WHAT IT IS NOW... AND THAT IS WHY COOKERY IN SPAIN IS WHAT IT IS NOW... AND HERE WE ARE, EYE-WITNESSING IT ALL IN 1st PERSON!

AU PIED DE COCHON

MONTREAL, CANADA

RASPBERRY VIRGIN MOJITOS

AU PIED POUTINE

MUSHROOM, ONION, AND
SCALLION PIZZA

REDHEAD TEMPURA MAKI ROLLS

CREAMY SMOKED STURGEON
PAPPARDELLE

About an hour before midnight, the quiet stone streets of Montreal's historic city center are frigid and moonlit. It is a night seemingly built for simple pleasures: a cracked leather chair, a dog-eared Dickens novel, perhaps a small dram of whiskey, neat. Then we cross the threshold of Au Pied de Cochon (literally meaning "of the pig's foot") into a culinary bacchanalia of epic proportions. As our coats come off, a blast of heat and noise from the jubilant—nearing possessed—crowd hits us. Packed tight in the small dining room bordered by an open kitchen, customers ogle their neighbor's fatty, oozing, crackling pork dishes, then brazenly introduce themselves in hopes of getting a taste or, at the very least, a closer look. They are here, as we are, to be trampled by chef and owner Martin Picard's personal breed of the Four Horsemen: foie gras, fat, pork, and booze. And we wonder: Does a staff that cooks with such gastronomic excess eat with a reckless abandon, too? We had our theories.

The cooks in the Au Pied de Cochon kitchen are all young men with a certain woodsman swagger about them. As a long, fierce service draws to a close, they simultaneously prepare the last of the ticketed orders, flirt with customers passing by the open kitchen, and pull together the staff meal. It is all happening at lightning speed, and we're not entirely sure what the staff will be eating and what is destined for the dining room. The inclusion of pork is no barometer. Be it bacon, trotters, snout, or lard, it seems to be going into absolutely everything. Ditto butter, cream, and cheese. It is in fact looking like excess is the rule for both paying customers and employees. A trend that successfully negates our first theory: that cooks who serve more than ten different foie gras dishes and fry in duck fat all day long would somehow prefer salad at the end of their shift.

As a whole roasted pig's head—skewered with a knife, holding a whole three-pound lobster in its mouth, and gilded here and there with edible gold—makes its way to a gleeful-looking couple, line cook Vincent Dion Lavallée tips his neon orange hunting cap and says: "You need to meet the head of this circus show now." We assume it is Martin Picard, the wild-haired owner whose own eccentricities (among them a devotion to foie gras and a passion for hunting, as seen on his Food Network Canada show, *The Wild Chef*) set the pace for the restaurant. But as we walk toward the wood-fired oven, the sea of testosterone parts to reveal Emily Homsy. Petite and chestnut-haired with deep black eyes, she is the lone woman on the kitchen staff, and her job as sous chef is twofold: to keep the boys fed and—sometimes—in line.

With a wooden peel as long as she is tall, she begins to shove just-made pizzas to the back of the oven, a relic from the pizza parlor that used to inhabit the space. "On Saturdays we have pizza," she says. "We don't normally order that many things for the family meal, so you have to use your imagination." You also have to be cunning. We notice that in addition to mozzarella and a simple tomato sauce (the restaurant jars and sells its own, in addition to pickles, canned stock, and its iconic "duck in a can"), she has managed to do a little log-rolling to coax bacon, mushrooms, onions, and scallions from the line cooks' precious mise en place, all of it to top the pies.

As swollen, spent, and smiling customers finally start to depart, the family meal appears on the kitchen's counter. It is now close to one in the morning, but plates fill with the kind of food begging to be eaten in front of the hockey play-offs—maki rolls filled with shredded veal and deep-fried into burrito-sized tempura; cream-soaked pasta studded with fat slices of smoked sturgeon; doughy pizzas with char and chew. A lingering female diner eyes the heaping bowls of crispy salted fries topped with cheese curds and pork gravy—known collectively as poutine—and orders one. "So sorry, staff only," says a nearby cook. She stomps away in a dramatic, somewhat inebriated huff. Unfazed, he spins back to the now-seated staff with a loud "Dig in!" They do just that. And we should note, it is indeed with reckless abandon.

PINGOUIN VS COCHON.

STAFF MEAL BATTLE: "LA SALLE" IS WINNING. (OF COURSE)

A Conversation with MARTIN PICARD
Chef and Owner

Here's a hypothetical: A cook just earned his first executive chef position. What's your number one piece of advice to him or her on serving the staff a meal?

Don't throw anything away.

Most staff meals we've covered are before service; why do you host yours afterward?

Because it is our way of doing things.

Okay, so then, what keeps the staff fueled until the end of the night?

Red Bull, stress, and coffee.

It's clear Au Pied de Cochon reveres everything porcine. What do you consider the most under-appreciated part of the pig?

The tongue, head, and tail.

The most overrated?

Pork tenderloin.

Besides a great staff meal, what is another way you motivate your staff?

Alcohol.

Anything odd that has made it to the staff meal table?

Cod heads.

Greatest kitchen gadget that every person should own?

Scissor saw.

One cookbook that every home cook should thumb through?

Larousse Gastronomique.

A menu leftover that always appears on the staff meal table?

Au Pied de Cochon mashed potatoes [potatoes mashed with butter, garlic-infused cream, and cheese curds].

If you had to pick a soundtrack for your staff meal, what songs would it include?

Anything and everything from Les Cowboys Fringants.

Fill in the blank. Our staff meal is

_____.

Much needed.

RASPBERRY VIRGIN MOJITOS

This drink defines the Au Pied de Cochon family meal experience: surprising, unexpected, celebratory, and just shy of overly extravagant. Big batches of these faux cocktails are mixed and served out of repurposed wine carafes. Not too cloying nor too minty—the plague of many a bad mojito—this drink is balanced and thirst quenching. A shot or two of good rum would be its only improvement.

When raspberries are out of season, Au Pied replaces them with ½ cup (80 grams) of diced cucumber. It's unusual but divine.

Serves 2

¼ CUP (50 GRAMS) GRANULATED SUGAR

20 LARGE MINT LEAVES, PLUS MORE FOR GARNISH

¼ CUP (59 MILLILITERS) FRESHLY SQUEEZED LIME JUICE (ABOUT 2 LIMES)

½ CUP (100 GRAMS) FRESH RASPBERRIES (SUBSTITUTE ½ CUP/80 GRAMS DICED CUCUMBER)

HANDFUL OF CRUSHED ICE, PLUS MORE AS NEEDED

1 CUP (237 MILLILITERS) CLUB SODA OR SPARKLING MINERAL WATER

Bring ¼ cup (59 milliliters) water and the sugar to a boil and whisk until the sugar dissolves. Remove from the heat and cool the simple syrup to room temperature. In a large cocktail shaker, muddle the mint, lime juice, and ¼ cup (59 milliliters) of the syrup with a wooden dowel or wooden spoon until bruised and fragrant, about 30 seconds. Add the raspberries and ice (if you would prefer this to be a cocktail, now is the time to add the light rum to taste). Cover the shaker and shake vigorously for 30 seconds, or until the shaker turns icy cold and the liquid a deep pink. Pour without straining into glasses, top off each with equal amounts of club soda, stir briefly, and add crushed ice to each glass. Garnish with extra mint. Serve immediately.

AU PIED POUTINE

Poutine is simultaneously one of the world's best—and most terri-fying—combinations: fries topped with cheese curds (see Note) and smothered in meat gravy. A mid-century Canadian diner invention, it was and continues to be a cheap and filling snack for young rev-elers wanting a refuel between drinking sessions. Au Pied de Cochon adorns customers' poutine with a slab of foie gras. For the staff, however, it's the humble pig's feet that top the crisp fries. To prepare them, the feet are first covered in caul fat and then braised in the restaurant's wood-burning oven until falling-off-the-hoof tender. Here we substituted smoked ham hock, but diced spiral ham or slab bacon could play the stand-in.

Serves 6

AU PIED SAUCE

1 CUP (8 OUNCES/170GRAMS) SMOKED HAM HOCK MEAT, CUT FROM THE BONE

2 TABLESPOONS (28 GRAMS) UNSALTED BUTTER

½ MEDIUM YELLOW ONION, THINLY SLICED

1 MEDIUM TOMATO, QUARTERED AND DICED

2½ CUPS (592 MILLILITERS) PORK OR BEEF STOCK

1 CUP (237 MILLILITERS) HEAVY WHIPPING CREAM

1 TABLESPOON (15 MILLILITERS) DIJON MUSTARD

1 TABLESPOON (15 MILLILITERS) RED WINE VINEGAR

1 TABLESPOON (15 MILLILITERS) CANOLA OIL

KOSHER SALT AND FRESHLY GROUND BLACK PEPPER TO TASTE

POUTINE

2 QUARTS (851 GRAMS) BEEF FAT FRIES (SEE RECIPE, PAGE 180)

6 OUNCES (170 GRAMS) CHEESE CURDS, COARSELY CHOPPED (SEE NOTE)

For the sauce: In a food processor pulse the meat until very finely chopped; set aside. Melt the butter in a sauté pan over medium-high heat. When frothy, add the onion and sauté until golden, about 4 minutes. Add the meat and fry until crispy, about 2 min-utes. Add the tomato, stock, and cream. Simmer to reduce by two-thirds, or until sauce coats the back of a wooden spoon, about 25 minutes.

Meanwhile, combine the Dijon and vinegar. In a slow stream whisk in the oil; set aside. When the sauce has been reduced, whisk in 2 tablespoons (30 milliliters) of the Dijon vinaigrette, adding more to taste if desired. Season with salt and pepper, and keep hot but do not over-reduce. If the sauce does get too thick, thin with extra stock or cream.

For the poutine: Put half of the hot-from-the-fryer French fries into a large bowl. Scatter half the cheese curds on top. Add the remain-ing fries and sprinkle with remaining cheese curds. Pour the hot sauce over everything (the heat will soften the cheese curds into pillowy blobs). Eat immediately with forks. Poutine is a communal dish, so encourage guests to eat straight from the same bowl.

Note

Cheese curds are soft Cheddar nuggets pulled out early from the ched-daring process—their brethren go on to being blocked and aged into wheels. They are slightly salty, fairly flavorless, and when fresh have a pleasant squeak between the teeth. Their audible quality is an accurate indicator of freshness: the fresher the curd, the louder the squeak. Cheese curds (plain or, more popular still, beer-battered and fried) are readily avail-able in cities and towns where cheese making is prevalent. If you cannot find cheese curds in your area, substitute coarsely chopped Cheddar, the milder, the better, or Greek halloumi. Halloumi doesn't melt that well but does have that magnificent squeak.

MUSHROOM, ONION, and SCALLION PIZZA

Sous chef Emily Homsy uses the restaurant's blazing hot wood-burning oven to produce pizza with both crispy wood-scented crusts and beautifully bubbling tops. While this is hard to achieve in most home ovens with thermostats that max out at around 550°F (288°C)—leaving the crust baked but not crispy, or the crust crispy and the topping burnt—the effects can be replicated to some degree with a pizza stone and a pizza peel. Both are inexpensive and readily available online and in stores. If you do not have either and need these pizzas stat, flip a large cast-iron skillet upside down in the oven, and dust the flip side of a sheet tray with cornmeal. The skillet becomes your pizza stone, the sheet tray your peel. (See the recipe for further instruction.) Be sure to keep your leftover dough: Emily turns hers into Beaver Tails (see Note), a funny name for an excellent fried dessert.

Makes six 8-inch/23 centimeter pizzas

DOUGH

2½ TEASPOONS (10 GRAMS) INSTANT YEAST

2 TEASPOONS (8 GRAMS) GRANULATED SUGAR

5 CUPS (625 GRAMS) ALL-PURPOSE FLOUR, PLUS MORE FOR DUSTING

1 TABLESPOON (20 GRAMS) FINE SEA SALT

1 TABLESPOON (15 MILLILITERS) OLIVE OIL, PLUS MORE FOR PROOFING

SAUCE

ONE (28 OUNCE/794 GRAM) CAN WHOLE PEELED TOMATOES, DRAINED

3 GARLIC CLOVES, MINCED

1 TABLESPOON (15 MILLILITERS) OLIVE OIL

4 THYME SPRIGS

4 LARGE BASIL LEAVES

1 TEASPOON (6 GRAMS) KOSHER SALT

PIZZA

1 MEDIUM YELLOW ONION, THINLY SLICED

12 OUNCES (341 GRAMS) ASSORTED MUSH-ROOMS, THINLY SLICED

1¼ POUNDS (567 GRAMS) MOZZARELLA, SLICED, GRATED, OR TORN

2 BUNCHES SCALLIONS (GREEN AND WHITE PARTS), CUT INTO 2-INCH (5 CEN-TIMETER) PIECES

KOSHER SALT AND FRESHLY GROUND BLACK PEPPER TO TASTE

OLIVE OIL AS NEEDED

½ CUP (70 GRAMS) COARSE CORNMEAL

For the dough: Stir together the yeast and sugar with 2 cups (473 milliliters) warm water. Let stand at room temperature until tiny bubbles form at the surface, about 2 minutes. (If bubbles do not emerge, your yeast is dead and will need to be replaced.)

Combine the flour and salt in the bowl of a mixer fitted with a dough hook. Add the yeast mixture and the oil and knead on low speed for 5 minutes. Lightly flour the work surface. Remove the slightly sticky dough from the bowl and knead by hand until smooth and elastic, about 5 minutes. Brush the bowl with oil, return dough to it, and cover with plastic wrap. Set the bowl aside at room temperature until the dough has doubled in size, about 1 hour.

Divide the dough into six equal–sized balls, arrange on a parchment paper–lined sheet tray, and cover with plastic wrap. Allow the balls to double in size, about 1 hour. The dough can now be stored overnight, wrapped in plastic wrap, in the refrigerator. Allow the dough to sit at room temperature for at least 1 hour before preceeding with the recipe.

For the sauce: Using a food mill, blender, or food processor, pulse the tomatoes for about 30 seconds to form a chunky sauce. Transfer to a jar and add the garlic, olive oil, thyme, basil, and salt. Cover tightly. Shake—hard!—for 30 seconds. That's it. Easiest tomato sauce you'll ever make.

For the pizza: Place a pizza stone or upside-down 12-inch (31 centimeter) cast-iron skillet on the oven's middle rack. Preheat the oven to as high as it will register (most top out at 550°F/288°C). Dust the pizza peel (or the back of sheet tray) generously with cornmeal.

Gently shape one dough ball by hand into an 8-inch (20 centimeter) pizza round directly on the pizza peel. Spread a thin layer of sauce all the way to the edges. Top the pizza with onions, mushrooms, cheese, and scallions. Finish by seasoning with salt and pepper, then drizzle lightly with olive oil. Transfer the pizza onto the stone from the peel or sheet tray using a flick of the wrist; it should slide off easily if you used enough cornmeal.

Bake for 12 to 14 minutes, until the crust on the sides and bottom is just slightly charred and the cheese is beginning to bubble and brown. Remove from the oven using the peel (if using a skillet and a sheet tray, remove the skillet using a kitchen towel and tip off the pizza), then transfer to a cutting board. Cut into rustic slices and serve piping hot, although it's also tasty cold the next day. Repeat the pizza-making process with the remaining dough.

Note

No dough gets trashed at Au Pied de Cochon. Any less-than-perfect pizza-tossing attempts get turned into "beaver tails," fried dough sprinkled with sugar. To make them at home, heat 2 quarts (1.9 liters) canola oil in a heavy-bottomed pot to 350°F (177°C). Flatten any leftover dough balls into large, thin, and oblong "tails" about the width and length of your hand and the thickness of your pinky, and carefully fry them—individually—in the hot oil until puffy, golden on the outside, and cooked in the middle, about 10 minutes. Sprinkle with maple sugar to taste, and serve immediately.

REDHEAD TEMPURA MAKI ROLLS

This state-fair interpretation of the Japanese sushi roll—braised veal sprinkled with oreilles de crises (the Canadian version of pork rinds made with pork jowl), rolled with rice, dipped in a buttery batter, and deep-fried—is the loopy invention of sous chef Emily Homsy. The lightbulb went off when she was asked to use up extra nori from the restaurant's steak tartare dish, and she named it after the cook who was working the fryer that night. "We always call him 'Le Roux' which means 'the redhead' in French," she said. We're told he's a good sport about his nickname and resulting namesake dish. As well he should be: fresh from the fryer they are unlike anything you've ever had, and just like everything you want.

Makes 6 large rolls

ROLLS

2 CUPS (420 GRAMS) SUSHI RICE

**2 TABLESPOONS (30 MILLILITERS) SEASONED
RICE VINEGAR**

6 SHEETS NORI (DRIED SEAWEED)

**1 POUND (454 GRAMS/ABOUT 1½ CUPS)
PULLED VEAL, BEEF, OR PORK (SEE NOTE)**

**½ CUP (16 GRAMS) CRUSHED OREILLES DE
CRISES OR PORK RINDS**

**1 SMALL CUCUMBER, PEELED AND THINLY
SLICED**

KOSHER SALT TO TASTE

TEMPURA BATTER

3 CUPS (375 GRAMS) TEMPURA FLOUR

**2 CUPS (473 MILLILITERS) CLUB SODA, AT
ROOM TEMPERATURE**

**4 OUNCES (1 STICK/113 GRAMS) UNSALTED
BUTTER, MELTED**

¼ TEASPOON (1.5 GRAMS) PAPRIKA

1 TEASPOON (6 GRAMS) FINE SEA SALT

**3 LARGE EGG WHITES, WHIPPED TO SOFT
PEAKS**

TO SERVE

1 QUART (946 MILLILITERS) SAFFLOWER OIL

KOSHER SALT TO TASTE

**SOY SAUCE OR PONZU SAUCE (PAGE 283),
FOR DIPPING**

For the rolls: Cook the sushi rice according to package instructions. Sprinkle with the vinegar and spread out on a sheet tray to cool slightly.

Lay out one nori sheet, shiny-side up, on a bamboo sushi rolling mat. With wet fingers, flatten ¼ cup (60 grams) of cooked rice into the center of the sheet, leaving a 1-inch (2.5 centimeter) border on all sides. On top of the rice, flatten about ¼ cup (60 grams) of the meat perpendicularly across the center of the rice, then sprinkle the meat with pork rinds and top with a layer of cucumber slices. Season with salt. Fold the nori in at the two opposing sides, then roll it from the bottom, using the mat to assist you, just as you would a burrito. Wet the top end of the nori with water, then press the two sides together to seal the roll. Repeat with the remaining nori sheets and ingredients to make 6 rolls total. Set aside, seam side down.

For the batter and to serve: Heat the oil in a wide, heavy-bottomed deep pot to 350°F (177°C). Line a baking sheet with paper towels. In a wide metal bowl big enough to fit the rolls lengthwise, whisk together the flour and soda water until there are no dry spots. Whisk in the melted butter, paprika, and salt. Gently fold in the egg whites. The batter will be light and airy but should also thickly coat a wooden spoon. (This batter must be used immediately.) Using a pair of tongs, dip one roll in the tempura batter to fully immerse. Lift out gently, allowing excess batter to drip back into the bowl, and carefully place the roll in the hot oil. Deep-fry until golden, light, and crispy, 3 to 5 minutes. Remove with a second pair of tongs, draining excess oil over the fryer, then drain on the paper towels. Season with salt while hot.

Repeat the process with the remaining rolls, coating and frying each one individually, to avoid crowding. Slice each roll into thick "sushi-style" pieces, layer onto a serving platter, and serve with soy sauce or ponzu sauce for dipping.

NOTE

While any pulled meat would work in this recipe, we used leftover Mr. Pickles's Pulled Pork (page 238) tossed with BBQ sauce (page 240). The sweet hit of the sauce was a welcome addition to the ingredient mash-up inside the rolls. The braised veal (page 106) from Craigie on Main would work well too.

CREAMY SMOKED STURGEON PAPPARDELLE

We've learned that if a restaurant invests the manpower to make fresh pasta from scratch, not a single strand goes to waste. So when sous chef Emily Homsy found herself with leftover pasta sheets at the end of the night, she cut them into extra-wide noodles called pappardelle. Having leftover slices of pricey smoked sturgeon on hand as well, she married the two with a simple thyme-scented cream sauce: a dish whose sophistication on the plate hides its simplicity on the stove.

Serves 6

2 TABLESPOONS (28 GRAMS) UNSALTED BUTTER

1 SHALLOT, FINELY CHOPPED

½ CUP (118 MILLILITERS) DRY WHITE WINE

2 THYME SPRIGS

1 QUART (946 MILLILITERS) HEAVY WHIPPING CREAM

1 CUP (95 GRAMS) FINELY GRATED PARMIGIANO-REGGIANO

FRESHLY SQUEEZED LEMON JUICE TO TASTE

KOSHER SALT AND FRESHLY GROUND BLACK PEPPER TO TASTE

1 POUND (454 GRAMS) FRESH PAPPARDELLE (SEE PAGE 140 FOR PASTA RECIPE)

8 OUNCES (227 GRAMS) SMOKED STURGEON, SLICED (OR SUBSTITUTE SMOKED MACKEREL OR TROUT)

2 TABLESPOONS (10 GRAMS) MINCED PARSLEY OR CHIVES

Heat a medium sauté pan over medium-high heat. Melt the butter and, when frothy, add the shallots and cook until translucent, about 2 minutes. Add the white wine and reduce until no liquid remains. Add the thyme and cream. After bringing to a boil, lower the heat and briskly simmer until the liquid has reduced by half, about 20 minutes. Stir occasionally (especially towards the end) to avoid scorching.

Add the cheese and stir until melted. Season with a squeeze of lemon, salt, and pepper. Keep warm but do not over-reduce or the cream will break. (This is when the oil and the solids separate, leaving behind a grainy yet greasy sauce.)

Bring a large pot of salted water to a boil. Warm your guests' pasta bowls in a low oven—this dish congeals quickly on cold plates and tastes best warm. Boil the fresh pasta to al dente (about 4 minutes), then drain. Portion the pasta into the warm bowls and layer a few slices of sturgeon on top; spoon the sauce over everything, and sprinkle with parsley. Serve immediately.

In the Kitchen, we always eat with our hands! Emily.

THE BRISTOL

CHICAGO, ILLINOIS

DEEP-FRIED CHICKEN FEET

BEEF HEART AND WATERMELON SALAD

PICKLED GREEN GRAPES

BREAD AND BUTTER JALAPEÑOS

STEAK AND VEAL KIDNEY PIE

CHARRED CABBAGE WITH MORNAY SAUCE

ffal. Mention it casually to a dining companion—a term that rhymes with *awful*—and a shudder may follow. Many modern diners consider fried liver, deviled kidneys, and other entrails a tough sell. Despite this, a handful of young, hip chefs are working to create a legion of "fifth quarter" converts (the other four quarters of the beast comprising the routine roasts and ribs) by transforming what is commonly considered scrap into coveted menu items. Since opening in 2009, The Bristol, a neighborhood eatery in Chicago's up-and-coming Bucktown district, has been playing a winning hand in this game. Their eclectic, ever-changing, wall-spanning blackboard menu highlights daily off-cut options such as stewed tripe and seared beef heart. Not surprisingly, offal holds center court on the family meal table too—as it most certainly does the afternoon of our visit.

Admittedly, offal is an ill-omened class of ingredients: the German translation, *abfall*, literally means "garbage," and in Britain the origin of the word derives from the term *falloff*, as in the pieces that tumble out of the carcass during the butchering process, including the liver, kidneys, heart, stomachs, and intestines. Today "organ meat," as it is sometimes called in the United States, has expanded beyond entrails to include trotters, tails, and snouts: inexpensive proteins that were staples a few decades ago in many American homes.

The Bristol challenges these modern cynics by adhering to a simple offal philosophy: they cook it because they love it and believe those courageous enough to try it

will love it, too. It certainly doesn't hurt that offal is cheap. On their way out of town, farmers depleted of their choicest cuts, thick steaks, and even thicker Midwestern chops, literally come knocking at The Bristol's back door with hearts, livers, and stomachs in hand. In this last-ditch effort to empty their trucks, they sell their wares for a song. Chef and owner Chris Pandel, a black-bearded self-proclaimed "fat, hairy chef," is quick to point out that while offal is inexpensive, it should still have integrity. "I'm not going to go to the local crappy grocery store to buy veal kidneys from them," Chris warns. "God knows where they came from!" Chris purchased the beef hearts for the evening's family-meal menu from a local farmer who stopped by the restaurant that morning. The dark burgundy orbs (which can weigh up to eight pounds, depending on the size of the animal) were covered in a lacy shift of fat and veins and, after being trimmed and grilled for just a moment, play the lead role in a salad brightened with watermelon and pickled grapes.

Not one to let anything go to waste,

Chris has also added a gargantuan pie of savory steak and kidneys to the staff meal menu. He explains that it makes good use of the seasonal root vegetables on hand as well as the restaurant's glut of kidneys, a by-product of the many animals they butcher in-house. "If we're not going to use the kidneys on the menu," he says, "they absolutely go into the family meal."

In The Bristol kitchen, there are no titles, no set duties, and somehow, no egos. Chris's guiding manifesto for his young and energetic staff in this laissez-faire environment is simple: "Let's have fun and let's talk about food. Let's continually try to make things better." Not surprisingly, this has earned The Bristol the high honor of being the post-service hangout for cooks around the city. In fact, the night before our visit, chef Grant Achatz of Chicago's avant-garde institution Alinea was dining in the corner. His presence at The Bristol pays out on the restaurant's gamble with guts and gore, and confirms that what some once considered "garbage" has now become the toast of the town.

A Conversation with Chef and Owner CHRIS PANDEL

If you had only one word to describe family meal, what would it be?

Sustenance. Most of the servers either walk or take the bus to work, so they deserve a nice hot meal when they get here. And my guys in the kitchen work twelve, fourteen hours a day. By the time service starts, they've been here for at least six hours, so the shift after that is heavy. A little meal goes a long way.

With both a growing staff and a growing family to feed daily, what's your advice for people who say they don't have time to cook?

My wife and I are expecting a baby soon, so we're trying to figure that out ourselves and decided it's got to be a group activity, from the shopping to the cooking. When we do everything together, we can bulk up our freezer and refrigerator for the week and call it a day.

Have any of your family recipes made it onto the family meal menu?

My grandma's lazy pierogi and her sour cream cukes.

Why serve offal at the staff meal?

It's practically free! Veal kidneys are about a dollar a pound. But you have to have a relationship with the people you're going to buy them from. My advice? If there's a local butcher down the block, get your off-cuts from him.

What do you consider a "starter" off-cut for those squeamish about such things?

I'd start with chicken livers. They're not overly offensive as far as flavors go. Sautéed with bacon, the flavor is masked, so you can't even tell they're there. But it's still giving you nutrients and what you need to get through the day, on the cheap.

And what do you suggest for the offal adventurous?

Heart is my favorite. I tell these guys: "Okay, you want to taste what an animal tastes like? Eat their heart." It sounds all Indiana Jones, but it's the purest muscle in the animal. It's surrounded by really clean fats and is working the entire time, so it is just a rough, tough, angry muscle. Surprisingly, it is both supple and "steak-y." For example, take chicken hearts. They have a little squeak to them, but beyond that they're really, really tasty—the best dark meat you'll eat in a chicken.

As far as references, my all-time favorite is *The Good Cook* series by Time-Life Books. I have the entire series, and there is a specific book on offal cookery that helped me through my trials.

What's one food scrap that you will never throw away?

All of them; we don't waste anything. We serve fried bones . . . mmm.

What's one ingredient that you use in your restaurant that no home cook should be without?

Patience. But if that's too corny, vinegar. Love that vinegar.

DEEP-FRIED CHICKEN FEET

Chicken feet are so plentiful in The Bristol's prep kitchen that they practically stampede. "They are used to create a base stock for our galantines en gelée," explains Chris Pandel, adding flavor as well as huge amounts of gelatin to the liquid, which allows the jellied meatloaves to hold their shape. After the stock is strained, however, the chicken feet stay behind. Now properly tenderized, a quick deep fry transforms them into the perfect game-day food: crispy, salty, and fatty with a deep chicken flavor. They are also unapologetically informal, as they require you to use your hands to eat them, and then spit out their tiny bones.

Serves 4

3 POUNDS (1.4 KILOGRAMS) CHICKEN FEET

2 MEDIUM CARROTS, QUARTERED

1 LARGE CELERY RIB, QUARTERED

1 LARGE YELLOW ONION, QUARTERED

1 BAY LEAF

1 TABLESPOON (16 GRAMS) KOSHER SALT, PLUS MORE AS NEEDED

2 QUARTS (1.9 LITERS) SAFFLOWER OIL

1 TABLESPOON (6 GRAMS) SHICHIMI TOGARASHI (JAPANESE SEVEN SPICE, SEE NOTES)

FOR SERVING

1 LIME, QUARTERED

½ CUP (120 MILLILITERS) SWEET CHILI SAUCE

Place the chicken feet, carrots, celery, onion, and bay leaf into a large pot and cover with cold water. Bring to a boil, then strain through a fine-mesh sieve. Discard the liquid and scrub the pot of any grayish scum.

Return the chicken feet and vegetables to the pot and cover with fresh water. Bring to a boil, reduce the heat to medium-low, cover, and maintain a gentle simmer; the water should maintain a constant bubbling. Simmer for 3 hours, then test doneness by giving one foot a shake: it should wobble like a rubber chicken.

When the feet are tender, strain the stock through a fine-mesh sieve and set aside the feet and stock separately to cool. Cool the stock to room temperature and freeze for later use. Once the feet are cool enough to handle, pluck out the nails with a pinch and a twist (this is optional). If you suspect your guests might recoil at the sight of whole chicken feet on their plates, chop the feet into "fries" using a heavy knife or cleaver to separate the feet into individual toes.

Arrange the feet on paper towels to dry completely. At this stage they can be refrigerated overnight, uncovered in a single layer on a sheet tray.

Preheat the oven to 200°F (93°C). Heat the oil in a heavy-bottomed pot to 375°F (191°C). Ready a splatter guard.

Using tongs, carefully place 6 to 8 chicken feet (or a handful of "fries") into the hot oil and immediately cover the pot with the splatter guard. (The chicken feet will shoot small blobs of oil into the air, so use extreme caution.) Fry the feet until the bubbling subsides, about 3 minutes. Remove the splatter guard, stir to ensure even cooking, and continue to fry until the feet are golden, slightly puffed, and super crisp, 2 to 3 minutes more. Drain the feet of excess oil on paper towels. Season the feet with salt and shichimi togarashi, if using. Arrange them on a sheet tray and place in the oven to keep warm while you fry the next batch.

Heat the oil back up to 375°F (190°C) and continue to fry the feet in batches until all are golden brown. (See Notes for controlling the temperature of the oil.) If you cut your feet into "fries," the pieces will stick together during the frying process, but will easily break apart.

Once the frying is complete, arrange all feet on a platter and garnish with lime wedges. Serve with bowls of sweet chili sauce for dipping and small plates to dispose of the bones.

Notes

Shichimi togarashi, also known as Japanese seven spice, is a blend of chiles, sesame seeds, seaweed, orange peel, and ginger. In this recipe, it adds a nuanced spice to the chicken feet, but it can be hard to come by outside Japanese specialty stores or online. A few pinches of cayenne along with a tablespoon or two of toasted sesame seeds (black, white, or both) will serve as a sufficient approximation.

Controlling the temperature of your oil while deep-frying can be frustrating, especially if using a sluggishly responsive electric stove. The simple solution is to have a clean spray bottle of cold water at the ready. If the temperature darts above the smoke point—for most oils at around 400°F (204°C)—remove the pot from the heat and spray the outside of the pot with cold mist. Aim toward the bottom to avoid any water landing into the oil; a few blasts will return the oil to its optimal temperature.

BEEF HEART and WATERMELON SALAD

Most people assume beef heart shares a level of funk and fat similar to liver, kidney, or gizzard. It decidedly does not. Full bodied yet lean, beef heart tastes—and chews—much like hanger steak. When seared and sliced thin as it is here, it could certainly be mistaken for pricier cuts of beef, but close observation would eventually reveal its telltale: the absence of any real grain to the flesh. Selling for about $2.00 a pound (if you can find a farmer to haul one to the market for you), it is a thrifty stand-in for steak, and when lightly poached and puréed, it makes an excellent protein-packed baby food.

Serves 4

1 POUND (454 GRAMS) BEEF HEART, TRIMMED INTO 3 STEAKS, EACH APPROXIMATELY 4 X 6 INCHES (10 X 15 CENTIMETERS; SEE NOTE FOR TRIMMING INSTRUCTIONS)

KOSHER SALT AND FRESHLY GROUND BLACK PEPPER TO TASTE

2 TABLESPOONS (30 MILLILITERS) CANOLA OIL

4 OUNCES (113 GRAMS) RICOTTA SALATA CHEESE (OR SUBSTITUTE FETA)

3 CUPS (450 GRAMS) CUBED WATERMELON (1-INCH/2.5 CENTIMETER CUBES)

1 CUP (214 GRAMS) WHOLE PICKLED GRAPES AND ¼ CUP OF THEIR PICKLING LIQUID, RESERVED SEPARATELY (PAGE 72)

½ BUNCH CILANTRO, LEAVES ONLY, COARSELY CHOPPED

½ CUP (70 GRAMS) PITTED KALAMATA OLIVES

¼ CUP (88 GRAMS) THINLY SLICED BREAD AND BUTTER JALAPEÑOS AND ¼ CUP (59 MILLILITERS) OF THEIR PICKLING LIQUID, RESERVED SEPARATELY (PAGE 73)

¼ CUP (59 MILLILITERS) EXTRA-VIRGIN OLIVE OIL

Generously season the heart steaks with salt and pepper. In a large cast-iron skillet, heat the oil over high heat. Once it is smoking, sear the steaks on one side until a golden brown crust has formed, about 3 minutes. Flip the steaks and sear for another 3 to 5 minutes, or until medium-rare (they should be bright red in the center, rimmed by about ¼ inch (6 millimeters) of seared meat). Remove from the pan and let rest on a cutting board for 8 minutes.

Shave the ricotta salata with a vegetable peeler into thin, delicate strips and set aside. Combine the watermelon, grapes, cilantro, olives, and jalapeños in a large bowl. In a separate bowl, whisk together the pickling liquids and olive oil.

After the heart steaks have rested, cut them into thin, long slices and arrange on a platter. Dress the watermelon salad with half the dressing, then season with salt, pepper, and additional dressing to taste. Spoon the watermelon salad over the beef heart and top with the shaved ricotta salata. Serve while the beef heart is still slightly warm.

Note

To turn a fresh or completely defrosted beef heart into steaks, first trim off any large amounts of hard, white fat and veinlike ventricles visible on the outside of the heart. Leaving some fat behind is fine, as it helps lubricate the lean meat. Split the heart open (but not in two) by cutting down one side, starting from the hole on the top. Using small, quick strokes of a sharp knife, release any internal structures holding the heart together to allow it to lie flat. Once it is butterflied, two-thirds of the heart will lie flat, and one-third will stick up from the center. Using this natural delineation, cut the heart into three "steaks," all approximately the same size. Now faced with more manageable pieces, trim off any fat and ventricles, including the slightly opaque silver skin on both sides of each steak. It helps to use the sharpest, thinnest knife you own. Continue trimming until you have uncovered the smooth, shiny, dark maroon flesh that lies underneath, at which point the heart steaks are ready for the pan.

PICKLED GREEN GRAPES

To accelerate the cure time for these unique pickles to a mere 24 hours, The Bristol calls for peeled grapes. (They use green table grapes, but any color will work as long as they are very crisp.) With no real shortcuts to quickly peel one, we can only assume this task falls to the lowest cook on the totem pole. If you find your Zen in repetitive kitchen tasks, by all means peel away, but slicing off the stem end of skin-on grapes will work just as well (though they will require a few more days in the brine). Skin on or off, once pickled, these grapes just about explode with the sweet-tart freshness of summer and make a surprising olive substitute in winter salads and on holiday cheese plates.

Yields 1 quart (946 milliliters)

1 CUP (237 MILLILITERS) APPLE CIDER VINEGAR

½ CUP (118 MILLILITERS) RICE VINEGAR

½ CUP (100 GRAMS) GRANULATED SUGAR

1 SMALL CINNAMON STICK

1½ POUNDS (680 GRAMS) SEEDLESS GREEN GRAPES

Scrub a 1 quart (946 milliliters) glass jar and its lid in hot soapy water. Rinse well and air-dry.

In a small pot combine the vinegars, sugar, cinnamon stick, and 1 cup (237 milliliters) water. Bring to a boil, lower the heat, and simmer until the sugar is dissolved, about 5 minutes. Remove from the heat and cool to room temperature.

Wash and dry the grapes, discarding any moldy or mushy suspects. Remove the stems, and using a small, sharp knife, cut a thin slice off the stem end to expose the flesh. Cram as many grapes as will fit snugly into the jar.

When the liquid is cool, ladle it over the grapes almost to the top of the jar, making sure to include the cinnamon stick. Screw on the lid, label the contents, and refrigerate for a minimum of 72 hours. The longer the grapes pickle, the better they taste (but the less crisp they become), and they can be stored in your refrigerator for up to 2 months.

BREAD AND BUTTER JALAPEÑOS

"We pickle pretty much everything we can in the summer. From chanterelles to raspberries to rhubarb, even wasabi," confirms Bristol cook Joseph Frillman. This pickled jalapeño recipe in the "bread and butter" style—as sweet as it is sour—was invented after a summer market windfall left The Bristol with more than 200 pounds of the spicy peppers. On Sundays they costar in The Bristol's "Bloody Breakfast," a handy hangover remedy that serves up pickles, cheese, and cured meats alongside a Bloody Mary and a High Life.

Yields 1 quart (946 milliliters)

16 TO 20 GREEN (ABOUT 8 OUNCES/227 GRAMS) JALAPEÑO PEPPERS

¾ CUP (177 MILLILITERS) WHITE WINE VINEGAR

½ CUP (100 GRAMS) GRANULATED SUGAR

½ TEASPOON (2 GRAMS) WHOLE YELLOW MUSTARD SEEDS

½ TEASPOON (1 GRAM) WHOLE CORIANDER SEEDS

½ TEASPOON (1 GRAM) WHOLE FENNEL SEEDS

½ TEASPOON (1 GRAM) BLACK PEPPERCORNS

1 BAY LEAF

Scrub a 1 quart (946 milliliters) glass jar and its lid in hot soapy water. Rinse well and air-dry.

Wash and dry the jalapeños. Prick each one several times with a fork. Stuff the jar with as many peppers as you can.

In a small pot, combine the remaining ingredients with ¾ cup (180 milliliters) water. Bring to a boil, reduce the heat, and simmer until the sugar is dissolved, about 5 minutes. Remove from the heat and carefully pour the hot liquid and spices over the jalapeños to almost the top of the jar. (A large-mouthed funnel may be useful here.)

Seal the jar tightly with the lid, label with the date of creation, and refrigerate for a minimum of 1 week. The brine becomes spicier over time and makes excellent vinegar for dressings. The peppers can be stored for up to 2 months in the refrigerator.

Note

Both the grape and jalapeño pickles are of the refrigerator variety, meaning that all of their curing happens in your icebox. Unfortunately, this fact renders them unsafe for pantry shelf storage, but they will store for 2 to 3 months at 35°F (2°C).

STEAK AND VEAL KIDNEY PIE

Finding a pastry crust languishing in the back of their freezer was all the encouragement The Bristol needed to make this savory pie. To save time, feel free to use two store-bought frozen pie crusts. Let them thaw slightly and, using your fingertips, weld them together to form one crust large enough to spill over the cast-iron skillet it is baked in. Keep in mind that this pie is huge! The Bristol made theirs in a Dutch oven, but we shrank it down to a cast-iron skillet. Still, it feeds a crowd quite easily.

Serves 8

CRUST

1 CUP (220 GRAMS) BEEF SUET (PAGE 181), CHILLED AND CUT INTO 1-INCH
    (2.5 CENTIMETER) CUBES

3 CUPS (375 GRAMS) ALL-PURPOSE FLOUR, PLUS MORE FOR DUSTING

¼ TEASPOON (2 GRAMS) KOSHER SALT

4 TO 6 TABLESPOONS (30 TO 90 MILLILITERS) ICE WATER

2 LARGE EGGS

FILLING

1 POUND (454 GRAMS) BEEF TOP ROUND, CUT INTO ½-INCH
    (13 MILLIMETER) CUBES

8 OUNCES (227 GRAMS) VEAL KIDNEYS (SEE NOTE)

4 TABLESPOONS (56 GRAMS) UNSALTED BUTTER, DIVIDED

4 MEDIUM CARROTS, COARSELY CHOPPED

2 LARGE ONIONS, COARSELY CHOPPED

2 CUPS (200 GRAMS) BUTTON MUSHROOMS, HALVED

2 CELERY RIBS, COARSELY CHOPPED

1 LARGE TURNIP, PEELED AND COARSELY CHOPPED

1 LARGE RUTABAGA, PEELED AND COARSELY CHOPPED

½ CUP (63 GRAMS) ALL-PURPOSE FLOUR

3 CUPS (710 MILLILITERS) IRISH STOUT BEER

2 CUPS (473 MILLILITERS) BEEF STOCK

2 THYME SPRIGS, 1 ROSEMARY SPRIG, AND 1 BAY LEAF,
    TIED TOGETHER WITH KITCHEN TWINE

KOSHER SALT AND FRESHLY GROUND BLACK PEPPER TO TASTE

For the crust: In a large bowl, using your hands, work together the suet, flour, and salt until it resembles coarse sand. Slowly add the ice water, 1 tablespoon (15 milliliters) at a time, mixing with a fork and adding more water until the dough forms a shaggy ball; it should not be too dry, as it will be very difficult to roll out without cracking. Add more water 1 teaspoon at a time as needed. Knead briefly, about 2 minutes, to bring together into a smooth, tight ball. Wrap the dough in plastic wrap, flatten, and chill in the refrigerator for 1 hour.

For the filling: Split the kidneys open down the middle, and using a sharp, small knife, cut out the white core and any other tough structures inside. Cube the organs using the natural delineation of the lobes. Season the beef and kidneys, keeping separate, with salt and pepper.

In a 12-inch cast-iron skillet, melt half the butter over medium-high heat. After the foam subsides, sear the beef until golden brown on all sides, about 6 minutes. Remove with a slotted spoon and set aside.

In the same pan, add the remaining butter, melt, and when the foam subsides, sear the kidneys until lightly golden on all sides, 3 to 5 minutes. Remove with a slotted spoon and set aside.

Add the vegetables to the skillet and sauté until the onion is translucent, about 5 minutes. Sprinkle with the flour and cook, stirring constantly, until the mixture smells lightly toasted, about 5 minutes.

Add the stout and scrape the bottom of the skillet with a wooden spoon to release any brown bits. Bring to a boil, then return the beef and kidneys to the skillet. Add the beef stock and the herb bundle. Bring the liquid back to a boil, then reduce the heat to medium-low. Simmer gently until the beef is tender and the liquid is thickened to just beyond stew consistency, about 40 minutes. Season the filling to taste.

Position a rack in the middle of the oven and preheat to 350°F (177°C). Remove the dough from the refrigerator at least 15 minutes before rolling out.

Shortly before the stew is ready, roll the dough on a well-floured surface into a circle about ¼ inch (6 millimeters) thick and 14 inches (36 centimeters) in diameter. Carefully wind the pastry dough around the rolling pin, then unwrap it over the skillet, allowing excess dough to fall over the sides. Pinch the crust shut around the circumference of the skillet with your fingertips to seal, but leave the overhanging crust in place. (This creates a rustic, and delicious, finish.) If the crust breaks apart when you attempt to top the skillet, do your best to mend it by pinching the pieces together. It will bind during baking.

In a small bowl, whisk together the eggs with 1 tablespoon (15 milliliters) of water. Brush the entire crust with the egg mixture and make several small slits in the crust with a sharp knife to allow steam to vent. Bake the pie on the middle rack until the crust is golden brown and crispy, 25 to 30 minutes.

Remove from the oven and let rest at room temperature for 10 minutes to allow the filling inside to set before serving.

Note

When purchasing kidneys, follow The Bristol's advice and take a deep sniff. A good-quality kidney will have no smell and should not require overnight soaking in milk. Sweet and vaguely beefy up front, kidneys impart an earthy, deeply primal vibe to the pie's filling. If pristine kidneys are not available, pass altogether and replace them with an equal amount of top round or extra uncooked beef heart (see page 70).

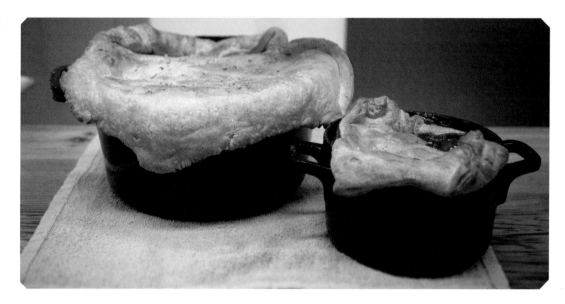

CHARRED CABBAGE with MORNAY SAUCE

The secret to this recipe is in the cut of the cabbage. The tough core is kept intact so that each half of the head can be cut into lengthwise "steaks" about 1 inch (2.5 centimeters) thick. The small portion of the hard, white core holds the slices together. Given a brief turn in a very hot cast-iron skillet, the slices take on a dark, crispy, caramelized crust, just like a good steak.

Amanda Rockman, The Bristol's gregarious pastry chef, added a ring of brandy-soaked prunes around the platter. Also known as "French kisses," the prunes are whimsical additions to her dessert plates, but in this dish they add a sweet counterpoint to the creamy sauce. Be sure to save the brandy after you've plucked out the prunes; it's a thick, robustly plum-flavored pre-dinner nip reminiscent of an aged Port.

Serves 8

PRUNES

15 PRUNES, PITTED (ABOUT 6 OUNCES/170 GRAMS)

1 CUP (237 MILLILITERS) BRANDY

MORNAY SAUCE

4 TABLESPOONS (56 GRAMS) UNSALTED BUTTER

¼ CUP (31 GRAMS) ALL-PURPOSE FLOUR

2 CUPS (473 MILLILITERS) COLD WHOLE MILK

4 OUNCES (113 GRAMS) COCOA CARDONA CHEESE, RIND ON AND CUT INTO CUBES (SEE NOTE)

GROUND NUTMEG (OPTIONAL)

KOSHER SALT AND FRESHLY GROUND WHITE PEPPER TO TASTE

CABBAGE

1 LARGE HEAD SAVOY CABBAGE

KOSHER SALT TO TASTE

¼ CUP (59 MILLILITERS) CANOLA OIL

For the prunes: Cover the prunes in the brandy and set aside at room temperature for 1 hour. Drain and set aside.

For the sauce: Melt the butter in a small saucepan over low heat. Add the flour and whisk vigorously to create a thick paste. Continue to cook, stirring occasionally, for 5 minutes or until the mixture starts to smell like pancakes.

Whisk in the cold milk, ¼ cup (60 milliliters) at a time, adding more milk only after the previous addition is completely incorporated. Increase the heat to medium-high and bring to a boil. Stir constantly until the sauce is thick enough to coat the back of a wooden spoon, 6 to 8 minutes.

Add the cheese and stir until melted, about 4 minutes. Season with salt and pepper, adding a fresh grate of nutmeg, if desired. Cover the surface of the sauce with plastic wrap to prevent a skin from forming, and keep warm.

For the cabbage: Slice the cabbage in half. Without removing the hard white core, slice each cabbage half like a sun radiating light—vertically but on a slight diagonal so each cut gets a bit of core to hold it together—into ¾-inch (2 centimeter) "steaks." (This yields about six steaks per large cabbage half.) Brush the steaks with oil on both sides and season with salt.

Heat a large cast-iron skillet over high heat. Once it is smoking, arrange steaks in a single layer and sear until charred, about 3 minutes. Flip each steak over and cook until just tender, about a minute more. Transfer to a platter and move on to the next batch of steaks.

To serve: Coat the cabbage steaks with the cheese sauce and dot the prunes around the platter. Serve immediately on to hot plates, with extra sauce on the side. If the sauce thickens past the pourable point, thin it down to the desired consistency by whisking in a little hot milk.

Note

Cocoa Cardona cheese is an award-winning wheel made by master cheesemaker Sid Cook of Carr Valley Cheese Company in Wisconsin. An aged goat cheese, it has a semisoft texture and a mellow tang, but the real magic happens on the rind. Sid coats the entire wheel in a thick layer of dark cocoa powder. Consequently, leaving the rind on while cooking infuses a faint hint of roasted chocolate into the Mornay sauce. The Bristol had scraps of Cocoa Cardona on hand, but if you cannot find it, substitute an aged goat cheese and a pinch of unsweetened cocoa powder.

CITY GROCERY

OXFORD, MISSISSIPPI

CHICKEN AND DUMPLINGS

CUCUMBER AND SWEET ONION SALAD

BANANAS FOSTER BREAD PUDDING
WITH BROWN SUGAR–RUM SAUCE

As at any restaurant worth its salt, the staff of City Grocery is fiercely loyal to the things that define them. They buy their stone-ground grits from boutique granary Anson Mills in Columbia, South Carolina. They swear by the rounded earthiness of tupelo honey harvested for more than a century by the Lanier family of Florida. They are loyal fans of the local literati—William Faulkner, food writer John T. Edge, and John Grishman among them—and direct customers to their Oxford Square neighbor, Oxford Books, for signed copies. They enjoy the creative craft-brewing efforts of Lazy Magnolia Brewery, one of the only brew houses in the world to tap into the beer potential in pecans, and are fervent supporters of the University of Mississippi–based Southern Foodways Alliance, an organization dedicated to preserving the food and food memories of the South. Thanks to our visit, one more allegiance was born: the staff meal.

City Grocery started life as a nineteenth-century livery stable, later taking a spin as a grocery store and finally, in 1992, a place to eat. We heard time and time again that the restaurant—held in tight embrace by the locals for its refined Southern menu—maintains a happy, motivated, and talented stable of cooks. They stay for years, even relocate from afar, and are fiercely devoted to their self-described "big bad chef" John Currence (aka Johnny Snack), who is indeed big in personality as well as physical appearance.

He sports the freshly shaven head of a pro wrestler and is as forthright as he is charming. "Bad," however, is a bit of a misnomer since John is also one of the nicest chefs around. He is deeply committed to fostering community, whether in Mississippi, his hometown of New Orleans, or beyond. Back in 2007 he helped spearhead the painstaking rebuilding of fried chicken nirvana Willie Mae's Scotch House in the aftermath of Hurricane Katrina and most recently proved his Quickfire mettle on *Top Chef Masters* to raise money for the No Kid Hungry campaign.

With the good omens mounting, it was clear to us that the City Grocery staff meal had to be stellar and so we set about our due diligence to make sure. A few days after sending our preliminary email, we received John's surprising response: "I am embarrassed to say that we do not do a regular staff meal. We have talked about it for years, and it is something that has bubbled back up as recently as the last week, but we have not yet engaged the wheels. Your book would be a great excuse for us to kick it in the rear." We agreed, a date was set, and just like that, the City Grocery staff meal was born.

Just a few weeks after our exchange, on a mild winter night in December, the employees of City Grocery sat down for their first family meal: big bowls of chicken and dumplings. So when we visited well into the new year, we were thrilled to find John measuring out flour, cornmeal, and butter for an encore presentation of the dish that would launch a thousand staff meals. While cutting out the dumplings, John admits that when he first announced there was going to be a

daily staff meal, most everyone was nonplussed: "It was just sort of an 'eh.'" But then again, John knew of no other restaurant in Oxford serving a staff meal. "Nobody else is attempting to do anything exceptional at all," so John has made it his mission to set the bar. Over the four months leading up to our visit, City Grocery kept us apprised of their early staff meal successes: pancakes flecked with bacon, venison sliders made with a deer shot by a line cook herself, and duck jambalaya courtesy of a beauty John flushed and bagged. At first the staff may not have known what they were missing, but now everyone has come to fully comprehend the perk. Cook Kasey Coleman is perhaps the most blunt about its benefits: "It helps

set the right tone for the night, and it beats not having a staff meal."

Under ceiling fans spinning lazy circles, the staff gathers around the table. With less than an hour before service, everyone vacuums up the plumped dumplings, then slurps the broth until just droplets are clinging to porcelain. It's then that we start to experience an overwhelming sense of déjà vu. It is as if we've enjoyed this meal before, eaten off these plates that are dinged and chipped in all the right places. And we realize that this is a good thing, a sure sign that the birth of a City Grocery staff meal tradition was inevitable, already part of this restaurant's DNA. It just happened to need a gentle kick in the rear.

A Conversation with JOHN CURRENCE
Chef and Owner

Some restaurants rely on the staff meal to form the ties that bind. You just started your staff meal program, yet your staff has stuck with you for years. What is your secret to cultivating a sense of contentment and loyalty?

Creating a unique place to work. When we opened, it was important to provide an atmosphere that people could thrive in physically and emotionally. I've been at restaurants that drain the life out of people, watched restaurants ruin a person's spirit by chewing them up and spitting them out. So we fattened the payroll to swell our ranks in the kitchen. This meant that the guys weren't getting absolutely massacred, spending four hours before service working as feverishly doing prep as they would be on a Friday night. You can't have all of your faculties in line working like that. It's kind of like doing calisthenics before doing a sport. You don't play a game before you play a game.

Why no staff meal until now?

I always, always thought about it. And always felt like it was a huge missing piece of the puzzle, particularly considering the experience we try to create for our staff here. I think it's a lovely experience, and it was one of those things that, when we opened, we crashed into it all so quickly. We thought about staff meal, but it got pushed to the side.

After watching the staff meal come alive over the past few months, what do you feel it now adds to your employees' work day?

The experience at family supper forces us to take that pause before the battle, a moment to stop and dine together. It's not cheap. But I just feel like it is important that we give the staff an opportunity to sit down at the table together so we can share with them some of what we're trying to do every day for the customers.

Has anyone balked at the extra work a staff meal requires? Or are all the cooks generally on board with making the meal?

None of them have suggested to me that it's just a pain in the ass. I think they all really like the challenge.

What is one cookbook every cook (professional or home) should read?

For everyone that comes to work for me, I encourage them to read *The Omnivore's Dilemma*. But even I know that the odds of getting people to sit down and read a 400-page book are pretty slim, so they can watch one of our copies of *Food, Inc.* Taking an hour to understand why we get beef pastured from Georgia or why we're buying lamb from Craig Rogers in Virginia, that's part of the experience.

Is there a system that you use to make the best of what is in your refrigerator? Something simple that a home cook could apply in his or her kitchen?

Oh yeah. We keep a whiteboard in the back that lists the things that can be used for the staff meal, some direction on what the supper should be, and what needs to be used right away.

So we have to ask, how does it feel to finally have a staff meal up and running?

It feels great. And I find that the question that's asked more regularly than anything else now is "What are we having for staff dinner today?" Thank you, guys, for the final kick in the butt.

CHICKEN and DUMPLINGS

When John Currence asked for suggestions for the inaugural City Grocery staff meal, chicken and dumplings was the first idea thrown into the ring. It was a hit, and thus the cornerstone of the City Grocery staff meal was laid. Comforting and filling, chicken and dumplings is what would happen if matzoh ball soup moved south. It is first and foremost a deeply flavored chicken soup made of simple vegetables, a rich broth, and shredded meat. At the last minute, dumplings (in this case made of cornmeal and flour) are dropped into the soup to poach gently before serving.

To achieve dumplings with a slick exterior and a densely chewy, slightly nubby interior, John briefly and gently kneads the dough before rolling it out like a pie crust and cutting it into dozens of small, thin squares. He is emphatic that overworking the dough at any point results in dumplings that rhyme with *luck*, but sadly do not benefit from it.

Serves 4 to 6

CHICKEN SOUP

1 WHOLE 3- TO 4-POUND (1.4 TO 1.8 KILOGRAM) CHICKEN

KOSHER SALT AND FRESHLY GROUND BLACK PEPPER TO TASTE

¼ CUP (59 MILLILITERS) OLIVE OIL

2 TABLESPOONS (30 MILLILITERS) BACON FAT (SEE NOTE)

2 SMALL YELLOW ONIONS, FINELY CHOPPED

2 CELERY RIBS, FINELY CHOPPED

2 MEDIUM CARROTS, FINELY CHOPPED

3 GARLIC CLOVES, MINCED

1 CUP (237 MILLILITERS) DRY WHITE WINE

¼ CUP (59 MILLILITERS) DRY VERMOUTH

GRATED ZEST OF 1 LEMON

2 TABLESPOONS (6 GRAMS) FINELY CHOPPED THYME

2 TEASPOONS (2 GRAMS) FINELY CHOPPED ROSEMARY

1 TEASPOON (1 GRAM) FINELY CHOPPED OREGANO

2½ QUARTS (2.5 LITERS) CHICKEN STOCK

DUMPLINGS

½ CUP (70 GRAMS) CORNMEAL

½ CUP (63 GRAMS) ALL-PURPOSE FLOUR, PLUS MORE FOR KNEADING

1 TEASPOON (5 GRAMS) BAKING POWDER

¼ TEASPOON (1 GRAM) FINE SEA SALT

2½ TABLESPOONS (35 GRAMS) UNSALTED BUTTER, CHILLED AND DICED

½ CUP (118 MILLILITERS) WHOLE MILK

For the chicken: Cut the chicken into 8 skin-on, bone-in pieces and sprinkle liberally with salt and pepper. Heat half the oil and half the bacon fat in a large pot over medium-high heat until smoking. Add half of the chicken pieces and brown on all sides, about 2 minutes per side. Remove and drain on paper towels. Add the remaining oil and fat and, once smoking, brown the remaining chicken pieces, then drain on paper towels.

Add the onions, celery, carrots, and garlic and sauté until the vegetables are barely caramelized and stick slightly to the bottom of the pan, about 6 minutes. Add the wine and vermouth, scrape up the brown bits at the bottom of the pan, then reduce the liquid by half, about 2 minutes. Add the lemon zest, thyme, rosemary, oregano, stock, and chicken to the pot. Bring to a boil, then reduce the heat to a simmer and cover. Cook until the chicken is very tender, about 1 hour, occasionally skimming fat and impurities as they rise to the surface.

Remove the chicken from the liquid. Once the chicken is cool enough to handle, remove and discard the skin. Strip the meat from the bones and shred it into bite-sized pieces. Return it to the stock in the pot.

For the dumplings: Combine the cornmeal, flour, baking powder, salt, and butter in the bowl of a food processor, and pulse until the mixture resembles coarse sand. (This can also be accomplished by hand with a bench scraper or your fingertips.) Add half of the milk and incorporate quickly. If the dough does not easily come together into a shaggy ball, add small amounts of milk until it does.

Knead the dough on a floured surface until smooth, about 5 minutes. (While you don't want to overknead the dough to stave off toughness, the dumplings will fall apart in the broth if not enough gluten is developed.) Let the dough rest for 15 minutes at room temperature.

Using a rolling pin, roll the dough to a uniform sheet about 7 inches (18 centimeters) square and ¼ inch (65 millimeters) thick. Using a sharp knife, cut the sheet into approximately 25 two-inch (5-centimeter) squares. The dumplings can be set aside in the refrigerator for up to an hour before poaching.

To serve: Bring the soup to a brisk simmer; add the dumplings carefully to the soup, adding more than one layer if necessary. They will initially sink but begin to expand and rise as they cook. Cover the pot and gently simmer the dumplings until they are tender and cooked through, 10 to 12 minutes. Season the soup with salt and pepper and serve immediately.

Note

City Grocery saves all their bacon drippings for an inexpensive, and very flavorful, alternative to oil. After your next Sunday brunch, strain cooled bacon fat through a fine-meshed sieve into a jar. Screw on the lid and store in the refrigerator for several weeks. Bacon fat can be used in Piccolo's Maple Butter (page 236) as well as the McCrady's Elvis-Inspired milkshake (page 182). Three strips of thick-cut bacon yield about 2 tablespoons (30 milliliters) bacon fat.

CUCUMBER and SWEET ONION SALAD

In 1990 Vidalia onions became Georgia's state vegetable, and for good reason: almost candy-sweet, they are the mildest onion on the market. Their lack of bite—in part due to the variety but also because they are grown in low-sulfur soil—makes them the foundation of this lightly sweet and refreshingly tart City Grocery salad. Sliced red onions, rinsed under cold water, can be substituted if Vidalias or other sweet onions are not available.

Serves 6

4 MEDIUM CUCUMBERS

1 LARGE VIDALIA ONION, HALVED AND THINLY SLICED

KOSHER SALT AND FRESHLY GROUND BLACK PEPPER TO TASTE

¾ CUP (178 MILLILITERS) RED WINE VINEGAR

¼ CUP (59 MILLILITERS) APPLE CIDER VINEGAR

½ CUP (118 MILLILITERS) OLIVE OIL

3 TABLESPOONS (36 GRAMS) GRANULATED SUGAR

1 TABLESPOON (4 GRAMS) HERBES DE PROVENCE

Decoratively peel each cucumber, alternating one strip of skin with one strip of peeled flesh. Cut off and discard the ends and cut the cucumbers in half lengthwise. Scoop out the seeds with a spoon and thinly slice the cucumbers into half moons. Combine the cucumber and onion slices in a plastic bowl with a tight-fitting lid, season with salt and pepper and set aside. In a separate bowl, whisk together the vinegars, oil, sugar, and herbes de Provence. Pour the dressing over the cucumbers and onion, season liberally with salt and pepper, mix well, and cover. Refrigerate for 1 hour, frequently turning the bowl upside-down to redistribute the dressing.

This salad is most refreshing served chilled and tastes great the following day, although it will lose a lot of its crunch.

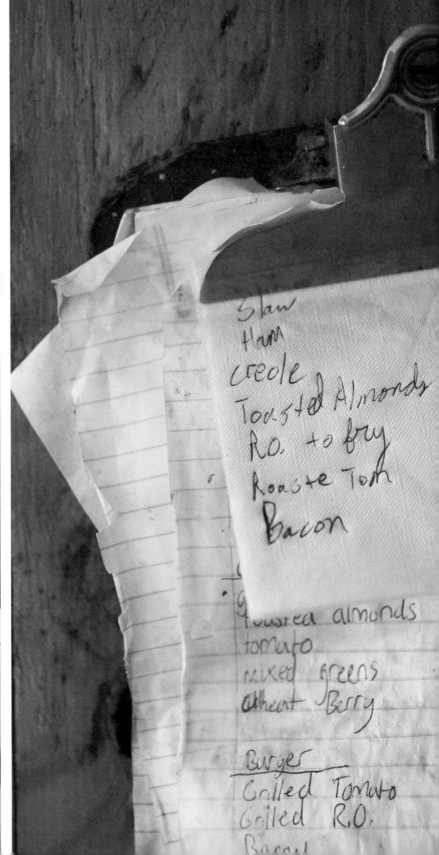

BANANAS FOSTER BREAD PUDDING
with BROWN SUGAR–RUM SAUCE

Never actually on the menu, customers lucky enough to know about this booze-soaked comfort bomb of a dessert can place an off-menu order. "It's kind of an under-the-table thing that people ask for," says veteran pastry chef Dwayne Ingraham, who always keeps a hotel pan in the walk-in. "It's a favorite."

It is easy to understand why. It welds together two of New Orleans's most famous desserts: bread pudding and Bananas Foster, the latter a tableside spectacle invented in 1951 at Brennan's in New Orleans, in which bananas and rum are ignited, then poured over vanilla ice cream. When we ask John Currence (himself a New Orleans native and a former employee in the Brennan family of restaurants) about the fusion, he says it was born out of anxiety: "I knew I could never trust anybody in the dining room to flambé bananas. So if we were going to have Bananas Foster, it was going to require a reinvention of it."

Serves 6 to 8

BREAD PUDDING

8 LARGE EGGS

1½ CUPS (355 MILLILITERS) HEAVY WHIPPING CREAM

1 CUP (237 MILLILITERS) WHOLE MILK

1¾ CUPS (350 GRAMS) GRANULATED SUGAR, DIVIDED

6 OUNCES (1½ STICKS/170 GRAMS) SALTED BUTTER, MELTED

1½ TABLESPOONS (11 GRAMS) GROUND CINNAMON

1 TABLESPOON (15 MILLILITERS) VANILLA EXTRACT

2 TEASPOONS (4 GRAMS) FRESHLY GRATED NUTMEG

½ CUP (118 MILLILITERS) BANANA LIQUEUR

10 CUPS (382 GRAMS) 1-INCH (2.5 CENTIMETER) STALE BREAD CUBES (SEE NOTE)

2 RIPE BANANAS, THINLY SLICED

SAUCE

4 OUNCES (1 STICK/113 GRAMS) SALTED BUTTER

1½ CUPS (330 GRAMS) PACKED DARK BROWN SUGAR

1 TABLESPOON (15 MILLILITERS) VANILLA EXTRACT

1 CUP (237 MILLILITERS) DARK RUM

½ CUP (118 MILLILITERS) HEAVY WHIPPING CREAM

For the bread pudding: In a large stainless-steel mixing bowl, lightly beat the eggs. Add the cream, milk, and 1½ cups (150 grams) of the granulated sugar. Whisk until the sugar dissolves, then add the butter (if your cream and milk are cold, the butter will congeal, but it's nothing to worry about). Add the cinnamon, vanilla, and nutmeg, then whisk in the liqueur.

In a large bowl, toss together the bread cubes and banana slices. Add the custard and mix well with your hands. Pour into a high-sided 11 x 9-inch (28 x 23 centimeter) baking pan, making sure to include all the liquid. (City Grocery uses a squatter, deeper square container and adjusts baking time accordingly.) Cover and place in the refrigerator for 4 to 5 hours, or overnight.

Preheat the oven to 375°F (191°C). Cover the baking pan with aluminum foil. Bake for 35 minutes; remove the foil. Sprinkle the top of the pudding evenly with the remaining granulated sugar. Bake for another 20 to 30 minutes, or until the pudding has risen high in the middle and on all sides (a sign that the custard has set) and is a crunchy golden brown on top. Allow to set and cool for 20 minutes before serving.

For the sauce: In a small pot over medium heat, melt the butter and bring to a simmer. Whisk in the brown sugar and vanilla until the sugar is dissolved. Stirring continuously, cook for 10 minutes; the mixture will become a deep mahogany color and will begin to resemble wet sand. Add the rum slowly and carefully. The mixture will sputter and seize up, but don't panic, just keep stirring. Cook until the alcohol has burned off, about 5 minutes. Swirl in the cream, return to a simmer, and cook until slightly reduced, about 10 minutes, stirring constantly to prevent it from boiling over. The sauce may seem too thin when it's hot, but it thickens as it cools, so best to cool slightly before serving. Yields about 2½ cups (500 ml). Extra sauce stores for several days, covered, in the refrigerator.

To serve: Spoon warm pieces of bread pudding into bowls and drizzle each serving with a generous amount of warm sauce.

NOTE

City Grocery uses whatever bread they have on hand to make this bread pudding. White bread is the most neutral background, but whole wheat or sourdough can also be used. It is advisable to de-crust and cube fresh bread the night before, allowing the cubes to sit out, uncovered, overnight. Alternatively, a slow toast in a very low oven can approximate the stale state. Leave them in long enough so they lose their bounce but not all of their moisture.

COCHON

NEW ORLEANS, LOUISIANA

CHILI-BASIL WATERMELON
AND TOMATO SALAD

BLUE CRABS WITH
SRIRACHA BUTTER

CHICKEN AND EGGPLANT
RICE NOODLES

For those countless hours before dinner service—and the grueling hours during—the Cochon cooks must live and breathe the culinary vision of co-owner and chef Stephen Stryjewski, a mild-mannered Southerner with an infectious chuckle. Making family meal, however, remains the one exception to this rule. Unlike creating the same dish the same way for every customer, feeding the staff demands daily innovation. So while one might find it surprising that a Cajun-style restaurant located in a Creole-centric city would serve an Asian-influenced family meal, anyone who has eaten a staff meal knows that the cook who shoulders the task calls the shots.

For some, this creative freedom poses an exhilarating challenge. For others (especially those new to the profession), it can provoke a raging case of kitchen stage fright, and Stephen isn't always pleased with the lack of gumption: "I find it frustrating when a recent culinary school graduate feels qualified to work on the line in my kitchen but can't get it together to create a meal for our staff that is creative and delicious."

The day we visit Cochon, the Cajun-meets-charcuterie hot spot in the Warehouse District of New Orleans, the family meal reins have been turned over to seasoned line cook Hirofume Okada, "Hiro" for short. Using what has been set aside for the staff meal—two extra chickens, a couple oversized eggplants, one candy-sweet watermelon, and a bushel of blue

crabs—Hiro decides to create a meal with a vaguely Vietnamese profile, and darts about the pantry to find the chili-garlic sauce, ginger, and fish sauce always on hand. It is a meal that exudes Cochon's new-age philosophy on Cajun cooking, one that honors its origins in Louisiana's backwoods while enriching it—with cautious reserve—with the many cultures that call the South home. Hiro's blue crabs roasted in sriracha butter are the near perfect example of this type of twenty-first century Cajun cuisine.

By forging a link between Gulf Coast blue crabs and the flavors of Southeast Asia, Hiro elegantly narrates the story of Vietnamese cuisine infusing the Big Easy. (It is a tale that is not his own—Hiro is Japanese—but it is not an unfamiliar one in a city brimming with talented Vietnamese line cooks.) The first Vietnamese immigrants arrived in New Orleans in the early 1970s, escaping from the growing threat of Communist rule. Searching for the touchstones of home, early immigrants were attracted to the Southern city by the subtropical weather, the proximity to fishing waters, and the presence of the Catholic Church. Today, there are more than 15,000 Vietnamese residing in East New Orleans, creating a vibrant food culture that boasts outdoor markets, urban gardens filled with edible exotics, and banh mi sandwiches, locally known as Vietnamese po' boys, stuffed with pork, pâté, and pickles.

Food with an Asian twist is always a

hit at the Cochon staff meal, but tonight's gathering is made even more convivial when the crabs emerge blazing hot from the wood-fired oven. Nothing says "party" along the Gulf Coast like a tableful of shellfish, be it boiled crawfish, grilled oysters, or shell-on shrimp. This roll-up-your-sleeves-and-get-messy spirit makes the meal slightly rowdier than usual; the decibel level rises (and the jokes get racier) as the pile of crab carcasses grows. Thirty minutes before the first customers take their seats, the staff's fingertips glisten with chili butter, and Stephen admits he has let this meal run a little longer than most. "These are the opportunities to build that family feeling," he says, a truth to be remembered when we gather our own families at the table.

A Conversation with Chef and Co-Owner STEPHEN STRYJEWSKI

Why is family meal important?

Like most jobs, you never really get to pick who you work with in a restaurant. But around the table, the stress and tension of restaurant life gets put on hold: no fighting about who finished the coffee and didn't make more.

Cochon is a "from scratch" restaurant right down to the hot sauce and yeasted biscuits: a time-consuming but rewarding way to feed your paying costumers. Who finds time to make the staff meal?

Any cook employed in the restaurant. The Honduran staff is known for their incredible dinners where they all team up and create great expanses of food.

What ingredients are the cooks asked to use when making the staff meal?

We make sure to figure in the extra bits— like the two spare chickens that come in our order. Meat-processing regulations disallow us from receiving less than a case. Strange. But whatever, we'll use it. Leftovers play an important role, too.

Leftovers are a four-letter word in some households. Can you always work them into a meal with decent results?

I've had some awful leftover-based family meals. One chef I worked for saved all of the fish trimmings for the Friday fish fry. Greasy tuna blood line, skin-on trout, and salmon belly all on the same plate? At least I learned what not to do. But many times the tiny quantities combine to form some of the most interesting dishes I've ever had. Believe it or not, meatloaf is always exciting. It can contain any number of ground meats with different vegetables and binders.

Any meatloaf epiphanies?

Avocado and couscous meatloaf works.

We'll take your word on that one. What are your go-to cookbooks for family meal if you're needing some inspiration?

Le Répertoire de La Cuisine by Louis Saulnier (Barron's Educational Series, 1977) is probably the best cookbook for professionals; it quickly inspires a dish or influences a flavor combination. It also proves that most everything has been done before.

Have you witnessed any family meal disasters?

One cook, new to the South, thought the grits needed some help and added a large quantity of garlic to the pot. Big mistake. Later that day I saw several of the dish crew corner him and threaten physical harm for ruining their breakfast.

What is your advice to a young cook given the family meal responsibility for the first time?

This is their time to get creative. I control the menu that they cook every day but give them free rein to cook for their fellow employees. Surprisingly, it can be a battle to get some of them to do it. The people who embrace the challenge are still here; it is a great indicator of a cook's ability and respect for ingredients, techniques, and fellow workers.

*Foodies are killing good times
Meals are about good company
Enhanced by good food & good wine*

CHILI-BASIL WATERMELON and TOMATO SALAD

The traditional Southern custom of a savory shake of salt on a slab of sweet watermelon is the departure point for this Southeast Asian inspired dish. However, the delicate Vietnamese alchemy of salty, sour, bitter, sweet, and spicy will be lost if this salad gets too soggy. To prevent the salt from leeching liquid from the melon as it sits, douse the salad with the dressing right before serving, and encourage your guests to eat posthaste.

Serves 4

DRESSING

2 TABLESPOONS (30 MILLILITERS) WHITE VINEGAR

2 TABLESPOONS (30 MILLILITERS) FISH SAUCE

¼ TEASPOON (.5 GRAM) CAYENNE PEPPER

JUICE OF 1 LIME

1 TEASPOON (5 MILLILITERS) HUY FONG CHILI-GARLIC SAUCE

¼ CUP (59 MILLILITERS) EXTRA-VIRGIN OLIVE OIL

½ CUP (16 GRAMS) BASIL LEAVES, LIGHTLY PACKED

½ CUP (16 GRAMS) MINT LEAVES, LIGHTLY PACKED

KOSHER SALT AND FRESHLY GROUND BLACK PEPPER TO TASTE

SALAD

1 QUART (24 OUNCES /675 GRAMS) CUBED SEEDLESS WATERMELON (1-INCH /2.5 CENTIMETER) CUBES

2 MEDIUM TOMATOES, CUT INTO 1-INCH (2.5 CENTIMETER) DICE

2 SMALL CUCUMBERS, PEELED, SEEDED, AND CUT INTO 1-INCH (2.5 CENTIMETER) DICE

½ LARGE RED ONION, HALVED AND THINLY SLICED

FRESHLY GROUND BLACK PEPPER AND LARGE FLAKE SEA SALT TO TASTE

For the dressing: In a large bowl, whisk together the vinegar, fish sauce, cayenne, lime juice, chili-garlic sauce, and oil. Tear the basil and mint into small pieces, then add to the bowl. Season with salt and pepper, and set aside for the flavors to meld, about 5 minutes.

For the salad: Right before serving, toss the diced salad ingredients with the dressing. Season with pepper to taste, toss again, then sprinkle the top with sea salt for crunch. Serve immediately.

BLUE CRABS with SRIRACHA BUTTER

"We have great crabs in abundant supply here in Louisiana," but as certain as Stephen Stryjewski is of the quality of his local crustaceans, he wasn't convinced the diners at Cochon would want to invest the time—and make the mess—required to pick the meat from their armored bodies. "I figured if the staff loved them, then everything would be fine." Stephen was right. The crabs were a big hit with his staff and consequently became the evening's bestseller. As for any leftover butter rub, it tastes great melted and tossed with popcorn.

Serves 4

SRIRACHA BUTTER

4 GARLIC CLOVES, MINCED

GRATED ZEST OF 1 LEMON

1 TABLESPOON (15 MILLILITERS) OLIVE OIL

1 TABLESPOON (6 GRAMS) TARRAGON LEAVES, LIGHTLY PACKED

¼ CUP (8 GRAMS) MINT LEAVES, LIGHTLY PACKED

¼ CUP (8 GRAMS) FLAT-LEAF PARSLEY LEAVES, LIGHTLY PACKED

¼ CUP (8 GRAMS) BASIL LEAVES, LIGHTLY PACKED

1 POUND (4 STICKS/448 GRAMS) UNSALTED BUTTER, ROOM TEMPERATURE

1 TABLESPOON (15 MILLILITERS) HUY FONG CHILI-GARLIC SAUCE

3 TABLESPOONS (45 MILLILITERS) SRIRACHA

½ CUP (118 MILLILITERS) FRESHLY SQUEEZED LEMON JUICE (ABOUT 2 LEMONS)

1 TEASPOON (5 MILLILITERS) SHERRY VINEGAR

KOSHER SALT AND FRESHLY GROUND BLACK PEPPER TO TASTE

CRABS

16 LIVE LARGE BLUE CRABS (SEE NOTE)

KOSHER SALT AND FRESHLY GROUND BLACK PEPPER TO TASTE

1 LEMON, CUT INTO WEDGES, FOR SERVING

For the sriracha butter: In a large mortar, with a pestle, crush together the garlic, lemon zest, and olive oil, until a uniform paste is achieved, about 1 minute. Add the tarragon, mint, parsley, and basil and continue to pulverize until the leaves are decimated, about 1 minute more. For a speedy alternative, pulse all the ingredients together in a food processor.

In a large bowl, add the herb paste to the butter along with the chili-garlic sauce, sriracha, half of the lemon juice, and the vinegar. Whip together into a thick, wet spread. Taste and adjust the acidity with the remaining lemon juice to achieve a pungent zing. Season with salt and pepper. Store extra butter in an airtight container in the refrigerator for up to one week.

For the crabs: Preheat the oven to 450°F (232°C). Rinse the crabs under cold running water, scrubbing the shells clean.

In a pot large enough to hold all the crabs, add about 2 cups (473 milliliters) water, and bring to a boil. Add the crabs, cover, and steam over medium-high heat for 20 minutes. Stir midway through so they turn uniformly bright red by the end of the cooking time. Drain and place the crabs in a large roasting pan.

Carefully smear half of the butter rub on the hot crabs. Cover the pan with foil, and place in the oven. Bake for about 15 minutes, spooning the butter over the crabs occasionally to lacquer them with herbs and spice.

While the crabs are roasting, melt the remaining butter rub over low heat in a small saucepan.

Serve the crabs directly from the roasting pan, giving each guest a small crab hammer and metal pick to patiently extract the sweet meat. Lemon wedges and a small cup of the melted butter for dipping are flavorful accompaniments.

NOTE

Your fishmonger may ask "Male or female?" when you are ordering your crabs. Choosing between the two is a personal taste preference. Some pickers enjoy the meatier back fin and claws on the males while others savor the added bonus of the bright red, unctuous roe that lines the interior of a female's shell. But how can you tell boy from girl? One of our interns, Erica Johnson, a Washington, D.C. native and no stranger to the Chesapeake blue crab boil, gave us a memorable pointer for distinguishing between them. Smack in the middle of the crab's white underbelly, a small flap—embedded like a jigsaw piece—gives you the clue. If this flap is shaped like the Washington Monument, tall and columnar, your crab is a guy. If it looks more like the Capitol building, domed with a slight protrusion on top, you've got yourself a gal.

CHICKEN and EGGPLANT RICE NOODLES

Restaurant staffers around the world wholly embrace the stir-fry. Cheap and quick, it requires only a deft hand and a few choice condiments—in this case, the flavors of Southeast Asia—to turn odds and ends into a meal. Cochon stretches the extra two chickens that come in their poultry order each week to make this dish, but you can get a jumpstart by using a store-bought roasted chicken. A liberal topping of homemade toasted brown rice powder gives the dish a nutty, Thai-style finish, but roasted and chopped peanuts or cashews would work nicely too.

Serves 4 to 6

ONE 3-POUND (1.4 KILOGRAMS) CHICKEN

2 QUARTS (1.9 LITERS) CHICKEN STOCK

½ CUP (94 GRAMS) BROWN RICE

¼ CUP (59 MILLILITERS) CANOLA OIL, DIVIDED, PLUS MORE AS NEEDED

3 SMALL ASIAN EGGPLANTS OR ½ LARGE ITALIAN EGGPLANT, COARSELY CHOPPED

½ LARGE YELLOW ONION, COARSELY CHOPPED

3 SCALLIONS, THINLY SLICED (BOTH WHITE AND GREEN PARTS)

1 TABLESPOON (14 GRAMS) MINCED GINGER

3 GARLIC CLOVES, MINCED

1 TABLESPOON (15 MILLILITERS) FRESHLY SQUEEZED LIME JUICE

2 TABLESPOONS (30 MILLILITERS) FISH SAUCE

1 TEASPOON (2 GRAMS) CRUSHED RED PEPPER FLAKES

4 OUNCES (113 GRAMS) THIN RICE NOODLES, COOKED ACCORDING TO PACKAGE DIRECTIONS AND COOLED

KOSHER SALT AND FRESHLY GROUND BLACK PEPPER TO TASTE

FOR SERVING

LIME WEDGES

HOT SAUCE

Cut the chicken into 4 bone-in pieces. Remove the skin from the chicken pieces, and discard. In a large pot, combine the chicken and stock and bring to a boil. Immediately reduce the heat to low, cover, and simmer gently until the meat is falling from the bones, about 90 minutes.

While the chicken is simmering, preheat the oven to 350°F (177°C). Spread the rice on a sheet pan and toast until golden brown, about 10 minutes, stirring occasionally. Cool to room temperature. Grind to a fine powder in a spice grinder or food processor. (Alternatively, use a mortar and pestle to smash it to dust.) Extra powder can be stored for several weeks, sealed in a glass jar, in a cool dark place.

When the chicken is done, transfer it to a sheet tray and let cool to room temperature. (Reserve the stock for another use after straining out the solids.) Pick the chicken meat from the bones and shred the meat into small pieces.

In a wok or large sauté pan, heat 2 tablespoons (30 milliliters) of the oil over medium-high heat until very hot. Add the eggplant and stir-fry until cooked through and golden brown on all sides, about 4 minutes. Remove, season with salt, and drain on paper towels.

In the same pan, heat the remaining 2 tablespoons (30 milliliters) of oil. Add the onion, scallions, ginger, and garlic and cook, stirring quickly, until everything is soft and fragrant, less than a minute. Add the lime juice, fish sauce, and red pepper flakes, and simmer another minute to slightly reduce the liquid. Return the eggplant to the pan along with the chicken and noodles, stir, and warm through, about 2 minutes. Season with salt and pepper.

To serve, heap the stir-fry fresh from the stove onto a large serving platter and liberally sprinkle with the rice powder. Serve immediately with lime wedges and hot sauce.

CRAIGIE ON MAIN

CAMBRIDGE, MASSACHUSETTS

NAPA CABBAGE AND APPLE SLAW
WITH SAMBAL DRESSING

CRISPY VEAL WITH HOMEMADE
HOISIN SAUCE

SPICY PICKLED PEANUTS

TOASTED CORIANDER BASMATI RICE

BUTTERMILK DOUGHNUT HOLES WITH
APPLE-HONEY CARAMEL SAUCE

"All right, everybody out. Let's go! Family meal time." The command crackles through the Craigie on Main kitchen like static electricity, though it's not an unexpected shock. No matter what is on the stove, how "deep in the weeds" a cook may be, or the number of reservations on tap that night, chef and owner Tony Maws insists that everyone working at Craigie on Main sit down together at 2:45 p.m. sharp. Today is no exception. The entire staff quickly wraps up the task at hand and heads to a small patch of green—a few trees, some concrete benches, and welcome sunshine—outside the kitchen's back door. Passing cars slow to gawk as the cooks, eating from plates balanced on their knees, sing verses of "Old McDonald" with Tony's two-year-old son, Charlie. Tony jokes that as the child of a chef, Charlie will eat almost anything. He's a welcomed regular at the restaurant's family meal.

Craigie on Main began its successful reign as the Boston area's premier nose-to-tail restaurant in 2002, then known as the Craigie Street Bistrot: a postage stamp–sized restaurant stuck to a corner of MIT's sprawling campus. The brainchild of Tony, a ruggedly handsome cook with a trim beard and a marksman's focus, the original Craigie was known for the epic line of customers snaking around the corner of its namesake street. If you did score a seat inside the basement-level dining area, elbow room was in as much demand as their crispy fried pigs' tails, and the kitchen fared no better in the square footage department. Most nights the family meal was shared on a makeshift table created by placing a wooden board over the kitchen's sink. It also functioned as the restaurant's "pastry department."

In 2008 it came as a great relief to staff and customers alike when Tony relocated the restaurant and its eclectic collection of pig-themed art to a street-level space nearly quadruple in size around the corner. The new restaurant, rechristened Craigie on Main, squarely places the diner's attention on the kitchen command center. It's an open floor plan showcasing a gleaming handcrafted Molteni range suite and the cooks who lovingly coax braised cockscombs and roasted pigs' heads from its fires.

Along with the bigger space comes a larger staff, but having to feed a few dozen more mouths each night has not diminished the quality of the family meal. In fact, so crucial is the tradition that Tony uses it as a kind of final test for new hires. "You simply cannot cook well for others if you can't cook well for yourself," says Tony. A glance above the prep area shelves reiterates this philosophy. A wide piece of masking tape, scrawled with black permanent marker, simply reads "No Compromise." Tony explains it was something a cook put up after a night of his braying throughout the service that there be no more concessions. Tony admits he was upset when he first saw the note—it made him feel more like a tyrant than a leader—but now he appreciates the motto. It is a constant reminder that there will be no compromise in his kitchen. Not in the food they prepare for their customers, and not in the food they make for each other. While they only moved a block away, Craigie has come too far for that.

A Conversation with Chef and Owner TONY MAWS

Why is the family meal important to the people on your staff?

You're working all these hours. It's high octane. It's sweat. It's blood. It's go, go, go. So from a cook's perspective, I need the fuel. I also need some downtime. I'm going to be better for it.

Why is staff meal important to you as the owner of the restaurant?

I've never understood the places that didn't do staff meal. As a boss, I need my staff not to keel over. I need them focused, as ready as possible, energized. This, of course, is a more selfish perspective.

Do you think the culture of the staff meal is more the exception than the norm in American restaurants?

I'm not sure if it's the norm, but I do feel that many that do serve staff meal don't take it that seriously—which falls in the same category as not serving it at all as far as I'm concerned.

We saw the small sign in your kitchen that reads "No Compromise." Can you explain what this means and how it may apply to the family meal?

It means we will make mistakes—that is simply inevitable—but we shouldn't ever do something that we know will limit our chances of success. This is not a switch that can be turned on and off. We can't cook for service with one set of rules (of passion, energy, and attention) and then cook for the staff with another. Staff meal doesn't need to be the most creative thing you do that day, but that doesn't mean it shouldn't be cooked correctly, seasoned correctly.

So what do you consider indispensable kitchen ingredients and equipment?

Banyuls vinegar, fish sauce, dashi, and a really solid cutting board.

If you had to make a staff meal using only four ingredients on hand in the Craigie kitchen right now, what would you make?

Pan-fried pork belly on rice—pork belly scrap, onion, fish sauce, and rice—I could eat this every day. Throwing away any pork by-product is grounds for serious public humiliation!

What is a quick go-to staff meal when time is tight?

Some days all we have time for is pasta with butter, parsley, and a little bit of cheese. That's a great pasta! When it's cooked right, seasoned right, and made with some care and love, what's wrong with that?

Has anyone ever gotten rewarded for making a great staff meal?

Do a few people move up because of stuff that they do in family meal? Hell yeah. I mean, it's cooking: show me what you can do.

NAPA CABBAGE and APPLE SLAW with SAMBAL DRESSING

This slaw is more akin to a Thai green mango salad, the green apples an equally crisp and sour American stand-in for the underripe tropical fruit. The dressing here is a marriage of the simple, clean flavors of Southeast Asia. It is conducive to experimentation so feel free to go heavier or lighter on any of the components to suit your taste. We squeezed a whole lime into ours and upped the heat factor with a generous spoonful of sambal.

Serves 6

DRESSING

JUICE OF ½ LIME, PLUS MORE TO TASTE

¼ CUP (59 MILLILITERS) RICE VINEGAR

¼ CUP (59 MILLILITERS) SOY SAUCE

2 TEASPOONS (10 MILLILITERS) FISH SAUCE, PLUS MORE TO TASTE

½ TEASPOON (3 MILLILITERS) SESAME OIL

½ TEASPOON (3 MILLILITERS) SAMBAL OELEK, PLUS MORE TO TASTE (SEE NOTE)

SLAW

2 MEDIUM GRANNY SMITH APPLES

½ SMALL RED ONION, THINLY SLICED

½ MEDIUM HEAD NAPA (CHINESE) CABBAGE, QUARTERED AND THINLY SLICED

½ BUNCH CILANTRO, LEAVES COARSELY CHOPPED, STEMS DISCARDED

KOSHER SALT AND FRESHLY GROUND BLACK PEPPER TO TASTE

For the dressing: Whisk together all the ingredients in a large bowl. Set aside at room temperature.

For the slaw: Cut the apples into thin julienne or matchsticks (see Notes, page 241), working quickly to avoid browning of the fruit. Add the apple, onion, cabbage, and cilantro to the dressing, and toss together. Season with salt and pepper and serve immediately—this salad will lose most of its snappy freshness after a couple of hours.

NOTE

Most Asian grocers carry sambal oelek by Huy Fong Foods (known as the brand with the bright green cap and rooster logo). Sambal oelek falls somewhere between a sauce and a paste, and is a simple combination of chile peppers and salt that can moonlight for Tabasco, cayenne, or sriracha. Native to Malaysia, Indonesia, Singapore, and Sri Lanka, there are over two dozen variations of sambal with ingredients ranging from salty (shrimp paste) and herbaceous (lemongrass) to just plain unusual (*petai* or green stinky bean). The common denominator for all of them is invigorating heat.

CRISPY VEAL with HOMEMADE HOISIN SAUCE

This recipe was created in an attempt to use the expensive but spent meat strained out of the restaurant's veal stock. A young cook tasked with the job of turning the dried-out hunks into the staff meal had the enlightened idea of first grating the meat, then dropping handfuls of the resulting shreds into hot oil. The veal clusters emerged from the fryer deeply caramelized and irresistibly crispy, unquestionably the best possible version of its once-miserable self. Crispy veal, as it is now known, has remained one of the family meal favorites since that serendipitous day.

We have given a recipe for braising veal to re-create the literal version of this dish, but Tony insists you can use any type of leftover braised meat including beef or veal from your own homemade stock, pot roast, turkey legs, or pork shoulder. If you do make the braised veal below, do not throw away the braising liquid: it is a spectacular stock for use in soups, stews, or sauces.

Serves 6

BRAISED VEAL

3½ POUNDS (1.6 KILOGRAMS) BONE-IN VEAL ROAST

KOSHER SALT AND FRESHLY GROUND BLACK PEPPER TO TASTE

2 TABLESPOONS (30 MILLILITERS) CANOLA OIL

½ CUP (118 MILLILITERS) WHITE WINE

6 CUPS (1.4 LITERS) BEEF STOCK

1 SMALL YELLOW ONION, QUARTERED

4 GARLIC CLOVES, CRUSHED

ONE (5-INCH/13 CENTIMETER) PIECE LEMON-GRASS, WHITE PORTION LIGHTLY CRUSHED

ONE (2-INCH/5 CENTIMETER) PIECE GINGER, PEELED AND QUARTERED

ZEST OF 1 LEMON, PEELED OFF IN WIDE STRIPS

½ TEASPOON (2 GRAMS) BLACK PEPPER-CORNS

HOISIN SAUCE

2 TABLESPOONS (16 GRAMS) CORNSTARCH

2 TABLESPOONS (30 MILLILITERS) CANOLA OIL

2 SHALLOTS, COARSELY CHOPPED

3 GARLIC CLOVES, CRUSHED

ONE (5-INCH/13 CENTIMETER) PIECE LEMON-GRASS, WHITE PORTION LIGHTLY CRUSHED

ONE (2-INCH/5 CENTIMETER) PIECE GINGER, PEELED AND QUARTERED

ONE (3-INCH/8 CENTIMETER) CINNAMON STICK

2 TABLESPOONS (30 MILLILITERS) SRIRACHA

¼ CUP (59 MILLILITERS) NUOC CHAM (SEE NOTE)

¼ CUP (59 MILLILITERS) SOY SAUCE

1 TABLESPOON (15 MILLILITERS) TOASTED SESAME OIL

½ CUP (118 MILLILITERS) FRESHLY SQUEEZED ORANGE JUICE

2 SCALLIONS, THINLY SLICED (BOTH WHITE AND GREEN PARTS)

½ CUP (35 GRAMS) COARSELY CHOPPED CILANTRO LEAVES

¼ CUP (8 GRAMS) COARSELY CHOPPED MINT LEAVES

JUICE OF 1 LIME

2 TABLESPOONS (30 MILLILITERS) MOLASSES

KOSHER SALT AND FRESHLY GROUND BLACK PEPPER TO TASTE

CRISPY VEAL

6 CUPS (1.5 LITERS) SAFFLOWER OIL

10 GARLIC CLOVES, THINLY SLICED LENGTH-WISE

½ CUP (35 GRAMS) COARSELY CHOPPED CILANTRO LEAVES

½ CUP (120 MILLILITERS) SPICY PICKLED PEANUTS (PAGE 109)

Note

Nu'ó'c châm is the slightly sweet, vinegary dipping sauce that usually accompanies Vietnamese spring rolls. Spiked with chile seeds and flush with notes of citrus, fish sauce, and garlic, it is readily available in Asian grocery stores in the Vietnamese section. A close approximation of the sauce can be made by combining equal parts white vinegar, water, fish sauce, and lime juice, then seasoning to your taste with sugar, minced fresh chiles, and minced garlic.

continues on next page

For the veal: Preheat the oven to 350°F (177°C). Trim the veal roast of excessive fat, leaving behind a thin layer for self-basting in the oven. Season generously on all sides with salt and pepper.

In a large oven-safe Dutch oven, heat the oil over high heat until it makes faint ripples in the pan. Using tongs, carefully position the veal roast in the pan, fat-side down, and sear until a golden crust forms, about 3 minutes. Sear an additional 2 to 3 minutes per side. (Considering the large cut of meat, this process can be a little tricky; turning the roast using a combination of tongs and a large carving fork will help.)

Once the browning is complete, remove the veal from the pot, pour out the fat, and add the white wine, scraping up any brown drippings stuck to the bottom. Return the veal to the pot and add enough beef stock to reach about three-quarters of the way up the roast. Add the remaining ingredients, cover, and bring to a boil. Remove the lid and place a piece of parchment paper over the pot, replacing the lid on top of the parchment (this ensures minimal moisture loss in the oven). Place the pot in the oven. Braise for 3 hours; the liquid should remain at a slow, lazy simmer.

The meat is done when a knife is easy to insert into the middle of the roast and strips of meat easily pull away. Remember, you can err on the side of overdone since meat pulled from an 8-hour stock is used at Craigie on Main. Transfer the veal to a cut-ting board to cool. Strain the flavorful brais-ing liquid through a fine-mesh sieve and reserve for another use. Discard the solids.

Once the veal is cool enough to handle, about 30 minutes, use your fingers or a fork to pull the meat into small shreds, no wider than a fettuccine noodle and no longer than a carrot stick. Try to remove fat from the meat during this shredding, as it can cause unnecessary splattering while deep-frying. Set aside.

For the sauce: Create a slurry by whisking together the cornstarch and 2 tablespoons (30 milliliters) water in a small bowl; set aside. Heat the canola oil in a saucepan over high heat. Once the oil is nearly smok-ing, add the garlic, ginger, lemongrass, and shallots, and sauté until the shallots are translucent, about 3 minutes. Add the remaining ingredients and bring to a boil. Lower the heat and simmer for 15 minutes.

Add the cornstarch slurry and whisk vigorously until the sauce is thick enough to coat the whisk, about 10 seconds. Once thickened to a hoisin sauce consistency, strain the sauce through a fine-mesh sieve, pushing hard on the chunky bits with the back of a wooden spoon to extract all the flavors. Keep the sauce warm until the veal is fried, but be careful not to reduce it any further, as this could make it too salty. Yields 1½ cups (355 milliliters) sauce which can keep, covered, in the refriger-ator for several days.

To crisp the veal: Heat the safflower oil in a high-sided, heavy-bottomed pot to 375°F (177°C).

Carefully drop the garlic slices into the hot oil. Fry until dark golden (but not brown) and the bubbling subsides, about 30 seconds. Transfer with a slotted spoon to paper towels.

Ready a splatter guard. Using tongs, pick up a hefty tongful of the shredded veal and carefully place into the hot oil. Immediately place the splatter guard over the pot. (If the veal is not overcooked, as it would be in the stock, the moisture and fat in the meat can be explosive when it hits the hot oil, so be very careful with this step.) Fry the veal until deep golden, about 45 seconds. Carefully lift the splatter guard, remove the veal using a slotted spoon, and drain on the paper towels. It is okay if the pieces stick together, creating fritters of fried veal; they will be broken up during the next step. Continue frying in batches for a total of 5 to 6 frying sessions.

Once the frying process is complete, combine the crispy veal and half of the warm sauce in a large bowl; toss to coat, breaking up any very large clumps of veal. Arrange on a platter and sprinkle with the crispy garlic, chopped cilantro, and pickled peanuts. Serve with the extra sauce on the side, and heaping scoopfuls of fragrant Toasted Coriander Basmati Rice (page 110).

SPICY PICKLED PEANUTS

Spicy and sweet, these Asian-inspired pickled peanuts are somewhat of a distant cousin to the American South's boiled version. They add a pleasantly soft crunch and nuttiness to stir-fries and salads and also make a nice bar snack when drained, sautéed in duck fat, and salted.

Yields one 12-ounce (355 milliliter) jar

1¼ CUPS (188 GRAMS) ROASTED UNSALTED PEANUTS

⅓ CUP (79 MILLILITERS) CIDER VINEGAR

2 TABLESPOONS PLUS 1 TEASPOON (29 GRAMS) GRANULATED SUGAR

2 TABLESPOONS (28 GRAMS) PACKED LIGHT BROWN SUGAR

1½ TABLESPOONS (22 MILLILITERS) FISH SAUCE

1 TABLESPOON (15 MILLILITERS) SOY SAUCE

2 TEASPOONS (10 MILLILITERS) SAMBAL OELEK (SEE NOTE, PAGE 105)

¼ OF A SMALL YELLOW ONION

ONE (3-INCH/8 CENTIMETER) PIECE GINGER, PEELED AND QUARTERED

1 GARLIC CLOVE, CRUSHED

½ TEASPOON (4 GRAMS) FINE SEA SALT

Clean, sterilize, and dry a 12-ounce (355 milliliter) glass jar and its lid. Preheat the oven to 325°F (163°C) and line a sheet tray with parchment paper.

Roast the peanuts on the sheet tray until dark brown, 14 to 16 minutes, stirring occasionally and rotating the tray twice during roasting. Set aside.

In a pot, combine the remaining ingredients with ¾ cup (180 milliliters) water and bring to a boil. Add the peanuts and boil for 2 minutes.

Drain, reserving the liquid and solids separately. Transfer the peanuts, onion, ginger, and garlic to the glass jar. Carefully pour the hot pickling liquid over the peanuts, filling the jar to the top. (The peanuts will not fill the jar to the top but will expand as they absorb the pickling liquid.) Seal tightly and refrigerate for 72 hours before using, and store in the refrigerator for up to two weeks. The longer these peanuts pickle, the spicier and sweeter they get.

TOASTED CORIANDER BASMATI RICE

Despite its simplicity, this is a deeply complex and buttery-tasting side dish. The extra TLC required to properly toast the coriander seeds makes all the difference.

Serves 6

2 TEASPOONS (4 GRAMS) WHOLE CORIANDER SEEDS

2 TABLESPOONS (28 GRAMS) UNSALTED BUTTER

2 TEASPOONS (12 GRAMS) MINCED GARLIC

1 TEASPOON (3 GRAMS) PEELED AND FINELY GRATED GINGER

¼ CUP (25 GRAMS) THINLY SLICED SCALLIONS (WHITE PART ONLY)

2 CUPS (390 GRAMS) WHITE BASMATI RICE

ONE (5-INCH/13 CENTIMETER) PIECE LEMONGRASS, LIGHTLY CRUSHED

1 TEASPOON (6 GRAMS) KOSHER SALT, PLUS MORE TO TASTE

FRESHLY GROUND BLACK PEPPER TO TASTE

¼ CUP (18 GRAMS) COARSELY CHOPPED CILANTRO LEAVES

Heat a small pan over high heat. Add the coriander seeds (no oil needed) and shake continuously until the seeds release a deep, woodsy fragrance and turn uniformly light brown. Remove them from the heat and cool slightly. Grind to powder in a spice grinder or with a mortar and pestle, or place the seeds in a heavy plastic bag and pulverize by rolling over them with a rolling pin or whiskey bottle.

In a 2-quart (2 liter) pot, melt the butter over medium-high heat. Add the coriander powder, garlic, ginger, and scallions and cook until just tender, about 2 minutes. Add the rice and stir until the grains are evenly coated in butter. Add 1 quart (946 milliliters) water, the lemongrass, and 1 teaspoon (6 grams) salt, and bring to a boil. Reduce the heat to low and simmer until most of the water is absorbed, about 20 minutes, stirring occasionally to prevent scorching.

Remove from the heat, cover, and let rest for 20 minutes.

When ready to serve, remove the lemongrass, season with salt to taste, and stir the rice with a fork to fluff. Pile the fragrant rice into a bowl, sprinkle with chopped cilantro, and serve while steaming hot.

BUTTERMILK DOUGHNUT HOLES
with APPLE-HONEY CARAMEL SAUCE

These doughnuts were a test for the restaurant's dessert menu. To everyone's delight, the experiments ended up on the staff meal table. They taste best when served piping hot and fleetingly crisp. So instead of frying a surplus of doughnuts, if you are left with extra dough, store it raw in the refrigerator, then cut and fry doughnuts to order throughout the week. They make an excellent, if indulgent, breakfast.

Yields 60 doughnut holes

DOUGHNUTS

6 TABLESPOONS (85 GRAMS) UNSALTED BUTTER, MELTED

1 CUP (120 MILLILITERS) BUTTERMILK

3½ CUPS (438 GRAMS) ALL-PURPOSE FLOUR

1½ TEASPOONS (7 GRAMS) BAKING POWDER

½ TEASPOON (2.5 GRAMS) BAKING SODA

½ TEASPOON (2 GRAMS) FINE SEA SALT

2¼ CUPS (450 GRAMS) GRANULATED SUGAR, DIVIDED

3 LARGE EGGS

2 QUARTS (1.9 LITERS) SAFFLOWER OIL, FOR FRYING

2 TEASPOONS (5 GRAMS) GROUND CINNAMON

CARAMEL SAUCE

1 LARGE CRISPIN (OR SIMILARLY TART) APPLE, CUT IN HALF AND CORED

¼ CUP PLUS 2 TABLESPOONS (90 MILLILITERS) APPLE CIDER

½ CUP (60 MILLILITERS) FLAVORFUL WILDFLOWER HONEY

2 TABLESPOONS (28 GRAMS) UNSALTED BUTTER, MELTED

⅛ TEASPOON (1 GRAM) KOSHER SALT

For the doughnuts: In a large bowl, whisk together the butter and buttermilk. In another large bowl, sift together the flour, baking powder, baking soda, and salt.

In the bowl of an electric mixer fitted with a whisk, whip 1¼ cups (250 grams) of the sugar and the eggs on high speed until the mixture reaches the ribbon stage, about 10 minutes. (The batter will run off the whisk in a very slow, ribbonlike stream and pile on top of itself as it falls back into the bowl, holding its shape for about 3 seconds before dissolving back into the rest of the batter.)

Switch out the whisk for the paddle and, on low speed, slowly add the flour mixture, about ½ cup (120 milliliters) at a time, until incorporated, about 2 minutes. Increase the speed to medium and slowly add the buttermilk mixture, mixing until just combined, about 30 seconds. The batter should be clumpy without any large, dry patches, and will be fairly wet and sticky.

Line a sheet tray with plastic wrap. Pour the batter onto the sheet tray, cover with a top layer of plastic wrap, and spread out to a ½-inch (13 millimeter) layer. Wrap tightly with more plastic wrap and chill for at least 2 hours or up to 12. (This allows the dough to set and readies it for doughnut hole punching.)

For the caramel sauce: Preheat the oven to 350°F (177°C).

Roast the apple in a baking dish, skin-side down, until the skin turns slightly brown and the flesh is puffed and mushy, about 40 minutes. Remove from the oven and set aside to cool.

When cool enough to handle, scoop out the insides of the apple and discard the skin. In a blender, purée the apple and ¼ cup (60 milliliters) of the cider until smooth, 2 to 3 minutes, adding the remaining cider if necessary to form a smooth purée.

Combine the honey and butter in a small pot and cook over high heat, stirring constantly. (The honey will foam.) When the bubbles turn a dark orange, about 12 minutes, remove the pot from the heat and whisk in the apple purée. It will foam up aggressively but keep whisking vigorously to cool it down. Season with salt and keep warm until you're ready to serve. This yields 1 cup (237 milliliters), and also tastes amazing on waffles or pancakes.

To fry the doughnuts: Heat the oil in large, high-sided pot to 350°F (177°C). Combine the cinnamon and the remaining 1 cup of sugar on a wide, shallow plate.

Using a 1-inch (2.5 centimeter) circular cutter (a shot glass will work in a pinch), punch out the doughnut holes ten at a time, returning the sheet tray to the refrigerator between batches. (Use a small amount of neutral oil on your hands and on the cutter to prevent the dough from sticking to either.) Carefully lower the holes into the oil using a slotted spoon and fry for 3 to 4 minutes, or until the doughnuts puff to almost twice their size and become deeply golden brown. Gently move the doughnuts around in the oil with the spoon as they fry; the dipping and bobbing ensures more uniform cooking and coloring.

Remove the doughnuts from the oil with the spoon, gently tapping along the side of the pot to remove excess oil. Immediately roll them in the cinnamon sugar. Set aside on a plate and move on to punching, frying, and sugar-coating the next batch. (Keep batches warm by placing them in a single layer on a sheet tray in a very low oven, about 200°F (93°C).) Serve immediately with caramel sauce on the side.

DILL

REYKJAVÍK, ICELAND

CREAMY BEET AND PICKLED
HERRING SALAD

PINE-INFUSED LANGOUSTINES

PICKLED RED CABBAGE IN RED
CURRANT JUICE

SPICE-STUDDED CRISPY PORK BELLY

CHARDONNAY GLÖGG

ead of winter in Iceland is a dark time. The sun sits on the horizon for a few struggling hours, reminding Icelandic citizens it still exists, before dipping into submission, leaving the cold, stark land dim again save for the oily green and indigo dance of the aurora borealis. The family meal happening in front of us at Dill, however, is full of brightness and intense warmth. This is, after all, a unique staff meal. Not only is it a holiday feast the day after Christmas, flush with traditional Icelandic delicacies; it is a way for executive chef Gunnar Karl Gíslason and his co-owner and sommelier, Ólafur Örn Ólafsson, to thank their staff for their unfaltering dedication to the restaurant despite some early bad luck. Dill opened at the exact moment that Iceland's economy collapsed.

Iceland has a tendency to do everything in a big way. Its waterfalls are the biggest in Europe. Its volcanoes are powerful enough to stop air traffic around the globe. And in 2008 the nation's bankruptcy amounted to one of the top ten in the history of the world. In October of that year the krona collapsed and the country amassed a debt exceeding six times the GDP of the nation. It wasn't a good time to be a restaurant in Iceland. Many went from a staff of several dozen to a workforce of one, maybe two, or closed their doors altogether. In Gunnar and Ólafur's case, they did the opposite, recruiting half a dozen of the hardest-working, multitasking workers in all of

Iceland to start their dream restaurant, Dill, in Reykjavik's historic Nordic House, a cultural center devoted to uniting the countries of the north, including Norway, Finland, Denmark, and Sweden.

As industrious as the redheaded Gunnar and red-bearded Ólafur (Gunni and Oli, respectively) might be, they are also the first to admit that the struggle following the collapse was exhausting. Adhering to the tenets of the New Nordic Cuisine movement (a style pioneered by Gunni's colleague and friend René Redzepi of Noma in Copenhagen), Dill's kitchen set out to execute hyper-local cooking. This included foraging from the wild larder outside their door

and sourcing every single ingredient, down to the last drop of vinegar, from local purveyors. The entire team worked nearly twenty hours a day, seven days a week, to keep the restaurant afloat, rarely taking breaks to keep themselves fed, and napping on the dining room banquettes. Slowly the glowing reviews came in. Then illustrious chefs the world over began paying their respects, and little by little, Dill was on top. Within a year it was labeled the best restaurant in Iceland. Gunni and Oli admit they would have called it quits if not for the almost super-human staff they had on their side.

They also knew that a time of thanks would come. And that their gift would be

in the form of a feast of gratitude: a staff meal like no other, planned for months in advance with friends and family invited to celebrate alongside the team. "We have had a very hard time here in Iceland since the economic collapse," says Gunni, "and tonight is finally a way to thank our staff for sticking with us through the difficult times." So here they sit at a long communal table sparkling with china, glittering with candlelight, and strewn with white lights entangled in pine boughs, giving off the faint scent of sap and Christmas. The evening celebration includes rare and coveted ingredients served only around the winter holidays: grouse smoked over hay, langoustines sautéed with pine and served with an oniony mayonnaise, dense sweet rugbraud bread, and herring—lots and lots of herring.

As the waiters and cooks gather round the table, their loved ones tucked in between them, there are only two people missing, Gunni and Oli. The chefs are busy personally serving thick slices of pork belly to their staff and guests from behind the buffet, thanking them all one by one for their loyalty, loss of sleep, and friendship. At last Gunni and Oli sit down next to each other and raise their glasses of ruby-colored aquavit (scented with dill and flavored with beets), shouting the traditional Icelandic toast: *Skål!* Everyone shouts back in unison and downs their shots, the darkness behind them, the feasting ahead.

Can you tell me us more about the Christmas buffets in Iceland like the one you are serving tonight?

Oli: Many restaurants all over Iceland have Christmas buffets each evening for about a month before Christmas. They are very popular here. They offer smoked lamb, smoked pork, and pork belly with a crispy skin like we are having today. There's pickled red cabbage and herring . . . a lot of herring. There's gravlax or smoked salmon and maybe some game as well. Just last week we took everyone out for a Christmas lunch and then we came back here [to the Nordic House] and we played Band Hero. It was fantastic.

So then within the traditional lineup of Christmas dishes, what is the most unique item on the staff meal menu tonight?

Gunnar: Well, the grouse is illegal. Hunters can give it to us, but we cannot sell it in the restaurant. The season for it is very short. It only lasts about three weeks.

Oli: Like you would say in New York, the ones we are having today "fell off the back of a truck." It's very rich meat. And you will always find birch berries in the grouse's neck when you butcher it. This is where the flavor of the grouse comes from actually.

What is Icelandic cuisine?

Oli: Up until about fifty years ago, Icelandic cuisine was about surviving. Taste and flavor was not a consideration. It's only in the past twenty years that restaurants have really started doing interesting things. It feels like a renaissance.

Gunnar: As for ingredients, herring is important, of course. Dill, cod, lamb, rye, and barley, too. There's also cabbage, beets, and onions. Horse is popular. Seal and puffin are not as popular as they used to be, but they still show up occasionally. At Dill we serve a smoked puffin dish. It's very rich, dark meat that tastes like the sea. Basically, we do the best we can do with limited resources. This is the Icelandic way.

Weeks before you opened Dill, Iceland fell into financial ruin. What happened next?

Oli: We had investors, people with money, and then the economic crisis hit. "People with money" all of a sudden became just "people" overnight.

Gunnar: Oli and I decided that we had to do it even without any money. Right before we opened, we talked to the producers and farmers who were selling us their ingredients. We couldn't afford to buy from them, but we said: "Believe in us and we will pay you back at the end of the month."

Despite the major challenges, do you feel there is a silver lining to opening during the financial meltdown?

Oli: It's nice because we can do exactly what we want. We can be eccentric and strange and people accept it. They want us to be ourselves. They want our staff to be themselves. It's very liberating.

What piece of cooking equipment should every home cook have in his or her kitchen?

Gunnar: The Icelandic leirpottur [a covered clay pot]. It's my favorite cooking vessel. It works fantastically, too. I use it a lot at home; I usually make lamb in it. You add everything to the pot and put it in a very low oven. The next day you have a wonderful meal. It's very easy but very delicious. When they were digging up the clay for these containers, they found lamb bones stuck inside the clay, so they decided to add the [decorative] bones to the lid, to remind us where it came from.

What makes tonight's staff meal so special?

Oli: Tonight is a way to thank our staff and loved ones for sticking with us through such hard times. We are a family and we want our guests to feel like they are a part of our family, too. It is all very important to us.

CREAMY BEET and PICKLED HERRING SALAD

Herring is as synonymous with Iceland as geysers. The ocean's stocks were an important lifeline, sustaining Scandinavian populations throughout the region's harsh winters with rich stores of vitamin D and healthy fats. At Christmastime herring and chopped roasted beets are combined in this creamy salad, traditionally served with slices of sweet Icelandic rye bread known as rugbraud. In addition to this classic recipe, Dill decided to push the boundaries by turning smoked herring into ice cream for the end of the meal. "It's not as bad as it sounds," says Gunnar. "It's actually really good if you just give it a try without thinking it might taste bad." In fact, it was surprisingly palatable, but not quite as good as this simple salad.

Serves 6

1 LARGE RED BEET

1 TABLESPOON (15 MILLILITERS) CANOLA OIL

1 TABLESPOON (15 MILLILITERS) WHITE VINEGAR

KOSHER SALT AND FRESHLY GROUND BLACK PEPPER TO TASTE

½ CUP (115 GRAMS) CREAM CHEESE, AT ROOM TEMPERATURE

½ CUP (115 GRAMS) CRÈME FRAÎCHE

2¾ CUPS (390 GRAMS) PICKLED HERRING, DRAINED AND FINELY CHOPPED

1 SMALL WHITE ONION, FINELY CHOPPED

2 TEASPOONS (8 GRAMS) MINCED DILL

FOR SERVING

THINLY SLICED RUGBRAUD (SEE NOTE)

SALTED BUTTER, AT ROOM TEMPERATURE

Preheat the oven to 400°F (204°C).

Scrub the beet vigorously under cold running water to remove any dirt, then trim the bottom and top. Whisk together the oil and vinegar, then brush over the beet. Season with salt and pepper, wrap tightly with aluminum foil, and roast until tender, about 45 minutes. (A wooden skewer will poke clean through without any resistance when it is done.)

Once the beet is cool enough to handle but still fairly hot, remove the skin. Cut the beet into ½-inch (1.3 centimeter) cubes. Refrigerate until chilled.

Whisk together the cream cheese and crème fraîche. Add the cubed beet and onion and stir until everything turns bright pink. Gently mix in the herring and dill and season with salt and pepper. Refrigerate until chilled.

Serve with rugbraud and softened butter on the side. Extra salad stores well for up to 3 days, covered, in the refrigerator.

Note

Somewhere between savory and sweet, a dense loaf of rugbraud is difficult to source outside of Iceland, but rustic whole wheat or rye bread can be substituted, as can the slightly sour Finnish ruis available at www.nordicbreads.com.

PINE-INFUSED LANGOUSTINES

Executive chef and co-owner Gunnar Karl Gíslason is a fanatical collector of the wild edibles that grow around him. So when he invited us to forage for the pine boughs that infuse these langoustines with the slightest hint of citrusy-tasting resin, we expected an epic outdoor adventure, one that would entail climbing centuries-old trees and dodging testy reindeer. Then he led us to the Christmas tree in the lobby of the Nordic House and began pruning its branches. With an impish grin he said: "If this isn't sustainable, I don't know what is."

While this dish may sound otherworldly, it is in fact quite simple once you find your own small pine branches. It certainly makes both an eye-catching and conversation-starting appetizer. For added dramatic effect, the cooks at Dill burn the langoustine tails just before serving so that they arrive flaming to the table.

Serves 6

CRISPY SHALLOTS

⅓ CUP (79 MILLILITERS) CANOLA OIL

5 SHALLOTS, THINLY SLICED INTO RINGS

2 TEASPOONS (8 GRAMS) MINCED DILL

KOSHER SALT AND FRESHLY GROUND BLACK PEPPER TO TASTE

ONION MAYONNAISE

3 LARGE EGGS

½ CUP PLUS 1 TABLESPOON (133 MILLILITERS) CANOLA OIL, DIVIDED

¼ CUP (50 GRAMS) FINELY CHOPPED RED ONION (ABOUT ½ MEDIUM ONION)

¼ CUP (45 GRAMS) FINELY CHOPPED LEEK, WHITE PORTION ONLY

2 SHALLOTS, FINELY CHOPPED

1 TABLESPOON (15 MILLILITERS) WHITE VINEGAR

KOSHER SALT TO TASTE

NORI SALT

2 SHEETS NORI SEAWEED, TORN INTO PIECES

1 TABLESPOON (18 GRAMS) KOSHER OR COARSE SEA SALT

LANGOUSTINES

TWELVE 6-INCH (15-CENTIMETER) FRESH PINE BRANCHES (SEE NOTE)

12 LARGE SHELL-ON LANGOUSTINES (OR JUMBO PRAWNS OR SHRIMP)

4 TABLESPOONS (56 GRAMS) UNSALTED BUTTER

KOSHER SALT TO TASTE

For the crispy shallots: In a heavy-bottomed sauté pan, heat the oil over high heat until it is hot enough for a loud sizzle to erupt when a single shallot slice is dropped into the pan. Add the remaining shallots and shallow-fry until golden brown and crispy, about 1 minute. Carefully remove the shallots with a slotted spoon and drain on paper towels. (Discard or save the flavored oil.) Season the shallots with salt and pepper, toss with dill, and set aside. Shallots can be made several days ahead of time and will keep in a covered container in the refrigerator.

For the onion mayonnaise: Fill a small bowl half full with ice and water. Bring a small pot of water to a boil and add the whole eggs, timing their cooking for exactly 4½ minutes. Quickly remove and immediately plunge into the ice bath. Chill for 2 minutes, then gently peel them under cold running water (try not to puncture the egg, since the yolk is still runny), returning to the ice bath before you move onto the next step.

In a sauté pan, heat 1 tablespoon (15 milliliters) of the oil and sauté the onion, leek, and shallots over high heat until translucent, about 3 minutes. Cool to room temperature, then combine with the whole eggs in a blender. Blend on high until smooth, about a minute, then begin adding the oil in a slow, steady stream until fully incorporated, about 3 minutes. The resulting mayonnaise will be thicker than most store-bought varieties. Add the vinegar and salt and blend until incorporated. Refrigerate until needed. Extra mayonnaise will keep in a covered container for up to 2 days.

For the nori salt: In a spice grinder, combine the nori and salt. Pulse until pulverized to a fine powder, about 1 minute. Extra salt can be jarred and stored in the cupboard for weeks.

For the langoustines: Using a sharp knife, score a slit on the back of each langoustine shell from head to tail, being careful not to puncture the flesh below. Season the langoustines with salt. Using butcher's twine, tie a prepared pine branch (see Note) to each langoustine on the side with the slit and trim excess twine. Repeat with the remaining langoustines.

In a large cast-iron pan, melt the butter until it begins to froth, then cook the bundles until the langoustine shells are bright pink, the flesh opaque, and the pine aromatic, about 3 minutes per side depending on size. (Use long tongs to keep your distance from the sap splattering in the pan.)

Immediately serve the langoustines on their boughs—offering guests scissors to cut the twine and remove the shell—with small cups of onion mayonnaise for dipping, and crispy shallots and nori salt for sprinkling on top. For the brave and dramatic, light the tails before serving to your guests as they do at Dill.

NOTE

To source the pine branches for this recipe, you will most likely need to do some foraging of your own backyard. Keep in mind that you don't have to travel far around the holidays to find pine; any unsprayed Christmas tree or wreath that is not too dehydrated will do. Once harvested, trim the branches into twelve 6-inch (15 centimeter) pieces. Each cut piece should have both a sturdy central stem as well as fragrant, fresh needles. Thoroughly rinse the cut pine boughs under hot running water for several minutes to remove any dirt and excess sap. This step will help prevent the sap from sputtering during the cooking process.

PICKLED RED CABBAGE in RED CURRANT JUICE

This pickled cabbage is of the simple and quick variety—it is really a braise rather than a preserve. The sweet-tart fruity flavors make it a mainstay on Iceland's Christmas buffets, cutting the richness of the accompanying meat dishes such as the pork belly recipe on page 125.

Serves 6

1 TABLESPOON (14 GRAMS) UNSALTED BUTTER

⅓ CUP (67 GRAMS) GRANULATED SUGAR

1 SMALL HEAD RED CABBAGE, OUTER LEAVES REMOVED, CORED, QUARTERED, AND THINLY SLICED

1¼ CUPS (296 MILLILITERS) WHITE VINEGAR

2 CUPS (473 MILLILITERS) RED CURRANT JUICE (SEE NOTE)

1 STICK CINNAMON

3 WHOLE CLOVES

3 JUNIPER BERRIES

In a sauté pan, melt the butter over medium-high heat. Add the sugar and cook until lightly caramelized, stirring constantly, about 6 minutes. Add the cabbage and cook until just tender, about 5 minutes. Add the vinegar, juice, cinnamon, cloves, and juniper and bring to a simmer. Reduce the heat to low and cook, uncovered, until the cabbage is very tender and the liquid has reduced slightly, about 30 minutes, stirring occasionally. Season with salt and cool to room temperature.

Remove the cinnamon, cloves, and juniper berries. Refrigerate until chilled. Serve chilled or reheat just before serving. Extra can be stored in a covered container in the refrigerator for up to 1 week.

NOTE

If red currant juice is not available, cranberry juice or Concord grape juice can be substituted.

Come In, We're Closed

While pork is not as prominent as lamb on Icelandic menus, at Christmastime it is always on the buffet line. Hangikjöt (smoked pork loin) is a national favorite, along with this roasted pork belly. Crispy skinned and stuck like a porcupine with bay leaves, cloves, and cinnamon stick shards, it makes a dramatic centerpiece on the holiday table, and a nice alternative to spiral-cut ham. The cooks at Dill render the skin extra-crispy by first roasting the pork belly, skin-side down, in a small amount of water, thus rendering out fat without burning the skin.

Serves 6

6 POUNDS (2.7 KILOGRAMS) FRESH PORK BELLY

½ CUP (144 GRAMS) KOSHER SALT

20 WHOLE CLOVES

16 BAY LEAVES, PREFERABLY FRESH

4 STICKS CINNAMON, BROKEN OR CUT INTO SHARDS

Preheat the oven to 400°F (204°C). With a very sharp knife, score the skin of the pork belly (going deep into the fat below but stopping just above the meat) about ¼ inch (6 millimeters) apart. Halve the pork belly into two long strips. Arrange the belly pieces skin-side down in a roasting pan and add a scant amount of water to just cover the skin, less than ¼ inch (6 millimeters). Roast for 15 minutes, then remove the pan from the oven, discard the water, and completely dry the pan. Pat the belly dry and rub the salt over the skin, ensuring that it fills the scores. Push the cloves into the skin and stick the bay leaves and cinnamon shards into the scored slits; they will stick out like spines. Return both pieces of belly to the roasting pan skin-side up, and roast until the skin is crackling and crispy and the meat easily pulls apart, about 2 hours.

Let the belly rest, uncovered, for 15 minutes.

Dill leaves the spices poking out of the crispy skin when bringing the pan directly to the table. Remove them before slicing and serving. Leftover pork belly can be diced into small cubes and used to fill the onigiri (Japanese rice balls) on page 281.

CHARDONNAY GLÖGG

Dill's co-owner, general manager, and sommelier, Ólafur Örn Ólafsson, prepared this mulled wine as a warming pre-dinner drink. Although the glögg is usually made with red wine, Ólafur uses Chardonnay, steeping it in a spice blend that includes cinnamon, cloves, cardamom, vanilla, and star anise. Ólafur extracts maximum flavor from the spices by first simmering them with a small amount of wine, then adding the remaining Chardonnay afterward, a technique that also helps prevent alcohol evaporation. After being refrigerated overnight, the glögg is reheated gently, at which point Ólafur's instructions are emphatic: "For those who want a little more punch in their punch, now would be a good time to add the aquavit. A splash would be perfect!" According to Ólafur, next comes the nicest part of glögg making: "Tasting to see if it's ready."

Makes about 3 quarts (3 liters)

THREE (750 MILLILITER) BOTTLES DRY WHITE WINE (SUCH AS CHARDONNAY)

6 TANGERINES, JUICED, PEEL CUT INTO WIDE STRIPS, PLUS EXTRA SLICES FOR SERVING

2 LEMONS, JUICED, PITH REMOVED, PEEL CUT INTO WIDE STRIPS

½ CUP (118 MILLILITERS) HONEY

2 STICKS CINNAMON, PLUS MORE FOR SERVING

10 WHOLE CLOVES

10 CARDAMOM PODS

1 STAR ANISE POD

1 VANILLA BEAN

¼ CUP (50 GRAMS) GRANULATED SUGAR

PINCH FINE SEA SALT

2 TABLESPOONS (30 MILLILITERS) AQUAVIT

Combine a half-bottle of wine, the tangerine and lemon juices and peels, honey, cinnamon, cloves, cardamom, star anise, and vanilla in a large saucepan and bring to a boil. Reduce the heat to medium and simmer until the liquid tastes strongly of spice and has reduced slightly, about 15 minutes.

Remove the peels and add the remaining wine. Over very low heat, gently warm until the temperature reaches 158°F (70°C); any higher and the alcohol may start to evaporate. Add the sugar and season with salt for balance, stirring until dissolved.

Remove from the heat, cover, cool to room temperature, and then refrigerate until chilled. Before serving, strain through a fine-mesh sieve, discarding the solids, and slowly reheat to 158°F (70°C). Add the aquavit, stir, and keep warm until ready to serve. Dill serves their glögg in goblets garnished with a cinnamon stick and a tangerine slice. Extra glögg can be stored, covered, in the refrigerator for up to 2 weeks.

THE FAT DUCK

BRAY, ENGLAND

WARM WHITE BEAN, BACON, AND SPINACH SALAD

RATATOUILLE

OLIVE OIL SMASHED POTATOES AND ROCKET

CREAM-BAKED COD WITH DILL

A Fat Duck stagiaire will never look at a grapefruit the same way again. On their first day on the job in the British village of Bray just down the road from Windsor Castle, they must break down four of the pink variety. Simple enough. Until they realize this is not a quick peel-and-slice operation. From each of the fruit's segments they must painstakingly remove every tiny pink teardrop of flesh, laying them out, one by one, on white toweling like sparkling citrus raindrops. (They are eventually used as garnish on a plate of salmon poached in licorice gel.) Referring to it as mind–numbing is generous. The tedious hours of cramp-inducing drudgery inspired a former stagiaire, the food and travel blogger Lennie Nash, to proclaim, "the urge to scream and hurl a grapefruit across the room is overwhelming." If not for the reprieve of staff meal twice daily, odds are that the prep room walls would be shellacked with pink juice.

The international team of unpaid stagiaires—often called "stages" for short and themselves taking part in a *stage*, a French term for a professional apprenticeship—are the indispensable prep room muscle behind The Fat Duck's experimental cuisine. The menu is a heady mixture of science and history spouting from the imagination of chef-owner Heston Blumenthal. The stagiaires themselves come for the cutting-edge experience of it all, hoping that through careful observation—and perhaps osmosis—they will absorb the secrets of what makes a restaurant rise to legendary status. What actually allows the dozen or so to make it through the eighteen-hour days of volunteer work is something a little less ambitious but equally important: comradeship, in large part forged around the family meal table, the remainder at the pub next door well after midnight, hard-earned lagers in hand.

The day of our visit, The Fat Duck's chef de cuisine, Jonny Lake, presides over the staff meal. He is a tall, thin Canadian known as a patient teacher by the stagiaires that fall under his command. Forming an orderly queue, they all look grateful to see him—or at least his promise of food and rest—as they step up and serve themselves dripping scoops of ratatouille, smashed potatoes whirled green with arugula, and cod fillets baked gently in a puddle of cream. The day is hazy but dry, so they eat at wooden picnic tables bumped up together like dominoes in the restaurant's fenced back garden. This is the first seat they've taken since sunrise. The relief is almost palpable. Even so, a mere twenty minutes later, the stagiaires cross the road to return to the prep kitchen with a slight spring in their step. It's not a long time, but it's just long enough.

"I recall the atmosphere; it was great. Like eating at the United Nations with all the different languages being spoken from cooks all around the world," says former stagiaire Tobin Boothe of the staff meal experience at The Fat Duck. (He himself is now in charge of creating more than a thousand staff meals three times daily at River Rock Casino Resort in British Columbia, Canada.) When we ask him if he would do it all over again—invest the grueling hours in exchange for culinary lessons he may or may not use in his lifetime—there is no hesitation, he absolutely would. "In a heartbeat," agrees Texas native Ryan Hernandez, who is best remembered as The Fat Duck stage who made an authentic Thanksgiving staff meal. "The energy to perform and the drive to perfection were incredible. It was infectious," he says. Former stagiaire Vito Mollica, now the executive chef at the Four Seasons in Florence, concurs: "Of course I would do it again. I was inspired by the entire experience, from Heston's philosophy to the organization of the team." He also ties it back to those picnic tables out back: "Most of all it was a chance to meet chefs from all over the world. People who were all there for the same reasons." Eating grapefruit, however, is an altogether different story. In that department, they may just be scarred for life.

A Conversation with JONNY LAKE

Head Chef

Fat Duck's research and development kitchen is the life force behind the restaurant's rare breed of hypermodern cuisine. Do any of your experiments ever find their way to the family meal table?

Fortunately our R&D kitchen receives many samples from different suppliers each week. Once we have tested them, they often end up being used in staff meals. It's also a great way for the team to try new and often pretty amazing ingredients. The best thing—and what the Lab is famous for, however—is their great potato salad. Sorry, not as exciting as what you probably imagine, but they are famous for it and we all love it.

Why is staff meal important?

Making a big deal of staff food helps build team morale and raises standards. It's about showing respect for the team. We spend an eternity sourcing the best possible ingredients and preparing the most delicious food we can for our customers, so it would be disrespectful to treat the team any other way. What kind of message would that be? From a chef's perspective, if you don't care enough to put up good-quality staff food, then what does that say about yourself? Are you a chef or what?

What is the one meal of the week your staff most looks forward to?

Saturday lunch, which normally consists of BLTs, scrambled or fried eggs, and croissants and chocolatines made by our pastry team. Also, the Lab's infamous potato salad.

Do you use the family meal as a time to educate your staff, or is it more about blowing off steam and getting some good grub?

Staff mealtime is definitely a meeting point for all staff, front of house and kitchen and administration, too. As we have staff working in different buildings, this can be the only time during the day that they get a chance to interact. We don't, however, turn it into a training session; it's very much downtime.

Considering that you use some pretty innovative ingredients on your menu, what is the most unique product that has graced your family meal table?

The whole pig cooked in a Jacuzzi for one of the *Feasts* [Heston Blumenthal's BBC production] episodes! It is Heston's world, after all.

If you had to make a staff meal using only four ingredients in the walk-in right now, what would you whip up?

Rice plus mushroom trimmings plus chicken bouillon plus Noilly Prat equals mushroom risotto.

Do you use any cookbooks for staff meal inspiration?

Heston's *Family Food*.

Have any special guests dropped by the family meal?

We have had Harold McGee eat with us a few times and also [*Guardian* food writer] Matthew Fort.

What are your favorite staff meal dishes in rotation right now?

Salmon pie, venison burgers, and I really can't say potato salad again or there will be no living with them.

WARM WHITE BEAN, BACON, and SPINACH SALAD

Whether fried to fragile crispness or ground to make a remarkable burger (see Double-Stack Burgers, page 178), bacon seems to be the only ingredient that nine out of ten cooks would feed each other. Consequently, staff meal is the stage upon which their bacon love affair unfolds. Here, The Fat Duck employs fried lardons—neat ⅜-inch (1 centimeter) rectangles cut from an enormous slab of Alsatian bacon—to weave a touch of smoke into tender white beans cooked in a pressure cooker (though we have given stovetop directions below). Part side dish, part salad, these beans partner well with slow-cooked roasts or swordfish steaks but also make a nice light lunch on their own.

Serves 4 to 6

1 POUND (454 GRAMS) DRIED CANNELLINI BEANS

KOSHER SALT TO TASTE

**1 POUND (454 GRAMS) SLAB ALSATIAN BACON, CUT INTO LARDONS
  (SEE RECIPE HEADER)**

10 SHALLOTS, THINLY SLICED

2 TABLESPOONS (30 MILLILITERS) CHAMPAGNE VINEGAR

8 OUNCES (227 GRAMS) BABY SPINACH

FRESHLY GROUND BLACK PEPPER TO TASTE

Note

Before being sliced, slab bacon must be stripped of its tough rind. Don't discard! It is an excellent stock and soup enhancer. Just add directly to the pot, and remove before serving. If slab bacon is not available, an equal weight of unsliced Italian pancetta can be substituted. If only sliced bacon is available, buy the thickest-cut slices for an approximate substitution.

In a large pot, cover the beans with cold water in excess of 3 inches (7.5 centimeters) and set aside overnight. (For a quick soaking method, bring the water to a boil over high heat and immediately take the pot off the heat. Set aside, covered, for 1 hour before proceeding.)

Drain the soaked beans, rinsing under cold water until it runs clear. Transfer them to a large pot with enough water to cover by 2 inches (5 centimeters), and enough salt to taste like the sea. Over high heat, bring to a boil, then reduce the heat to a simmer and cook until the beans are fully tender and creamy in the center, 1 to 1½ hours. Drain and keep warm.

In a skillet over medium-high heat, fry the bacon until golden and crispy, about 10 minutes. Reduce the heat to medium, add the shallots, and cook until very tender, about 20 minutes. Increase the heat, add the vinegar, and simmer until the liquid has evaporated, about 2 minutes. Add the cooked beans, stir to combine, and season well with salt and pepper.

Heap the spinach onto a serving platter and spoon the warm beans over the top. The heat from the beans will gently wilt the spinach below. Serve immediately.

Extra beans will keep in a covered container in the refrigerator for several days.

RATATOUILLE

Few dishes pack more vegetables into one pan than the classic French ratatouille, a stew-like side dish of vegetables braised in their own juices. While purists in the French tradition will insist on cooking all the components separately, head chef Jonny Lake finds no fault with saving time and dishes by sautéing and baking everything in the same skillet. And while those same purists may simper at any creative additions, seasonal vegetables do make memorable cameos, including pattypan squash, leeks, mushrooms, cauliflower, and fennel. As for the leftovers, they are as versatile as they come. Draining the ratatouille of excess liquid turns it into excellent omelet filler for the next morning, or the heart and soul of a lunchtime vegetarian burrito.

Serves 4 to 6

KOSHER SALT TO TASTE

1 LARGE ITALIAN EGGPLANT, CUT INTO ½-INCH (13 MILLIMETER) CUBES

3 TABLESPOONS (45 MILLILITERS) CANOLA OIL

6 ROMA TOMATOES, SEEDED AND COARSELY CHOPPED

2 MEDIUM RED BELL PEPPERS, COARSELY CHOPPED

2 MEDIUM YELLOW BELL PEPPERS, COARSELY CHOPPED

2 SMALL ZUCCHINI, CUT INTO ½-INCH (13 MILLIMETER) CUBES

1 BAY LEAF

FRESHLY GROUND BLACK PEPPER TO TASTE

FINELY CHOPPED BASIL, THYME, AND PARSLEY, AS DESIRED (OPTIONAL)

Preheat the oven to 350°F (177°C).

Lightly salt the eggplant. Place on paper towels and allow to rest at room temperature for 10 minutes to draw out excess water; press until dry with more paper towels.

In a large ovenproof skillet, heat the oil over medium-high heat. When hot, add the eggplant and sauté until barely tender, about 8 minutes. Add the tomatoes, peppers, and zucchini and sauté until everything is slightly softened, about 6 minutes. Add the bay leaf, season well with salt and pepper, and transfer to the oven.

Bake for about 1 hour, uncovered, until the vegetables are cooked through and swimming in their juices.

Remove from the oven, discard the bay leaf, and stir in the chopped herbs of your choice; we recommend at least a heaping tablespoon of each. This dish can be served immediately, or left to cool to room temperature.

Ratatouille holds up well covered in the refrigerator for several days. We are partial to sprinkling a thick layer of grated Gruyère over top before reheating in a 350°F (177°C) oven.

OLIVE OIL SMASHED POTATOES and ROCKET

These potatoes are a Fat Duck staple but are seldom made the same way twice. Arugula (known as rocket in England) is a favorite addition because of its subtle peppery bite, but head chef Jonny Lake also recommends using a mix of seasonal soft-stemmed herbs like basil, chervil, chives, and parsley. Fruity extra-virgin olive oil is used in place of butter, so this is a great time to bring out your best bottle. Fancy olive oils infused with aromatics would work well too. Note that caramelizing the onions helps to balance the spiciness of both the olive oil and the arugula, so be as thorough as possible. If you do not have the time to caramelize slowly, adding a tablespoon of honey to the onions after they have softened will help speed up the process. It's cheating, but it's fast.

Serves 4

½ CUP (118 MILLILITERS) EXTRA-VIRGIN OLIVE OIL, PLUS ADDITIONAL TO SERVE

2 LARGE WHITE ONIONS, THINLY SLICED

2 TEASPOONS (12 GRAMS) SEA SALT

1½ POUNDS (680 GRAMS) MARIS PIPER POTATOES, SCRUBBED CLEAN (SEE NOTE)

2 CUPS (2 OUNCES/57 GRAMS) ARUGULA, PACKED

KOSHER SALT AND FRESHLY GROUND BLACK PEPPER TO TASTE

In a large skillet, heat half of the oil over medium heat. When hot, add the onions and caramelize until deep golden brown in color, about 55 minutes stirring occasionally. (See recipe header to speed up this process.) Set aside.

Bring a pot of heavily salted water to a boil; add the whole, skin-on potatoes. Boil until a paring knife pierces cleanly through without resistance, about 40 minutes.

Drain the potatoes and cut each in half. (This is a hot job; use an oven mitt.) Immediately return the potatoes to the pot along with the onions in their oil. Using a potato masher, smash quickly—they should be more lumpy than smooth—then stir in the remaining oil and arugula until wilted with a heavy spoon. Add more olive oil to taste, and season generously with salt and pepper. Serve immediately straight from the pot.

NOTE

The palm-sized Maris Piper potato is the most widely grown spud in the United Kingdom. Its ability to maintain structure after cooking and its appealing, floury mouth feel are both due to its medium starch content. The Maris Piper is difficult to source in America, but Yukon Golds or German Butterballs can serve as suitable substitutes.

CREAM-BAKED COD WITH DILL

Heston Blumenthal's trio of restaurants—The Fat Duck, neighboring Hind's Head, and his London outpost, Dinner—are all known for resurrecting historic recipes, the earliest dishes dating from the 1300s. With Heston at the helm, however, one can expect authentic recreations with a twist. The night before our visit, the tasting menu included a dish of lamb with cucumber and onion, circa 1895. Though we doubt it was served with "fluid gel dill" back then. So when the cooks had leftover dill along with freshly caught cod, they brought the two together in this lovely little dish. It is almost like a baked version of fish chowder, but in half the time and with half the work.

Serves 4

FOUR 6-OUNCE (170 GRAM) SKINLESS COD FILLETS

SALT AND FRESHLY GROUND WHITE PEPPER TO TASTE

¾ CUP (178 MILLILITERS) HEAVY CREAM

1 TABLESPOON (6 GRAMS) FINELY CHOPPED DILL

1 LEMON, CUT INTO WEDGES

Preheat the oven to 350°F (175°C).

Season the cod with salt and pepper and arrange snugly in a single layer in a 9 x 11-inch (23 x 29 centimeter) baking dish. Pour in enough cream to creep one-third of the way up the fillets.

Bake until the cream has reduced slightly and the fish flakes easily with a fork, 16 to 20 minutes. Baste the fish midway through cooking to break up any skin that forms on the cream.

Remove from the oven, sprinkle with dill, and serve immediately, spooning the cooked cream over the top of the fillets. We recommend serving the fillets on top of a bed of Olive Oil Smashed Potatoes (page 134) to sop up the stellar sauce. Serve with lemon wedges on the side.

FRASCA FOOD AND WINE

BOULDER, COLORADO

Jared Sippel is on his third tour of duty at Frasca Food and Wine. A sous chef in the restaurant's scrupulous kitchen—organized like a pharmacy, everything is clearly labeled and spotless—he has a habit of punctuating his time at the Boulder restaurant with globetrotting cooking gigs. He has worked in multistarred kitchens around the world. Yet he always ends up right back in the heart of the American Rockies. When we press him about why he boomerangs back to this small but food-obsessed town, he gives us a shy, sweet, farmboy-like shrug as he coaxes penne from a bronze pasta extruder. "Bobby and Lachlan are just great restaurateurs to work for. They really take care of their staff," says Jared of the restaurant's owners, Bobby Stuckey and Lachlan Mackinnon-Patterson. The two first met while working at The French Laundry in Napa Valley and opened Frasca in 2003. "But really," continues Jared, an Iowa native, his eyes the color of a cloudless sky, "I missed living in Colorado."

As the day's fading sunshine casts a golden haze on soaring saw-toothed peaks, we can appreciate the sentiment. Blanketed in early winter snow, Boulder shimmers with the vitality of its adventure-seeking residents. If they're not skiing, they're probably biking (Bobby is a former professional cyclist); if they're not biking, they're probably running (several Frasca staff members train for road races together); and if they're not running, they're probably eating. Luckily, Frasca caters to this type of perpetually famished outdoor athlete, especially around the staff meal table.

"Family meal is about feeding the troops," says sous chef Matthew Perez, "but it is also about utilizing product." For example, the trim from cowboy ribeyes, thicker than paperback romance novels, becomes the base for the Bolognese sauce. "When you are in charge of executing family," says Matthew—using the shortened vernacular for the meal—"you need to make it all come together with your available resources."

Fortunately, these resources are all cut from the same cloth since the restaurant is built around a very specific culinary theme, the cuisine of Friuli-Venezia Giulia. A somewhat obscure region of northeastern Italy, Friuli borders the hills of Slovenia to the east, Austria's soaring mountains to the north, and the Adriatic Sea on its southern flank. As a border region, Friulian cuisine can best be described as Italian fare grounded in Eastern European sensibilities: more potato, dairy, and corn, and less pasta, olive oil, and wheat. Bobby and Lachlan fell in love with the region and its local frasches, seasonal in-home eateries offering homemade wine and food that place a green branch—a frasca—above the door when open for business. They took a gamble that this hearty fare, when elevated with exacting technique, would cater to Boulder's calorie-burning lifestyle. They were right on the money. Eight years after first open-

ing their doors, they have expanded both Frasca's kitchen and dining room as well their empire with a Naples-style pizzeria next door, complete with a pizza oven imported directly from the motherland.

It can be argued that Frasca's success is in direct relation to the care extended to its staff. In addition to a once-daily staff meal at 4 p.m., Bobby and Lachlan provide everyone who works at Frasca with healthcare and a retirement plan—benefits still rarely seen inside the culinary industry. They even invite their long-term staff members to join them on a ten-day trip to Italy in order to experience a frache in the flesh. So in Lachlan's mind, the staff meal is really just a small part of taking care of his team. "It's a long day, so it really is just a small concession," he says. "To spend thirty dollars a day to make a nice meal?" He lets his rhetoric linger with a squint and a shrug. Like any good mountain man, they wordlessly say it all.

A Conversation with BRIAN LOCKWOOD
Chef de Cuisine

You have been in the business since age thirteen and have worked at restaurants all around the world; have you always lucked out and had great staff meals like this to sit down to?

Actually, no. That's why it's really important to me. We all work thirteen, fourteen hours a day, so it's just really important that it's not overlooked. I feel strongly about it not being just a "clean out the fridge" thing.

So you don't use the leftovers, the scraps lying around, to make the family meal?

Of course we do! But I'm really adamant that the whole meal has to make sense, has to be composed, has to be thought out. I don't want a big smorgasbord of things that don't work together.

Let's say a new cook is making staff meal for the first time at Frasca; what advice do you give them?

Season really well.

Any other words of wisdom to the new cook on the line?

It's a grueling profession. If you don't come to terms with that, you really shouldn't be here. You really shouldn't. Fortunately, I got blessed with a great wife who understands.

Do you cook at home with her on your time off?

Yeah, all the time. It's different than what I would cook professionally; more home-style food, comfort food.

So what are your tips for the busy family who wants to cook a weeknight dinner but is short on time?

Honestly, it's about making time. That's what I love about European culture so much; it really revolves around the table. Family get-togethers center on the meal, and I think that's a big part of it.

Frasca recently doubled their kitchen staff. Has the expansion changed your staff meal?

We really used to be able to sit down together a bit more in the other restaurant, but since we've reopened, everybody's been so busy it's been hard to really find the time to. But everybody eats.

What Frasca staff meals do you find yourself hoping to find on the pass at 4:00?

Kinda hard question. I love pasta. Especially pasta bakes. I also love the tacos we make here.

Frasca is based on the cuisine of Friuli, Italy, a region through which you traveled to learn recipes for the restaurant. What makes that cuisine distinctive?

It has a lot of Austrian influence as well as Slovenian influence, but it is still super Italian. The Alps are right there, so you have the mountains, but the ocean is just a few miles away. It was also a major spice port back in the day. So they use curry, caraway, a lot of weird stuff that you wouldn't normally find in the rest of Italy. Although, I was really sent over there to learn how to make risotto.

So do you have any risotto words of wisdom for the home cook?

In the Friuli region they do a risotto that is almost soupy. They use a different grain of rice; it's a shorter, fatter grain, and it releases more starch into the risotto. It is an olive oil–based risotto with no cream, no butter. The finished dish is not heavy with cheese so it's really light. Unfortunately, I think the hardest dishes to cook have the least ingredients in them. With this risotto, you have to fail before you figure it out. But as they say, you usually learn more from your mistakes than your successes.

FRESH EGG YOLK PASTA

This pasta tastes incredibly rich due to a high ratio of egg yolks to whites, but its deep yellow color is thanks to the flour. Semolina pasta flour is made from the coarsely ground endosperm of durum wheat. Yellow-hued and high in protein (and therefore high in gluten), semolina produces a golden-colored fresh pasta that keeps its shape but remains light, not leaden, after cooking. Semolina requires more liquid than white flour, so if substituting with equal parts white flour, hold back on ¼ cup (59 milliliters) of egg yolks, then add it to the flour well as necessary. If it is your first time working with semolina, we recommend making this recipe by metric weight as written below; it will help remove some of the guesswork.

The recipe will yield longer pasta sheets than you will need to create a single lasagna (such as the Lasagna Bolognese, page 143) but not quite enough for two (although the recipe can easily be doubled by weight). Do what Frasca does and save the pasta trimmings: stuffed with extra ricotta, rolled, and then baked in a thin layer of tomato sauce (see the Tomato Sauce on page 146), they become excellent cannelloni—a dish that is trumped only by lasagna as Frasca's favorite staff meal.

Yields 8 to 12 lasagna sheets

3 CUPS (500 GRAMS) SEMOLINA PASTA FLOUR, PLUS MORE FOR DUSTING

1⅓ CUPS (330 GRAMS) EGG YOLKS (FROM 18 TO 20 LARGE EGGS)

2 TABLESPOONS (20 GRAMS) EGG WHITES (FROM ABOUT 1 LARGE EGG)

1½ TABLESPOONS (25 GRAMS) WHOLE MILK

2 TEASPOONS (10 GRAMS) OLIVE OIL

Place the flour in a large bowl, forming a deep well in the center. Whisk together the egg yolks, egg white, milk, and oil and pour into the well. With a fork, slowly incorporate the liquid into the flour, creating a firm but slightly sticky ball. Do not worry if it seems slightly more wet than pasta dough made with all-purpose flour; the extra liquid will be absorbed during kneading. If the mixture is crumbly, however, add more milk, 1 tablespoon at a time, until the dough comes together. Place the dough on a lightly floured surface. Knead for 10 minutes or until the dough is smooth and elastic, about the stiffness and tackiness of new Play-Doh.

Flatten the dough into a thick disk, cover with plastic wrap, and rest at room temperature for 1 hour. (At this stage, the dough can be wrapped well and stored in the refrigerator for up to 2 days.)

After resting, divide the dough into eight equal-sized pieces. Using a pasta machine according to the manufacturer's instructions, roll each piece into a single long lasagna noodle (see Note about thickness). Immediately after each rolling, dust both sides of the noodle with flour and lay out in a single layer to dry slightly. You will need at least six pasta sheets (two for each layer), cut to the length of your lasagna pan minus about ½ inch/1.25 centimeters (to account for expansion after blanching). Frasca advises to "roll a couple extra sheets, just in case." This same dough can be used to make any fresh pasta shape of your choosing, including fat strands of papparadelle for the recipe on page 62.

Bring a large pot of salted water to a boil. Fill a large bowl halfway with ice and water.

Blanch the sheets in the boiling water for 1 minute, then place in the ice bath to cool for about 2 minutes. Drain and pat dry with paper towels. Lay out in a single layer on a sheet tray covered in plastic wrap. Cover lightly with more plastic wrap, and set aside for later use.

DIY RICOTTA CHEESE

This whole-milk fresh cheese is your gateway into home cheese making. Once you start, you'll find it hard to stop. In very little time (and with very few ingredients) you are rewarded with a substantially creamier, smoother, and denser ricotta than you can normally buy. The only special items you will need are an instant-read thermometer, citric acid (see Note), and an abundance of cheesecloth. The key, however, is not to rush the process. Some will say that it can be made in 15 minutes or less, but allowing the milk to slowly heat up will yield a much creamier, less rubbery end product.

Technically, however, this is not true ricotta cheese. Ricotta is made with the whey collected after rennet-initiated curds have been used to make mozzarella. Ricotta cheese is made from this by-product by heating the already cooked whey to just below boiling, hence its literal meaning, "recooked." While this recipe does indeed yield a delicious fresh cheese that is similar to ricotta, it is more a cross between small-curd cottage cheese (made with acid, not rennet) and the German-style sahnequark (a farmer's cheese made of whole milk fortified with cream).

In any case, the end product is amazingly versatile, and leftover ricotta can be used to make Malfatti (page 270) or sweetened with lemon juice and confectioner's sugar, then topped with fresh berries for a simple dessert. And don't throw away the whey! The greenish liquid left behind in the pot after straining out the ricotta becomes the key ingredient in Ubuntu's Whey and Brine Braised Pork Shoulder, page 269. Extra whey can be kept in the refrigerator for up to a week or frozen for several months.

Yields about 1 quart (946 milliliters)

1 TABLESPOON (16 GRAMS) CITRIC ACID (SEE NOTE)
1 GALLON (3.8 LITERS) WHOLE MILK
1 QUART (946 MILLILITERS) HEAVY WHIPPING CREAM
2 TABLESPOONS (25 GRAMS) GRANULATED SUGAR
4 TEASPOONS (24 GRAMS) FINE SEA SALT, PLUS MORE TO TASTE
1 TEASPOON (5 MILLILITERS) FRESHLY SQUEEZED LEMON JUICE

Dissolve the citric acid in 1 cup (237 milliliters) warm water.

In a large pot, combine the citric acid, milk, cream, sugar, salt, and lemon juice, whisking briefly to dissolve. Over low heat, slowly bring the liquid to scalding (just below a boil), stirring the bottom occasionally with a wooden spoon to prevent scorching. At around 160°F (71°C), curds will begin to form in the pot; gently move them from the sides to the center to allow for more curds to form. Continue to slowly heat the liquid to 195°F (91°C), 45 minutes to 1 hour, then remove the pot from the heat. Allow to rest, unmolested by curious spoons, for 30 minutes. Gently scoop the curds using a spoon (not slotted) into a fine-mesh sieve lined with a single layer of cheesecloth sitting atop a bowl.

Allow the cheese to drip-drain in the refrigerator set over a bowl for about 30 minutes (longer if you desire a drier consistency). Salt if desired, and transfer the now-semisolid ricotta into a resealable container. Store in the refrigerator and consume within 5 days.

Note

Frasca uses dissolved citric acid to initiate the curd and whey separation. They believe it yields a cleaner taste in the finished cheese that they can later enhance with lemon juice. Other recipes use vinegar and lemon juice for the same curd-separating effect. For sourcing of citric acid and instructions for substitutions, visit www.cheesemaking.com.

LASAGNA BOLOGNESE

Like most traditional Italian recipes, lasagne alla Bolognese varies significantly from region to region. Using that logic, Frasca's version is a commendable interpretation using the dross about the kitchen, including the trim from their rib-eye steaks, to make the classic Bolognese meat sauce. However, since rib-eye is an expensive cut to buy whole and then grind to oblivion, feel free to substitute with any suitably fatty ground beef of your choice.

With everything made from scratch right down to the ricotta, this recipe creates best-in-breed lasagna. However, employing judicious shortcuts will help avoid an all-day cooking affair. Store-bought pasta is probably the easiest swap. We recommend using a variety that requires boiling (as opposed to the "no boil" kind) to retain better control over the final texture of the noodle. You'll want them al dente so they do not turn to mush during baking. They will also be less wide than their homemade counterparts so figure in at least 12 sheets per lasagna.

Serves 6 to 8

BOLOGNESE SAUCE

¼ CUP (59 MILLILITERS) OLIVE OIL

1 MEDIUM YELLOW ONION, FINELY CHOPPED

1 MEDIUM CARROT, FINELY CHOPPED

1 MEDIUM RIB CELERY, FINELY CHOPPED

2 OUNCES (57 GRAMS) PANCETTA, FINELY CHOPPED

2½ POUNDS (1.14 KILOGRAMS) GROUND RIB-EYE (SEE RECIPE HEADER)

2 LARGE GARLIC CLOVES, MINCED

¾ CUP (178 MILLILITERS) DRY WHITE WINE

ONE (28-OUNCE/794 GRAM) CAN PEELED ITALIAN TOMATOES, SEEDED AND FINELY CHOPPED, JUICES RESERVED

1 CUP (237 MILLILITERS) CHICKEN STOCK

½ TEASPOON (.5 GRAM) DRIED THYME

1 BAY LEAF

¼ CUP (59 MILLILITERS) HEAVY WHIPPING CREAM

SALT AND FRESHLY GROUND BLACK PEPPER TO TASTE

ROASTED FENNEL

3 MEDIUM FENNEL BULBS, HALVED AND THINLY SLICED

2 TABLESPOONS (30 MILLILITERS) OLIVE OIL

4 THYME SPRIGS

SALT AND FRESHLY GROUND BLACK PEPPER TO TASTE

LASAGNA

1 TABLESPOON (15 MILLILITERS) OLIVE OIL

6 TO 8 SHEETS FRESH EGG YOLK PASTA (PAGE 140)

1¼ POUNDS (567 GRAMS) AGED PROVOLONE CHEESE, GRATED

12 OUNCES (340 GRAMS) ASIAGO CHEESE, GRATED

2 CUPS (473 MILLILITERS) RICOTTA CHEESE (DIY, PAGE 142, OR STORE-BOUGHT)

1 QUART (946 MILLILITERS) TOMATO SAUCE (PAGE 146), PLUS MORE FOR SERVING

SALT AND FRESHLY GROUND BLACK PEPPER TO TASTE

continues on next page

For the Bolognese sauce: Heat half of the olive oil in a large, heavy stockpot over medium heat until shimmering. Add the onion, carrot, celery, and pancetta and cook, stirring occasionally, until the vegetables are softened and the pancetta is crispy but not browned, about 8 minutes. Scrape the mixture into a large bowl.

Add the remaining oil to the pot and heat again over high heat. Add the beef and cook until browned, 8 to 10 minutes, then carefully drain all but a few tablespoons of the resulting fat. Return the vegetable mixture to the pot. Add the garlic and sauté until fragrant, about 1 minute. Add the wine and allow to almost fully evaporate, about 4 minutes. Stir in the tomatoes and their juices, the stock, thyme, and bay leaf. Season with salt and pepper and bring to a boil. Cover partially, reduce the heat, and simmer for 1 hour, or until the liquid has reduced by not quite half. Discard the bay leaf. Stir in the heavy cream and cook until the sauce thickens again, 10 to 15 minutes. It should be a thick sauce that is easily spreadable. Yields approximately 2 quarts (1.9 liters). You'll use about a quart for the lasagna; reserve the remaining sauce for another use. It can be stored in the refrigerator for up to a week.

For the fennel: Preheat the oven to 450°F (230°C). Line a sheet tray with parchment paper. Toss the fennel with the olive oil and thyme and season with salt and pepper. Roast on the sheet tray until softened and lightly caramelized, about 35 minutes. Remove from the oven and set aside. Crumble the now-dried thyme on top of the fennel, and discard stems.

For the lasagna: Preheat the oven to 350°F (175°C). Lightly oil the bottom of a baking dish (see Note) and lay down the first layer of noodles; if necessary, cut to fit. Spread the noodles with 2 cups (473 milliliters) of Bolognese, then top with one-third each of the provolone and Asiago. Spread half of the ricotta on top of the cheeses, arrange half of the roasted fennel on top of the ricotta, and finally spread a thick smear of tomato sauce over top (about 1¼ cups/300 milliliters). Season the layer with salt and pepper.

Arrange the next layer of noodles and repeat the layering process. After laying down the final layer of noodles, spread with the remaining tomato sauce (there should be ample coverage to keep it moist) and a thick layer of provolone with a sprinkling of Asiago. Cover the baking dish with foil, tented up and away from the cheese layer, then place the baking dish on a parchment paper-lined sheet tray. Bake in the oven for 1 hour, until the center is hot and the edges are bubbling.

Remove the foil and continue baking until the top layer is browned, about 30 minutes. Allow to cool for 15 minutes before slicing and serving. Serve with extra tomato sauce on the side.

This lasagna tastes better over time so if you can plan ahead, try to make it the day before and refrigerate it overnight. Slice when completely cool, and then reheat in a 350°F (175°C) oven before serving.

Note

Frasca uses a full hotel pan with a depth of 3 inches (8 centimeters) to serve their entire staff. We cut the recipe in half and used a pan approximately 15 x 11 x 2½ inches (38 x 28 x 6.25 centimeters). Traditional ceramic lasagna pans will be slightly higher, allowing for an additional layer. If you choose to make yours mile-high, scale up the ingredients and allow for a slightly longer cooking time.

CAULIFLOWER, EGGPLANT, and FENNEL LASAGNA

To appease the meat-conscious members of the staff, Frasca creates a vegetarian twin of their beefy lasagna using whatever seasonal vegetables they have on hand. In this version, grilled eggplant adds a charred, almost meat-like heft, while the roasted cauliflower firmly ties in the early winter harvest. Feel free to substitute with whichever grilled or roasted vegetable you prefer. It's an especially creative way to use up your garden's zucchini and yellow squash, the ones that may have become unwelcome houseguests during their midsummer glut.

Serves 6 to 8

TOMATO SAUCE

¼ CUP (59 MILLILITERS) OLIVE OIL

FOUR (28-OUNCE/794 GRAM) CANS WHOLE PEELED TOMATOES, JUICE RESERVED (SEE NOTE)

1 MEDIUM ONION, FINELY CHOPPED

3 GARLIC CLOVES, THINLY SLICED

6 BASIL LEAVES (OPTIONAL)

GRILLED EGGPLANT

1 MEDIUM ITALIAN EGGPLANT

1 TABLESPOON (18 GRAMS) KOSHER SALT

3 TABLESPOONS (45 MILLILITERS) OLIVE OIL

FRESHLY GROUND BLACK PEPPER TO TASTE

ROASTED FENNEL

3 MEDIUM FENNEL BULBS, HALVED AND THINLY SLICED

2 TABLESPOONS (30 MILLILITERS) OLIVE OIL

4 THYME SPRIGS

SALT AND FRESHLY GROUND BLACK PEPPER TO TASTE

ROASTED CAULIFLOWER

1 LARGE HEAD CAULIFLOWER, CHOPPED INTO SMALL FLORETS

2 TABLESPOONS (30 MILLILITERS) OLIVE OIL

4 THYME SPRIGS

SALT AND FRESHLY GROUND BLACK PEPPER TO TASTE

LASAGNA

1 TABLESPOON (15 MILLILITERS) OLIVE OIL

6 TO 8 SHEETS FRESH EGG YOLK PASTA (PAGE 140)

1¼ POUNDS (567 GRAMS) AGED PROVOLONE CHEESE, GRATED

12 OUNCES (340 GRAMS) ASIAGO CHEESE, GRATED

2 CUPS (473 MILLILITERS) RICOTTA CHEESE (DIY, PAGE 142, OR STORE-BOUGHT)

SALT AND FRESHLY GROUND BLACK PEPPER TO TASTE

For the tomato sauce: In a food processor, pulse the tomatoes and their juices until very small chunks remain, about 30 seconds. In a large pot, heat the olive oil over medium high heat until shimmering. Sauté the onion and garlic until fragrant and translucent, about 4 minutes. Add the tomatoes and their juices, and bring to a boil. Lower the heat and simmer, uncovered, for 30 minutes, skimming any foam as it rises. Remove from the heat and set aside. We added a few leaves of fresh basil to the pot as it cooled for added flavor. Yields about 3 quarts (2.85 liters). Extra sauce can be frozen in an airtight container for several months.

For the eggplant: Slice the eggplant lengthwise into ¼-inch (1 centimeter) slices. Season both sides of each slice lightly with salt, set aside on paper towels to drain for 1 hour, then blot each slice with a paper towel to remove excess liquid. This step will help keep the lasagna from becoming watery.

Prepare a hot grill or heat a cast-iron grill pan until very hot. Brush the eggplant with olive oil, and season with pepper. Working in batches if necessary, sear the eggplant until branded with grill marks, about 2 minutes per side. Set aside until cool enough to handle.

For the fennel: Preheat the oven to 450°F (230°C). Line a sheet tray with parchment paper. Toss the fennel with the olive oil and thyme and season with salt and pepper. Roast on the sheet tray until softened and lightly caramelized, about 35 minutes. Remove from the oven and set aside. Crumble the now-dried thyme on top of the fennel, and discard stems.

For the cauliflower: (This can be roasted at the same time as the fennel.) Preheat the oven to 450°F (230°C). Line another sheet tray with parchment paper. Toss the cauliflower with the olive oil and thyme and season with salt and pepper. Roast on the sheet tray until softened and lightly caramelized, about 35 minutes. Remove from the oven, crush the thyme on top (discard the stem), and set aside to cool slightly (enough to handle with your fingers). Mix with the fennel to combine.

For the lasagna: Preheat the oven to 350°F (175°C). Lightly oil the bottom of a baking dish (see Note, page 145) and lay down the first layer of noodles; if necessary, cut to fit. Spread the noodles with 2 cups (473 milliliters) tomato sauce, then top with one-third each of the provolone and Asiago. Spread half of the ricotta on top of the cheeses, arrange all of the grilled eggplant on top of the ricotta, and spread a thick smear of tomato sauce (about 1¼ cups/300 milliliters) on top. Season the layer with salt and pepper.

Arrange the next layer of noodles and repeat the layering process with another 1¼ cups (300 milliliters) tomato sauce, half the provolone and Asiago, the remaining ricotta, all the cauliflower and fennel mixture, and another 1¼ cups (300 milliliters) tomato sauce.

After laying down the top layer of noodles, spread with the remaining tomato sauce (there should be ample coverage to keep it moist) and the remaining provolone and Asiago. Cover the baking dish with foil, tented up and away from the cheese layer to prevent sticking, then place the baking dish on a parchment paper–lined sheet tray. Bake in the oven for 1 hour, until the center is hot and the edges are bubbling; remove the foil and continue baking until the top layer is browned, about 30 minutes. Allow to cool for 15 minutes before slicing and serving. Serve with extra tomato sauce on the side.

Note

One taste tester declared this the best marinara she's ever had. So she was surprised to hear that it was the simplest, not to mention quickest, recipe for red sauce we've ever made. Using higher-quality canned tomatoes makes a big difference. At Frasca they use whole Solania San Marzano Tomatoes certified from the region in Italy and pass their tomatoes through a food mill to achieve the correct liquidity. You can use a food processor to achieve the approximate consistency, but we advise against buying chopped tomatoes; somehow they are not as flavorful as whole and retain a slightly "tinny" quality even after they are cooked.

GRACE

PORTLAND, MAINE

MAINE SHRIMP AND ANDOUILLE GUMBO

GHOST PEPPER HOT SAUCE

HOMEMADE CHICKEN AND SMOKED PAPRIKA SAUSAGE

PRESSURE-COOKED GARLIC DRESSING
WITH TURNIPS AND CARAMELIZED EGGS

Grace is a stunning restaurant, breathtaking even. An early Gothic Revival cathedral painstakingly restored in 2008, its massive, curved wooden beams bend and cross to create a soaring internal skeleton under which the diners sit. As at places of worship the world over, you look up and your heart lifts. But on the day of our visit, it is a humble pumpkin, not the historic nave, that steals the show. Lining the tables where pews once stood, the restaurant is filled with squashes of staggering variety, grown and delivered by the Crown O' Maine Cooperative, a consortium of local farmers who provide Grace with seasonal produce for their new American menu. Tied to each pumpkin's stem is a handwritten label. It identifies the species and farm of origin and also includes a quirky footnote. One especially fetching squash was bestowed the review: "A wacky, wild one! Eye candy and edible!" Bathed in multicolored sunbeams streaming in from the three-story stained-glass windows, the pumpkins sit like plump orange idols; and we realize just how devoutly Grace worships its local harvest.

Fitting, then, that the open kitchen is built on what was once the church's high altar, and only natural that local ingredients find their way into the staff meal. As midday light gives way to fog—Portland being a city notorious for its shifting sunshine—the smell of sausage, flour, and fat waft into the church. Executive Chef Eric Simeon, a young cook who sports the laid-back California attitude of his youth along with a crop of unruly dark curls, has decided to use the tiny local Maine shrimp to make his famous gumbo. Eric absorbed his version of this dish by standing at his Creole grandmother's side but admits kitchen detritus, not nostalgia, inspired this particular recipe: "We did a brunch a few weeks ago for some people from the South, and they wanted a Southern theme, so I bought a bunch of country hams. I was lucky to have the bones left over for the gumbo, which is nice because country hams are deeply intense."

As Eric chops vegetables, his even, measured staccato bouncing off the pipe organ looming above, he champions the significance of the gumbo's "trinity," the vegetable foundation of diced bell pepper, onion, and celery. Some cooks add garlic too, also known as "the pope." Representing the holiest of numbers, the trinity motif is echoed throughout the restaurant's details: carved delicately into wooden beams, hovering within the restaurant's stylized logo, even supersized via a massive glass fixture suspended over the central bar. Asked to elaborate on the umbrella-like feature, Eric clarifies the concept: "It's called a triquetra [a series of interlinking petals that form a rounded triangle]. The number three is important in Christianity, so we've incorporated the theme. Plus, it makes it a great bar to sit at."

Handfuls of the chopped raw trinity are dropped into the darkened roux, a slow-cooked mixture of fat and flour that

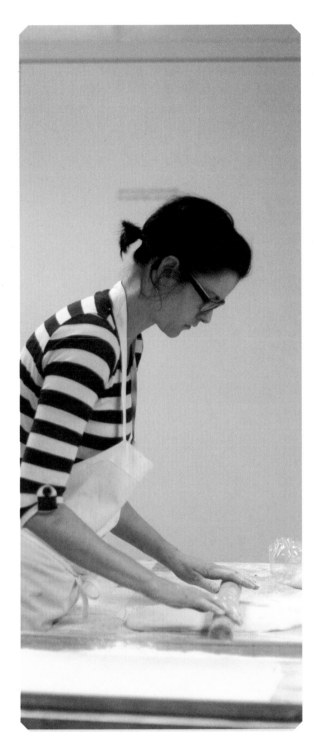

flavors and thickens the gumbo. Over the loud sizzle, Eric explains that this step prevents the roux from burning and becoming bitter. He prefers to add some fiery chile peppers at this stage but keeps things mild for the staff meal—just a few Mexican poblanos mixed in with the trinity, a trick he learned while at the California restaurant Postrio. "Gumbo wouldn't be the same without some heat," he says, "but I've found that people have a vast range of capsaicin tolerance."

Fitting then that right before the meal was served, Eric presents a surprise for the staff, homemade hot sauce. From behind the bar counter emerge three large mason jars in raging shades of crimson, labeled mild, medium, and spicy. Adam Bryant, a tall, wiry, and reserved line cook, eyes their contents. "What kind of peppers did you put in the hot one?" When Eric replies that ghost peppers are part of the equation—also known as Bhut Jolokia, the ghost pepper is the world's hottest chile, registering about one million on the Scoville heat scale—Adam wisely reaches for the sauce labeled "medium." At the end of the meal, he helps himself to another serving of gumbo, plopping a spoonful of rice into the center. This time he ladles a generous ribbon of ghost pepper sauce into the bowl. Returning to his seat, Adam slowly, methodically eats it all. When he hits the bottom of the bowl, he stands up and says to the silenced table, "Let's cook." No one can steal that thunder, not even the pumpkins.

A Conversation with Head Chef ERIC SIMEON

Why is the family meal important here at Grace?

For me, having to cook family meal is really what made me a good cook when I was starting out. I worked at this place called Postrio, which is a big Wolfgang Puck restaurant, and one of my main jobs was to do family meal every day. It was high pressure, you know. I had to make the staff meal and then I had to set up my station. It was always a lot to balance.

What lessons did you learn making the staff meals there?

I had to figure out how to manage my time, how to work with whatever ingredients that I was given: sometimes really crappy, sometimes really nice. I realized chickens were a big factor, so I started researching and trying out new chicken recipes: Asian style, Indian things, even gumbo once. That was in '96; I still remember thinking to myself, "I can't mess this up."

Do you have a family meal here at Grace every day?

We do, but honestly, we don't always sit down and eat together. Although we always make something nice, eat, hang out for a minute or two, and then, "Let's go!"

What's the best staff meal you've ever eaten?

Oh man. I've had a lot. When I was in Hawaii, I worked at this hotel that was right on the water. The family meals themselves were okay, but we sat at this table that was looking out over the ocean. To sit outside, eat family meal, and watch the sun set over the water? You can't really beat that.

What local ingredient always makes it into the staff meal?

Local Maine garlic, that stuff is awesome. It comes in still dirty, and the cloves are so juicy. Our farmer calls it "kitchen-grade."

What is one kitchen scrap you will never throw away?

I make a point of saving every kind of fat that I can, and thus have a steady supply of chicken, pork, beef, duck, lamb, and bacon fat. Like the fat that comes off roasted beef? We put it in a sous vide bag with our steak . . . you can't get any closer to what steak is supposed to taste like! Oh yeah, burgers, too. We sous vide the burgers first with beef fat, and then we finish them on the grill.

Do you feel that the spiritual aspect of a church-turned-restaurant plays into your food and the way you run your kitchen?

Well, I wouldn't say directly, but just being in this place, it really gives you a lot of peace. I love being up here in the kitchen when I'm alone; it feels so comfortable. You have the light coming in from the stained glass. It's really nice. We do some Gregorian chants sometimes, too. Just to calm down.

MAINE SHRIMP and ANDOUILLE GUMBO

"I learned to make gumbo by the sides of my father, aunts, uncles, and cousins," says Head Chef Eric Simeon, but never once did he see anyone refer to a written recipe. Growing up he believed there was a Yoda-like knowledge when it came to making the dish. "It actually took me many years before I worked up the nerve to make my own," he admits. "In reality it is very forgiving, with a million variations." This one makes excellent use of the local Maine shrimp—the rosy fingernail-sized variety bursting with sweetness—but any small shrimp would work in this recipe, including frozen Key West shrimp available all year long.

For authenticity, Eric recommends using Cajun andouille, a pork-based sausage that is fatty and heavily smoked but not heavily spiced. LaPlace, Louisiana has declared itself the andouille capital, hosting an annual festival every October, but when Eric returns to his family's home in Los Angeles to host their annual gumbo gathering, he frequents Pete's Louisiana Style Hot Links in Crenshaw. Says Eric, "We have to buy extra to make sure that there is enough left after everybody snacks on them." If none are available, any smoked pork sausage will work.

Serves 8

STOCK

1 WHOLE CHICKEN

KOSHER SALT AND FRESHLY GROUND BLACK PEPPER TO TASTE

8 OUNCES (227 GRAMS) ANDOUILLE SAUSAGE (SEE RECIPE HEADER)

1 SMOKED HAM HOCK (OR LEFTOVER HAM BONE)

1 GALLON (3.8 LITERS) CHICKEN STOCK

1 TABLESPOON (15 MILLILITERS) BACON GREASE

4 RIBS CELERY, COARSELY CHOPPED

2 LARGE YELLOW ONIONS, COARSELY CHOPPED

1 SMALL GREEN BELL PEPPER, COARSELY CHOPPED

1 LARGE RED BELL PEPPER, COARSELY CHOPPED

1 SMALL POBLANO PEPPER, SEEDED AND COARSELY CHOPPED

8 GARLIC CLOVES, MINCED

2 TEASPOONS (4 GRAMS) SMOKED HOT PAPRIKA

2 TEASPOONS (2 GRAMS) DRIED THYME

2 TEASPOONS (2 GRAMS) DRIED BASIL

2 TEASPOONS (2 GRAMS) DRIED OREGANO

1 TEASPOON (1 GRAM) DRIED GROUND SAGE

¼ TEASPOON (.5 GRAM) CAYENNE PEPPER

4 BAY LEAVES

1 CUP (237 MILLILITERS) CANOLA OIL

1¼ CUPS (156 GRAMS) ALL-PURPOSE FLOUR

1 POUND (454 GRAMS) SMALL MAINE RED SHRIMP, PEELED

1 TABLESPOON (8 GRAMS) FILÉ POWDER

2 TABLESPOONS (10 GRAMS) MINCED PARSLEY

1 TABLESPOON (4 GRAMS) MINCED OREGANO

2 TEASPOONS TABLESPOON (3 GRAMS) MINCED SAGE

FOR SERVING

I CUP (160 GRAMS) COOKED WHITE RICE PER PERSON

4 THINLY SLICED SCALLIONS (WHITE AND GREEN PARTS), OPTIONAL

GHOST PEPPER HOT SAUCE (PAGE 156)

Preheat the oven to 450°F (232°C).

Season the chicken liberally both outside and inside the cavity with salt and pepper. Tuck the wings underneath the bird (twist at the joint) and tie the drumsticks together with string or twist ties. Place breast-side up in a roasting pan. Roast to an internal temperature of 165°F (74°C), 45 to 55 minutes, or until the skin turns deep golden brown and juices from the center of the bird run clear into the pan when you tip them out.

Remove from the oven and rest for 25 minutes, until the chicken is cool enough to handle.

Meanwhile, lower the oven to 350°F (177°C).

Roast the andouille in a small roasting pan until fully cooked, about 20 minutes. Remove from the pan and set aside to cool, then slice into bite-sized pieces and set aside. (Grace saves the sausage fat left behind in the roasting pan to use for sautéing the trinity later on in the recipe.)

Return to the rested chicken and remove and discard the skin. Pull the meat from the carcass, chop into bite-sized pieces, and set aside. Return the bones back to the pan and roast in the oven until bones are deeply browned, about 25 minutes. This step is optional but adds depth of flavor to the finished stock.

Transfer the roasted bones to a large pot. Add about ¼ cup (59 milliliters) water to the drippings in the hot roasting pan and scrape up the browned bits clinging to the bottom. Pour the resulting liquid into the pot. Add the ham hock and chicken stock. Bring to a boil, then lower the heat to medium-low and gently simmer for 1 hour, skimming away fat and impurities that rise to the surface.

Strain the resulting stock through a fine-mesh sieve, reserving the liquid and the ham hock separately. Rinse the pot of any residue and return the stock to it. Discard the chicken bones. Once the ham hock is cool enough to handle, pick off the meat, chop into bite-sized pieces, and set aside.

In a large skillet over high heat, melt the fat. Add half the trinity (onions, celery, and peppers), reserving the rest for later. Reduce the heat to medium-high and sauté for 5 minutes, until the vegetables soften slightly. Add the garlic and continue to cook until the vegetables are tender, about 5 more minutes.

Add the vegetables to the stock along with the paprika, dried herbs, cayenne, and bay leaves. Bring to a boil, then reduce the heat. Simmer briskly for about 1 hour, until the liquid is reduced by one-quarter, then season with salt and pepper.

To make the roux, pour the canola oil into a large skillet, preferably cast iron, and whisk in the flour to create a wet paste. Cook over medium heat, whisking often and employing patience, until the roux darkens past the "peanut butter" stage, taking on a deep, dark chocolate color and a rich, nutty aroma, about 30 minutes.

Turn off the heat and carefully add the remaining chopped trinity vegetables to the roux, continuing to stir constantly until the vegetables stop spitting, 3 to 5 minutes.

Transfer the roux to a large mixing bowl and cool for 15 minutes.

Slowly whisk 2 cups (473 milliliters) of hot stock into the roux to thin the consistency.

Now it's time to pull the gumbo together! Pour the thinned roux back into the pot of hot stock (now properly reduced), whisking vigorously to incorporate it. Add the reserved chicken, ham hock, and sausage along with the shrimp, filé, and fresh herbs. Bring to a boil, then reduce the heat. Simmer until the gumbo has thickened and the shrimp are cooked, about 25 minutes. The final consistency should be somewhere between a soup and a stew, or as one cook describes, "muddy." If it is too thin, reduce the liquid until it reaches the desired consistency. Too thick? Add water or stock. When finished, season with salt and pepper.

To serve: Spoon gumbo into large, flat bowls, then spoon a liberal mound of rice in the center. Drizzle on as much hot sauce as you dare. Scallions are the authors' addition for color and texture; good Creoles or Cajuns would eat their bowls neat. Leftover gumbo tastes better the next day—even better the day after that—and can be saved for up to a week in the refrigerator.

GHOST PEPPER HOT SAUCE

If you're anything like Eric Simeon, a bowl of gumbo is naked without hot sauce. "Having a very fiery option allows the thrill seekers to have enough heat without making the gumbo too acidic," he says. This recipe is fiery indeed. The heat from the ghost peppers will linger for many minutes on the palate so warn guests who may assume it's only Tabasco. If you have a couple of heat-seeking friends who would perhaps like a jar, this recipe doubles easily.

Yields two 12-ounce jars

8 OUNCES (227 GRAMS) FRESH PAPRIKA PEPPERS OR OTHER MILD TO MEDIUM CHILE PEPPERS, STEMS REMOVED AND THINLY SLICED

4 OUNCES (113 GRAMS) SHALLOTS (ABOUT 4), THINLY SLICED

4 SUN-DRIED TOMATOES

3 DRIED GHOST PEPPERS, STEMS REMOVED (ABOUT 3 GRAMS), (SEE NOTES)

2 TEASPOONS (12 GRAMS) KOSHER SALT

1 CUP (237 MILLILITERS) APPLE CIDER VINEGAR

Clean, sterilize, and air-dry two 12-ounce glass jars.

Using tongs or wearing gloves, place the fresh peppers, shallots, tomatoes, ghost peppers, salt, and 1 cup (236 milliliters) water in a small pot. Bring to a boil, then lower heat and simmer until the peppers and shallots are tender, about 20 minutes. Be careful not to inhale the steam! It is potent with pepper spice.

Add the vinegar, increase the heat to high, and cook for 5 more minutes. Remove from the heat and cool the sauce to room temperature.

Transfer the sauce to a blender and purée on high speed until smooth, about 2 minutes. If the sauce is too thick to pour, add a little water to thin.

Transfer the sauce to the sterilized jars, seal tightly, and store in the refrigerator for up to a month.

NOTES

Ghost peppers are the world's hottest chile peppers, a little over 400 times hotter than Tabasco sauce. The more you add to this recipe, the more insanely hot the sauce will get. Tread lightly. For a much milder sauce, omit the ghost peppers altogether. For a medium-strength sauce, use only one or two. Dried ghost peppers can be purchased online.

HOMEMADE CHICKEN and SMOKED PAPRIKA SAUSAGE

Head chef Eric Simeon knows that making your own sausage is a time-consuming process, but he's adamant about its advantages: "Not only is homemade sausage more delicious, you have complete control over the freshness and quality of ingredients." In this recipe, sausage–making also serves as a catchall for the dark meat of the chicken not served on the customer menu. Note that this recipe is given solely in weight measurements for a reason: successful sausage-making requires precision.

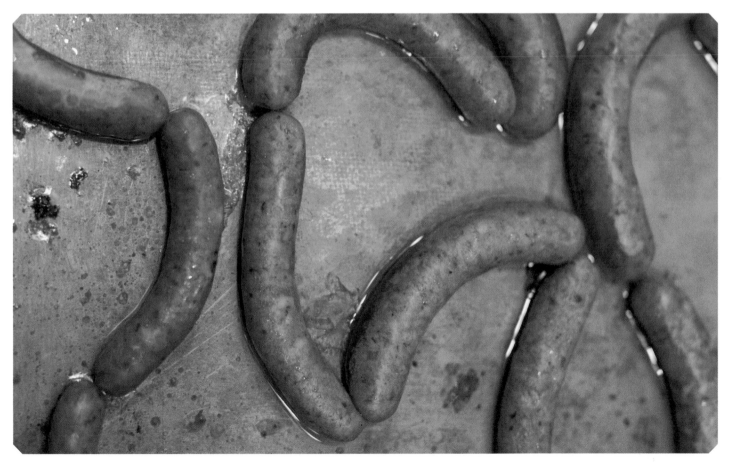

continues on next page

Yields about sixteen 3-ounce
(85 grams) patties

15⅞ OUNCES (450 GRAMS) PORK FATBACK

**31¾ OUNCES (900 GRAMS) BONELESS
CHICKEN THIGH MEAT, COARSELY
CHOPPED**

½ OUNCE (14 GRAMS) SMOKED HOT PAPRIKA

**½ OUNCE (14 GRAMS) PARSLEY, COARSELY
CHOPPED**

**½ OUNCE (14 GRAMS) OREGANO, COARSELY
CHOPPED**

⅜ OUNCE (12 GRAMS) GRANULATED SUGAR

¼ OUNCE (7 GRAMS) MINCED GARLIC

¼ OUNCE (7 GRAMS) KOSHER SALT

**⅛ OUNCE (3.5 GRAMS) FRESHLY GROUND
BLACK PEPPER**

**⅛ OUNCE (3.5 GRAMS) CRUSHED RED PEPPER
FLAKES**

**¼ CUP PLUS 2 TEASPOONS (70 MILLILITERS)
DRY RED WINE**

**2 TABLESPOONS PLUS 1 TEASPOON (35 MILLI-
LITERS) CHICKEN STOCK**

**2 TABLESPOONS PLUS 1 TEASPOON (35 MILLI-
LITERS) HEAVY WHIPPING CREAM**

CANOLA OIL, FOR TESTING AND SHAPING

**10 FEET (3 METERS) HOG CASINGS, SOAKED
AND RINSED THOROUGHLY INSIDE AND
OUT (OPTIONAL), (SEE NOTE)**

**SOFT ROLLS AND CREOLE MUSTARD FOR
SERVING**

Place all equipment, including the meat grinder (see Note, page 178), mixer bowl and paddle, and stuffing equipment (if using) in the freezer until thoroughly chilled. (This is key so the fat remains emulsified in the sausage.)

Freeze the fatback in the coldest part of your freezer for at least 12 hours. Coarsely chop the fatback, then grind along with the chicken meat through the small die of a meat grinder into the chilled mixer bowl.

Add the paprika, parsley, oregano, sugar, garlic, salt, pepper, red pepper flakes, wine, chicken stock, and cream. Fit the bowl into the electric mixer, and using the paddle attachment, mix on low speed for 1 minute, or until the liquid is fully absorbed and the mixture is tacky.

Test the sausage by forming a small patty and frying it over high heat in a skillet slicked with oil. Taste the cooked patty and adjust the salt, pepper, and spices if desired, mixing for another 15 to 30 seconds to incorporate. Work quickly! The more time you keep the sausage mixture at room temperature, the greater the possibility the fat will not emulsify correctly.

Using a light, oil-greased hand, gently shape the sausage mixture into loose 3-ounce (85 gram) patties about 3 inches (7.5 centimeters) in diameter and 1 inch (2.5 centimeters) thick. Arrange in a single layer on a sheet tray, cover, and refrigerate until needed.

Alternatively, stuff the sausage into casings using a sausage stuffer. If you do not have a stuffer, saw off the spout of a large-diameter funnel to the appropriate diameter of the casing. Fill the funnel with the sausage mixture and slip the empty casing around the spout. Using your hands and, if necessary, a dowel that fits into the spout, push the filling through the funnel and into the casing, twisting off sausages at the desired length. Try to avoid air pockets, as this can cause bursting when cooking; empty and restuff the casing should an air bubble occur or pierce the bubble with a sterilized pin.

To cook the links or patties, either brown in an oiled skillet over medium-high heat about 15 minutes, or bake at 350°F (177°C) about 20 minutes, until fully cooked.

Serve with soft rolls and spicy Creole mustard. Extra uncooked patties or sausages can be stored in the freezer, tightly wrapped, for several months.

NOTE

For home cooks who don't have time to hunt down casings (or are not up to the challenge of cleaning and stuffing them), forming sausage patties yields instant gratification. If you do decide to go the casing route, keep in mind that most butchers stock casings and would probably be willing to sell them for a song; just ask.

PRESSURE-COOKED GARLIC DRESSING
with TURNIPS and CARAMELIZED EGGS

Vampire novels aside, garlic breath is rarely considered a good thing. To skirt this front-of-the-house faux pas, Grace pressure-cooks whole heads in milk to soften and mellow the cloves. What was once an acrid bite gives way to a slightly sweet, almost roasted, creaminess. After puréeing, the pressure-cooked cloves become a useful paste to have on hand. Here it is turned into a great dressing, but whipped into softened butter along with finely grated Asiago it makes an easy spread for a marvelously mellow garlic bread.

Serves 8

GARLIC PURÉE

1 CUP (140 GRAMS) GARLIC CLOVES, PEELED AND LEFT WHOLE

2 CUPS (473 MILLILITERS) WHOLE MILK

DRESSING

½ CUP (120 MILLILITERS) MAYONNAISE

½ CUP (120 MILLILITERS) SOUR CREAM

1 TABLESPOON (15 MILLILITERS) DIJON MUSTARD

JUICE OF 1 LEMON

2 TABLESPOONS (30 MILLILITERS) EXTRA-VIRGIN OLIVE OIL

1 TABLESPOON (3.8 GRAMS) MINCED PARSLEY

1 TABLESPOON (3 GRAMS) MINCED CHIVES

1 TABLESPOON (3 GRAMS) MINCED TARRAGON

KOSHER SALT AND FRESHLY GROUND BLACK PEPPER TO TASTE

SALAD

1 HEAD RED LEAF LETTUCE

2 SMALL TURNIPS, PEELED AND VERY THINLY SLICED

8 CARAMELIZED EGGS, PEELED AND QUARTERED (PAGE 161)

KOSHER SALT AND FRESHLY GROUND BLACK PEPPER TO TASTE

continues on next page

For the purée: Combine the garlic and milk in the pressure cooker. Secure the lid closed and locked. If your pressure cooker has multiple pressure settings, set it to the highest pressure, 15 psi. Over high heat, bring it to pressure, about 5 minutes. (You'll know your cooker has reached pressure capacity when it starts violently, and very loudly, streaming steam from its release valve.)

Lower the heat to medium to maintain a steady "the kettle is ready" whistle. If you are using an electric stove, have another burner preheated to medium, and move the pressure cooker, carefully, to the second burner to avoid overcooking. Cook the garlic for 20 minutes.

Remove from the heat, and without releasing any steam or unlocking the lid, let the pot rest for 30 minutes.

After resting, release any remaining steam according to your cooker's directions, unlock, and remove the lid. Transfer the cooked milk and garlic, now soft and slightly caramelized, to a blender. Pulse several times with the lid cracked to vent hot steam (hold a dish towel over the vented lid to prevent any hot splatters). Blend until smooth and creamy, about 2 minutes. Refrigerate until chilled.

For the dressing: In a large bowl, combine 2 cups of the purée with the mayonnaise, sour cream, mustard, lemon juice, olive oil, and herbs. Whisk together and season with salt and pepper. Taste and add more purée if desired. The dressing will be very thick, about the consistency of Dijon mustard. Yields about 3 cups (710 milliliters) dressing. Extra dressing can be saved in a jar for up to a week in the refrigerator. It makes an interesting substitute for mayonnaise in dishes like tuna or chicken salad.

For the salad: Wash and dry the lettuce, then tear into pieces. Toss with enough dressing to coat each leaf then place the lettuce on a serving platter. Top decoratively with the turnips and eggs. Drizzle with more dressing, serving extra dressing on the side.

NOTE

A word about safe pressure cooker use from Eric: "The pressure cooker can be a very useful tool in the kitchen, but you should always operate it in a safe manner. Always inspect sealing gaskets on the lid before operating the cooker, and avoid using any that are torn or deteriorated. Make sure pressure release valves are kept clean and free of food particles. Never fill the cooker more than half full. Avoid violent movement of the pot, and never open the lid until the pot has cooled down and the pressure has been released."

CARAMELIZED EGGS

These eggs do take a bit more time than hard-boiled, but the end product is worth it. The typical sulfuric funk of hard-cooked yolks is replaced with a profound sweetness, and the whites of the eggs turn a surprising and beautiful light toffee color thanks to the caramelizing effects of the Maillard reaction—the same effect you get on a nicely seared piece of beef when protein and sugar molecules react. The texture is slightly firmer than a 12-minute egg, though not at all rubbery, and the yolk turns a tawny yellow.

This recipe can be scaled up or down quite easily. Just make sure that you add enough water to cover the eggs completely, especially if they are stacked up higher than a single layer. Extra pressure-cooked eggs will last for days, unpeeled, in the refrigerator, and can multitask throughout the week: turned into egg salad, sliced onto pork ramen, even transformed into "the most amazing deviled eggs," according to head chef Eric Simeon.

Yields 8 eggs

8 LARGE EGGS

2 TABLESPOONS (36 GRAMS) KOSHER SALT

Check the eggs to make sure they are free of cracks. Carefully place them in the pressure cooker. Fill with enough water to just cover the eggs. Add the salt.

Bring to a boil, remove from the heat, and secure the lid closed and locked. If your pressure cooker has multiple pressure settings, set it to the highest pressure, 15 psi.

Place the sealed pot back over high heat and bring the pot to pressure. (You will know your cooker has reached pressure capacity when it starts violently, and very loudly, streaming steam from its release valve.) Lower the heat to medium to maintain a steady "the kettle is ready," whistle. If you are using an electric stove, have another burner preheated to medium, and move the pressure cooker, carefully, to the second burner to avoid overcooking. Cook the eggs for 40 minutes.

Remove from the heat, and without releasing any steam or unlocking the lid, let the pot rest for 1 hour.

After resting, release any remaining steam according to your cooker's directions, unlock, and remove the lid. Drain the eggs and plunge them into an ice bath. When cold enough to handle, about 5 minutes, peel the eggs to reveal their mahogany interior and serve.

THE HERBFARM

WOODINVILLE, WASHINGTON

WHOLE HERB VINAIGRETTE WITH MIXED GREENS

IOWA-STYLE FRIED CHICKEN

STRAWBERRY SHORTCAKE WITH ORANGE AND
THYME BISCUITS

HOMEMADE TARRAGON AND CHERRY SODA

ittingly, The Herbfarm's family meal starts—and often ends—amidst the herbs. In fact, few staff meals here are ever created without the cooks first foraging in the quarter-acre of raised beds outside their back door. It is a time-worn tradition. Decades before the term "local" became a trendy restaurant catchphrase, The Herbfarm's founders, Ron Zimmerman and Carrie Van Dyck, used the Seattle seasons to craft their menus and educate their customers. With a near fanatical devotion to the harvest—some have even referred to The Herbfarm's style as "micro-seasonal"—the menus change bimonthly to accommodate local crops. Along with fruits and vegetables from their nearby four-acre farm, all the meals here are literally built from the ground up.

During our visit, we watch as Lisa Nakamura—a three-year veteran who has since left to open her own restaurant, Allium, on Orcas Island off the Washington coast—grabs a metal mixing bowl and wades into an expanse of fragrant blossoms just steps away from the kitchen. With softly crunching footfalls, the Hawaii native winds her way around the paths lined with hazelnut shells. She cuts long stems of bee balm, orange balsam thyme, and anise hyssop, whose thick spires of tiny purple blossoms smell faintly of licorice.

So when we return with Lisa to the kitchen and offer up our garden bounty, cooks quickly descend to wash, dry, and prep the ingredients with care. Within minutes the bee balm and anise hyssop

find their way into a homemade cherry soda while the thyme takes a spin in buttermilk biscuits as light as air. Lisa runs her fingers over a chorus of dark green, saucer-sized leaves: "This spinach is a tad too large to serve to customers," she says, "but they are just perfect for us." It's a simple statement that affirms the garden's role as both teacher and muse.

As the sun retreats, the raspy sputter of a pickup truck announces the arrival of a local farmer who has come to join the staff meal. The Herbfarm invites its purveyors to dinner once a week as a way of thanking them for supplying the restaurant. "It's family meal and they're part of our family," says Chris Weber, the restaurant's executive chef. Around 3:30 p.m., people pack the garden's well-worn picnic table wedged between a Douglas fir and a shaggy red cedar. As they pile plates high with fried chicken, buttermilk biscuits, and spinach salad doused in an herb vinaigrette born from the garden itself, the term "farm-to-table" has never seemed more appropriate—or more genuine.

A Conversation with Chef CHRIS WEBER

Why is the staff meal important?

It teaches our cooks to become chefs. It instills the importance of sticking to an allotted budget, creating continuity in a meal, and using time wisely.

How does the adjacent garden at The Herbfarm inspire your staff meals?

Anyone who has ever grown zucchini or tomatoes or greens knows that there is always a time when you will have more than you can use. For us, that surplus goes into our daily staff meals. Things can get pretty "creative" when it comes to utilizing the harvest, but we're committed to using everything that our farmers grow.

So how does The Herbfarm make good on the garden's surplus?

When it comes to using a surplus of ingredients, our goal is to concentrate flavors. One of the best soups I have ever had was a total contradiction of everything I had learned about zucchini—a roasted zucchini and garlic soup, simmered for hours. The intensity of the two flavors unified them and turned them into something completely new.

Do you handle the herbs, vegetables, and fruits from your garden differently than those purchased from a store?

It's important to harvest early while it's still cool but just after the dew dries so nothing is wet. If we harvest ingredients in the heat with dew still on them they can steam themselves and wilt. Back in the kitchen, we know everything is chemical–free so we just rinse it all in vinegar water—to get rid of the bugs—before using it.

What's one ingredient that you use in your restaurant that no home cook should be without?

I think fresh chives make just about anything taste better.

What was your most memorable staff meal? What made it so special?

Toby Kim's ma po tofu, a stew made of ground pork and tofu simmered in a garlic, chili, and bean sauce. It made me understand that no matter what the cuisine, a dish can be made over and over again without losing its integrity.

Are there any cookbooks that you use to inspire a good family meal menu?

Sunday Suppers at Lucques by Suzanne Goin is one of my favorites. Also, the original *The Herbfarm Cookbook* by Jerry Traunfeld. Though we no longer use most of the recipes in the book at the restaurant, it's a glimpse into some interesting flavor combinations, especially with lesser known herbs.

What's one cooking tool/piece of equipment that you use in your restaurant that no home cook should be without?

The sense of taste. It's good if you like it. A lot of times home cooks get hung up on the way things are "supposed" to be rather that what they actually are. Just enjoy and listen to your belly.

WHOLE HERB VINAIGRETTE with MIXED GREENS

In 1974, The Herbfarm opened its doors as an herbal nursery, supplying the Seattle area with hard-to-source botanicals. A decade later, an old garage on the property was transformed into a restaurant, appropriately named The Herbfarm. To ensure that no gardening effort—or flavor—is wasted, both the leaves and stems of herbs are used to make this dressing. Former chef de cuisine Lisa Nakamura noted, "The stems are often discarded, but they have a lot of flavor. I try to use them whenever possible." The added bonus here is that you get to skip the fiddly process of separating the leaves from stems.

Yields 1½ cups (355 milliliters)

VINAIGRETTE

½ CUP (118 MILLILITERS) CANOLA OIL

½ CUP (118 MILLILITERS) OLIVE OIL

2 TABLESPOONS (30 MILLILITERS) DIJON MUSTARD

⅓ CUP (79 MILLILITERS) RED WINE VINEGAR

1 TABLESPOON (15 MILLILITERS) FRESHLY SQUEEZED LEMON JUICE

1 TEASPOON (6 GRAMS) KOSHER SALT, PLUS MORE TO TASTE

6 TARRAGON SPRIGS

6 MARJORAM SPRIGS

4 THYME SPRIGS

SMALL BUNCH OF CHIVES, PARSLEY, OR BASIL

1 SHALLOT, MINCED

FOR SERVING

A LARGE HANDFUL OF MIXED GARDEN GREENS PER PERSON

KOSHER SALT AND FRESHLY GROUND BLACK PEPPER TO TASTE

For the vinaigrette: Combine the oils in a measuring cup with a spout. In a blender, combine the mustard, vinegar, 2 teaspoons (10 milliliters) lemon juice, and the salt and blend on high until the salt dissolves, about 10 seconds. Continue to blend while adding the oil in a slow, steady stream until the mixture is emulsified, about 1 minute. The dressing should be as thick as heavy whipping cream. Turn off the blender and add the herbs. Don't bother pulling off stems, as they impart just as much flavor as their leaves; just mash them as far down into the blender as possible with a long wooden spoon. Pulse for 20 seconds, then blend on high speed until the liquid takes on a vibrant green color, about 30 seconds more. Strain the vinaigrette through a fine-mesh sieve, pushing on the solids with the wooden spoon to extract as much liquid as possible. Stir the shallot into the dressing and season with salt and pepper. If you accidentally oversalt, neutralize the mistake with the remaining lemon juice. Set aside.

For the salad: In a large bowl, toss together the mixed greens with enough vinaigrette to coat but not drown the leaves. Season with salt and pepper, toss again, and serve immediately.

HOMEMADE TARRAGON and CHERRY SODA

The Herbfarm celebrates the short Northwest cherry season with this simple homemade soda. The day of our visit, licorice-scented anise hyssop and bee balm blossoms (also known as wild bergamot, with a flavor that is a cross between mint and oregano) was used, but tarragon and mint are reliable substitutes. For a more adult version of this drink, Cava, an affordable Spanish sparkling wine, makes an excellent stand-in for the club soda.

NOTE

If you don't have a cherry pitter at home, use a plastic straw to puncture the cherry's stem end, then push, hard, to drive the pit out the other side.

Yields 2 quarts (1.9 liters)

1 CUP (200 GRAMS) GRANULATED SUGAR

1 POUND (454 GRAMS) PITTED CHERRIES (CAN SUBSTITUTE FROZEN AND THAWED)

¼ CUP (8 GRAMS) TARRAGON LEAVES

¼ CUP (8 GRAMS) MINT LEAVES

1 QUART (946 MILLILITERS) CLUB SODA, CHILLED

CRUSHED ICE

1 LEMON, CUT INTO WEDGES

For the cherry syrup: Begin by making a simple syrup. Bring 1 cup (237 milliliters) water and the sugar to a boil, whisking until the sugar dissolves. Remove from the heat and cool to room temperature. Yields about 1½ cups (354 milliliters).

In a blender, combine the cherries, 1 cup (237 milliliters) simple syrup, and the tarragon and mint and blend on high until smooth, about 1 minute. Add more simple syrup to taste. Strain through a fine-mesh sieve, pushing on the solids to extract as much liquid as possible. Skim off any resulting foam; set aside. Yields about 3 cups (710 milliliters).

For the cherry soda: When ready to serve, pour the cherry syrup into a 68-ounce (2 liter) pitcher. Add the club soda very slowly (to avoid creating foam) and stir gently. Serve over ice, garnished with a lemon wedge.

IOWA-STYLE FRIED CHICKEN

A short-term kitchen intern created this dish using her mother's "Iowa Style" recipe, where hot-from-the-fryer chicken is served with sumptuous amounts of honey and hot sauce. An addictive combination. With "no herb left behind" as the restaurant's guiding principal, she also used up leftover leaves by stirring them into the buttermilk marinade. The end result was succulent fried chicken with an unexpected herbal hit. And by finishing the pieces in the oven instead of the fryer, time at the stove was greatly reduced—a handy trick when cooking for a large crowd.

Serves 4

1 QUART (946 MILLILITERS) BUTTERMILK

2 GARLIC CLOVES, MINCED

1 CUP (160 GRAMS) COARSELY CHOPPED ASSORTED HERBS (THE HERBFARM USES A MIX OF THYME, SAGE, ROSEMARY, AND WINTER SAVORY)

KOSHER SALT AND FRESHLY GROUND BLACK PEPPER TO TASTE

ONE (3- TO 4-POUND/1.4 TO 1.8 KILOGRAM) CHICKEN, CUT INTO 8 PIECES

1 CUP (140 GRAMS) ALL-PURPOSE FLOUR

5 LARGE EGGS, BEATEN

2 CUPS (140 GRAMS) PANKO BREADCRUMBS

1 QUART (946 MILLILITERS) CANOLA OIL

HONEY AND HOT SAUCE, TO SERVE

The night before frying, whisk together the buttermilk, garlic, and herbs in a large bowl. Lightly salt each chicken piece and arrange in a large, resealable plastic bag. Pour the buttermilk bath over the chicken to cover completely. Refrigerate overnight, or for at least 12 hours.

Preheat the oven to 350°F (177°C). Drain the chicken, discarding the buttermilk bath. Pat the chicken pieces dry with paper towels. Season each piece with salt and pepper.

Assemble your breading station by placing the flour, eggs, and panko in three separate bowls, and setting out a clean wire rack. Dredge one piece of chicken in flour, dip in the egg bath, and finally coat thoroughly in panko, shaking off excess between coatings. Place the dredged pieces on the rack to maintain a crispy bottom coating.

In a Dutch oven, heat the oil to 375°F (191°C). Using tongs, carefully place as many chicken pieces as will fit inside in a single layer without touching. The oil should just cover the pieces. Fry the chicken, turning with tongs once or twice, until all sides are golden brown, about 10 minutes. Drain the chicken on the paper towels. Arrange the pieces in a single layer on the sheet tray and season with salt and pepper. Fry the remaining chicken, making sure the oil returns to 375°F (191°C).

Bake the fried pieces for 25 to 30 minutes, or until the flesh in the center of a breast is opaque white, and the leg pieces register 165°F (74°C) on an instant-read thermometer.

The coating is delicate and light and flakes off easily, so be careful when you transfer the chicken from the sheet tray to a platter. Serve piping hot with bottles of honey and hot sauce for passing around the table.

Note

A deep-fry thermometer is always the most reliable method for gauging the temperature of frying oil. However, if yours has gone missing, drop a single popcorn kernel into the heated oil. (Don't worry about popcorn flying out of the pot. As long as you drop in one kernel at a time, it will just float to the top.) When the kernel pops into a billowy bloom, the oil is between 350°F and 390°F (177°C and 199°C), spot-on deep-frying territory. The oil is too hot (above 400°F/204°C) if the kernel turns into a shriveled, almost CornNut-like piece of popcorn. If this is the case, remove the pot from the heat and allow the oil to cool or use the trick on page 69 for a quicker fix.

STRAWBERRY SHORTCAKE
with ORANGE & THYME BISCUITS

This dessert is known in-house as "Anna's Shortcakes" after their original creator and can incorporate any seasonal berry or stone fruit the restaurant may have on hand. Light and cake-like with a hint of citrus, these biscuits pair well with sliced strawberries and whipped cream but could just as easily be slathered with salted butter and served alongside the fried chicken. To save time during the berry-laden summer months, make the dough in multiple batches. Cut out the biscuits, place in a single layer on a sheet tray, and freeze until solid. Place the frozen disks in a resealable plastic bag and store in your freezer, baking them from their frozen state as you need them. They should only take a minute or two longer in the oven.

Serves 6

BISCUITS

1 LARGE EGG

¾ CUP (177 MILLILITERS) BUTTERMILK, PLUS MORE FOR BRUSHING

2½ CUPS (315 GRAMS) ALL-PURPOSE FLOUR, PLUS MORE FOR DUSTING

⅓ CUP (67 GRAMS) GRANULATED SUGAR

1 TABLESPOON (14 GRAMS) BAKING POWDER

½ TEASPOON (3 GRAMS) KOSHER SALT

4 OUNCES (1 STICK/112 GRAMS) UNSALTED BUTTER, COLD AND CUT INTO CUBES

FRESHLY GRATED ORANGE ZEST FROM 1 MEDIUM ORANGE

2 TEASPOONS (2 GRAMS) THYME LEAVES, MINCED

BERRIES

1 POUND (454 GRAMS) STRAWBERRIES, SLICED

¼ CUP (50 GRAMS) GRANULATED SUGAR

JUICE OF 1 MEDIUM ORANGE

TO SERVE

PLENTY OF FRESHLY WHIPPED CREAM

For the biscuits: Place a rack in the middle of the oven and preheat the oven to 400°F (204°C). Line a sheet tray with parchment paper.

Whisk the egg and buttermilk together; set aside. Sift the flour, sugar, baking powder, and salt into a bowl. Work the butter in with your hands until pea-sized granules form, about 2 minutes.

Make a teacup-sized well in the flour and fill with the buttermilk mixture, zest, and thyme. With a fork, mash the wet and dry ingredients together for 1 minute, or until the dough just comes together. Quickly and gently knead the mixture with your hands until a ball forms, about 30 seconds. (The dough should be fairly wet, and will stick slightly to your hands and bowl.) Work quickly! The less you work the dough, the less your butter will melt, which leads to a lighter biscuit.

On a clean work surface dusted liberally with flour, flatten the dough with a rolling pin until ½ inch (13 millimeters) thick. Using a 3-inch (6 centimeter) ring cutter (a clean tuna can or water glass lightly oiled on the inside can be used instead), punch out as many biscuits as you can. Gather together the scraps of dough until they form one cohesive piece, then dust, roll, and cut out again.

Transfer the biscuits to the prepared sheet tray and brush the tops with buttermilk.

Bake on the middle rack for 13 to 15 minutes, or until the tops are light golden brown and the bottoms are crisp. Remove from the oven and allow to cool slightly on the tray before serving.

For the berries: When the biscuits are in the oven, toss together the berries, sugar, and orange juice in a bowl. Set aside at room temperature to macerate until the fruit is slightly softened and oozing juice, about 20 minutes.

To serve: Split a warm biscuit in half through the middle. Place the bottom half cut-side up on a dessert plate and top with a generous spoonful of berries plus a drizzle of the juice, to moisten the biscuit. Load on the whipped cream and crown with the top half of the biscuit. Serve immediately.

McCRADY'S

CHARLESTON, SOUTH CAROLINA

DOUBLE-STACK CHEESEBURGERS
WITH SPECIAL SAUCE

BEEF FAT FRIES

THE ELVIS PRESLEY MILKSHAKE

Winburn Carmack is the kind of cook every head chef dreams of having on staff. Fair-skinned and flaxen-haired with a toothy, megawatt smile, she is the young Executive Pastry Chef at McCrady's, one of Charleston, South Carolina's most celebrated restaurants. She is known for putting her head down and getting the job done. When she finally comes up for air after hours of intense baking, she is as delightful as a slice of her huckleberry clafouti. The portrait of the perfect Southern hostess.

So when we ask Winburn what chef and owner Sean Brock does to inspire employees like her to stay on year after year—like most on staff, she is a near-ten-year veteran—we are expecting a handful of rote answers. Because Sean is first and foremost a Southern cook, verging on scholarly when it comes to the region's culinary history and committed to the South's pantry of local ingredients. Because he traverses the region finding rare seeds to add to his collection of endangered edibles that he then grows at nearby Thornhill Farm. Because he applies modern culinary technique with a deft and subtle hand, coaxing the sublime from the staples of his Southern childhood, from Carolina Gold Rice to huckleberries. Or because he believes in the power of true Southern hospitality, a value he reiterates daily to his staff in the form of an abundant family meal, often making it himself if the cooks are short on time. We get none of these answers.

"The thing I appreciate about him versus other chefs I've worked for," says Winburn, "is that he's not snobby. He'll eat Doritos and like, drink a Coca-Cola." Living in the image of his idol in music and in life, Elvis Presley, Sean Brock is equal parts everyman and culinary royalty.

He is also exhausted. His ambitious new restaurant, Husk, opened just four days earlier and is becoming a locavore's paradise; nothing will be served there that does not come from within a couple day's drive. Fueled by fifteen-minute catnaps in his car, Sean flits down the cobblestoned palm-lined alleyways between the two restaurants while we nip at his heels and ask him what will keep the staff fed tonight. He seems to be keeping the menu a secret, peppering us with hints but no real answers. Instead, he distracts us with his new bar toy: a Japanese ice machine that molds shiny, wet, golf ball–sized spheres of ice. "How does it work?" we ask. Sean grins and says, "I have no idea, but isn't it the coolest thing you've ever seen?" The day passes quickly like this. We are completely caught up in Sean's whirlwind of food and drink, his facts and observations: "Every single day I get up, I'm extremely happy. How can

shoulders is swapped for a giddy energy. When we ask for Sean's secret for juggling so much, so successfully, he lays his keys out with a clatter and points to the keychain. A black lightning bolt hovers frozen in perpetual strike above the letters "T.C.B." We ask about the acronym. "They stand for Elvis's trademark phrase," says Sean. "Taking Care of Business." From the many memorable sound bites that Sean could have pinned his extraordinary success on, we are heartened (and not surprised) that he found the King's humblest words to live—and cook—by.

you not be? Look at this!" But still no staff meal is in sight.

When we finally return to the McCrady's kitchen around 1 p.m., Sean heads to the back, out of plain view. A moment later he is bouncing around the kitchen placing white In-N-Out Burger paper hats—sourced specially for our visit—on the heads of each of his cooks. His round cheeks now flushed pink, Sean announces the all-American staff meal menu: burgers, fries, and shakes inspired by Elvis Presley. There's a shout from the back: "Right on!" Then the entire staff

sets to work, shaping custom-blended beef into dozens of burger patties to be griddled, smothered, and stacked two at a time onto the "cheapest buns you can find," according to Sean. Next it's on to the shakes. Thick as a low-country swamp, they are a blend of vanilla ice cream, bananas, peanut butter, and bacon fat, plus a generous splash of bourbon, "For Elvis!" shouts Sean over the whirring Vitamix.

Around 2 p.m. the cooks dive into the burgers. Grease drips down their arms, and the stress hiding in hunched

A Conversation with SEAN BROCK
Chef and Owner

What inspires your staff meals?

I'm inspired by drive-ins and dive bars, and cool places where a dude can smoke a cigarette while he cooks a hamburger for you, ashes falling in there. Gives a whole new meaning to cooking with ashes.

You are deeply committed to the ingredients of the South. How does this play out in your restaurant and why is it so important to you?

I believe that the South has the most beautiful produce in the world. Our raw ingredients are just the most beautiful in the world, too. I think if we can just use those ingredients and shape them in a certain way, we can show people that there's more to Southern cuisine.

If you could invite any living chef to your staff meal, who would it be?

I would love to eat lunch with Michel Bras. I'd cook the veg that we have around here, show him our stuff. I think that would be wonderful.

The burgers you are serving today are out of this world. What makes a good burger great?

We grind in Benton's bacon from Madisonville, Tennessee, into the meat. You don't see the bacon, but you taste it. I do this because I know how important cooking with a wood grill is, but we just have an indoor griddle. We need that smokiness, that fiery grill flavor, and it is the bacon that really adds that. We also use the Keating Miraclean, which is a really cool griddle that, ironically, is the same one Shake Shack uses. Also, the beautiful thing about a double-stack burger is that the melted cheese allows for that emulsification between the patties.

Do you ever experiment on the staff during staff meal?

Yeah, I made massaman [Thai curry] once and nobody on staff had had it before. So here you have this dish with coconut and lime and all these wacky spices like cinnamon and peanut that taste incredible together. We go eat these dishes at Thai restaurants all the time and think, "Hey, this is really good," but it never goes past that; it kinda stays there. So that was the conversation over staff meal: why don't we look at beef dishes a little differently? From there, we took all those components of massaman and did a really cool dish that was familiar on the plate but had all these ingredients. When customers ate it, they were like "Oh, that's familiar." It stayed on the tasting menu for four months.

What are some of your favorite staff meals here at McCrady's?

We have special days. One cook used to work at Momofuku, so he shares dumplings with us sometimes. Or sometimes we'll just do straight-up noodle bowls with ramen.

If you could eat family meal anywhere in the world, where would you go?

Here!

DOUBLE-STACK CHEESEBURGERS
with SPECIAL SAUCE

We can just about promise these burgers will be the best you ever make. Soldering the two patties together with molten cheese helps, of course, but grinding Benton's bacon—a specialty of Madisonville, Tennessee—directly into the custom beef blend is the real secret. The resulting burgers are flush with smoke, salt, and fat, and despite being thin patties, don't lose beefiness or succulence when cooked to medium-well. The pickles and special sauce are the only two components necessary to complete this McCrady's masterpiece; adding lettuce and tomato would be considered sacrilege.

Makes 10 double cheeseburgers

2¾ POUNDS (1.3 KILOGRAMS) BEEF CHUCK STEAK

12 OUNCES (340 GRAMS) BEEF FLANK STEAK

5 THICK-CUT STRIPS SMOKED BACON, PREFERABLY BENTON'S

2 TEASPOONS (12 GRAMS) KOSHER SALT, PLUS ADDITIONAL TO TASTE

FRESHLY GROUND BLACK PEPPER TO TASTE

3 TABLESPOONS (42 GRAMS) UNSALTED BUTTER, AT ROOM TEMPERATURE

10 WHITE HAMBURGER BUNS

1 YELLOW ONION, SLICED PAPER-THIN

20 SLICES AMERICAN CHEESE

1 CUP (237 MILLILITERS) SPECIAL SAUCE (PAGE 179)

1 CUP (170 GRAMS) DRAINED BREAD AND BUTTER PICKLE SLICES, PLUS MORE AS NEEDED

NOTE

Should you have a KitchenAid mixer in your home, we recommend purchasing the meat grinder attachment (it can be found online) to make the raw burger blend. It is easy to use and clean and takes up a lot less storage space than a hand-cranked version. You can also ask your butcher to custom-grind your beef. He or she will probably refuse to incorporate the bacon (it cross-contaminates the machine), but a few pulses in your food processor will pulverize it enough to then incorporate it—gently—into the ground beef by hand.

Place all the components of your meat grinder in the freezer until well-chilled, about 3 hours (see Note). Cut the beef into strips small enough to fit through the grinder; keep the beef and the bacon very cold until you are ready to grind.

Grind the beef and the bacon through the large die. Add 2 teaspoons of salt, then gently and quickly mix together by hand, working the mixture no more than 30 seconds. (The key to a tender patty is to handle the meat as little as possible.) Divide the mixture in half. Grind only one half through the small die. Combine the two ground meat mixtures by hand very briefly, no more than 30 seconds. Using your hands, portion the mixture into twenty 3-ounce (85 grams) loosely formed balls. Next, using your fingertips, gently press the balls into patties, approximately ½ inch (1.25 centimeters) high and 4 inches (10 centimeters) in diameter. (If you are not cooking all of the patties, stack the extras between sheets of parchment paper, tightly wrap in plastic wrap, then aluminum foil. They freeze beautifully for up to 3 months.) Season both sides of the patties with salt and pepper, then refrigerate until needed.

When ready to serve, heat a large cast-iron skillet over high heat. As the skillet is heating, generously butter the cut sides of the buns and toast quickly, cut-side down, on the skillet until golden brown. Spread both sides of the toasted buns with a thick coat of Special Sauce, place a layer of pickles on the bottom buns, and set aside within arm's reach of the stove.

When the skillet is smoking, place about 4 patties in the pan, avoiding overcrowding. Sear for about 90 seconds, until the patties have a dark, almost black char, then flip them over. Working quickly, place a small mound of shaved onions on two of the patties, then top every patty with a slice of cheese. Cook until the cheese melts, about 90 seconds more, then stack a non-onion patty on top of an onion patty and remove the stacks from the skillet. If you are cooking in batches, place the double-stacks on a sheet tray and cover with aluminum foil to keep warm.

Sandwich the burgers between the waiting buns and serve immediately with a generous amount of napkins and extra Special Sauce on the side.

SPECIAL SAUCE

This is the sauce that brings these burgers home. It is easy to make and stores well in the refrigerator for several days (or in the freezer for several months, just stir briskly after thawing to reemulsify). Slather it on the burgers or drizzle it over a plateful of beef fat–cooked fries; plain old ketchup on the table is a pale substitute.

Yields approximately 3 cups (710 milliliters) sauce

1¾ CUPS (414 MILLILITERS) DUKE'S MAYONNAISE

1 CUP (237 MILLILITERS) YELLOW MUSTARD

3 TABLESPOONS (45 MILLILITERS) KETCHUP

½ CUP (128 GRAMS) DRAINED AND MINCED BREAD AND BUTTER PICKLES

¼ CUP (75 GRAMS) DRAINED AND MINCED BREAD AND BUTTER JALAPEÑOS (PAGE 73)

¼ CUP (50 GRAMS) GRANULATED SUGAR

1 TEASPOON (5 MILLILITERS) FRESHLY SQUEEZED LEMON JUICE

1 TEASPOON (5 MILLILITERS) WHITE VINEGAR

HOT SAUCE TO TASTE

KOSHER SALT AND FRESHLY GROUND BLACK PEPPER TO TASTE

In a large bowl, stir all the ingredients together until blended. Season with hot sauce, salt, and pepper, refrigerate until chilled, and serve.

BEEF FAT FRIES

For frying potatoes there is nothing like rendered beef fat, also known as suet, to create an extra crispy fry with a pronounced depth of flavor. At McCrady's, making and using suet is also a way to utilize the fat trimmed from an expensive side of heritage beef. See the note on the next page for instructions on how to render fat for yourself. It's easy, versatile, and if you can sweet-talk your butcher for their fat trimmings, it's free.

At McCrady's they sous vide the potatoes before frying. After vacuum-sealing them into a plastic bag, they are placed in a thermal circulator at 180°F (82°C) for 4 hours. This technique results in potatoes with a near-mashed tenderness yet enough structure for the fryer. For those without this setup, the simmering method below is the closest approximation. When properly executed, these thrice-cooked potatoes are like mashed potatoes coated in a potato chip, at once extra-creamy and extra-crispy.

Serves 6

6 LARGE RUSSET POTATOES (ABOUT 3 POUNDS/1.4 KILOGRAMS), UNPEELED

KOSHER SALT AS NEEDED

1½ QUARTS (1.4 LITERS) RENDERED BEEF FAT (SEE NOTE)

2 CUPS (473 MILLILITERS) PEANUT OIL

Scrub the potatoes under running water to remove dirt. Dry well, then cut into ½-inch-thick fries (1.25 centimeters). After cutting, immediately transfer the fries to a bowl of heavily salted water. Cover the bowl and refrigerate the fries for at least 12 hours to help remove excess starch. Drain and set aside.

Fill a large bowl halfway with water and ice; set aside. Place the potatoes and bring to a boil. Immediately reduce the heat to a very low simmer and cook the fries until just tender, about 10 minutes. Be careful not to overcook or they will fall apart. Carefully remove the potatoes from the pot with a slotted spoon and immediately transfer to the ice bath. Chill completely, drain carefully, and arrange on sheet trays in a single layer. Freeze until solid, about 30 minutes.

Heat the beef fat and oil in a high-sided, heavy-bottomed pot to 260°F (127°C). Line sheet trays with paper towels. Remove the potatoes from the freezer, and working in batches, carefully deep-fry them for 6 minutes. They will develop little or no color during this fry but an outer "skin" will form. Gently remove the potatoes from the fat, drain on paper towels, and freeze again in single layers until solid, about 30 minutes. Once frozen, they can be transferred to a plastic freezer bag and stored in the freezer for several weeks.

When ready to serve, reheat the beef fat to 370°F (188°C). Remove the potatoes from the freezer, and working in batches, carefully fry them for 4 to 7 minutes, moving around with a slotted spoon to achieve a deep golden-brown and extra-crispy exterior. Drain on paper towels and season with salt while still hot. Serve immediately. The beef fat can be cooled, strained, and stored in the refrigerator for future frying.

NOTE

To make your own rendered suet, you must first find 6 pounds (2.7 kilograms) of beef fat. This is an easy task since most butchers or farmers will save their fat trimmings for you if you ask. Chill the fat until very cold, cube into pieces, then pass through the smallest die of your meat grinder (see Note, page 178). Alternatively, use your food processor to pulse beef fat cubes into a chunky paste. Place the ground fat in a heavy-bottomed stockpot over medium-low heat. When the fat is first starting to melt, stir it up from the bottom every 10 minutes to avoid sticking and burning. Slowly render the fat for about 2 hours. When the fat has rendered completely into a clear, golden liquid, strain out the now-caramelized and crispy cracklings through a fine-mesh sieve. (Reserve the beef cracklings; they make an excellent addition to a stir-fry or a topping for nachos.) Ladle the fat through a funnel into clean and sterilized glass jars. Allow to cool completely with the lid off (it will turn into a creamy white semisolid), then seal with the lid and store in the refrigerator for up to 1 month. Replace half the butter with cold beef fat in your next pie crust; it yields incredible flakiness. Yields about 2 quarts (1.9 liters).

THE ELVIS PRESLEY MILKSHAKE

Several years ago Sean Brock had the good fortune of spending time with Elvis Presley's personal cook, Mary Jenkins Langston, who shared with him some of the King's deviant indulgences. "One of his favorite things was to take two pieces of white bread and spread them with peanut butter and sliced bananas," Sean explained. Harmless enough until Sean lets us in on the dark side of the dish: sautéing the sandwich until crispy in enormous amounts of butter and bacon fat.

This milkshake is Sean's loose interpretation of the sandwich. The generous slosh of Southern bourbon is his personal touch. It is very thick, incredibly rich, and somehow all the ingredients, despite the odds, taste fit for the King.

Serves 4 to 6

5 THICK-CUT STRIPS OF SMOKED BACON

2 VERY RIPE BANANAS

½ CUP (129 GRAMS) SMOOTH PEANUT BUTTER

¼ CUP (60 MILLILITERS) BUFFALO TRACE BOURBON

3 CUPS (440 GRAMS) VANILLA ICE CREAM, SOFTENED SLIGHTLY

In a large skillet over medium-high heat, fry the bacon until very crispy, about 6 to 8 minutes. Drain the bacon on paper towels. Reserve the rendered bacon fat separately, allowing it to cool slightly.

Place the bananas, peanut butter, and bourbon in a blender. Add the cooked bacon and 3 tablespoons (45 milliliters) of the reserved bacon fat and blend until smooth, about 45 seconds, scraping down the sides if necessary. Add the ice cream and pulse to incorporate into a smooth shake, about 30 seconds. If you'd like, you can also incorporate the ice cream by hand by mixing it in with a whisk or an immersion blender; this will help keep the shake in a more frozen state. Serve immediately. Transfer any extra shake to a lidded container and reserve in the freezer. Because the alcohol prevents it from completely freezing, it turns into a scoopable ice cream.

MICHEL ET SÉBASTIEN BRAS

LAGUIOLE, FRANCE

FRESH TOMATO AND CAPER
SALAD WITH CONFIT OF CHICKEN
HEARTS AND GIZZARDS

POTATOES BRAISED IN
VEGETABLE BROTH

BRINED PORK LOIN WITH
CARAMELIZED VEGETABLES

We first notice the honeybees. Hundreds of them, maybe thousands, their collective buzz giving the vegetable gardens surrounding restaurant Michel et Sébastien Bras an electric charge. It could be said that these loyal pollinators are the key to the restaurant's success, now a cult culinary pilgrimage nearly four thousand feet above the Aubrac region of France. Michel, after all, is famous for his self-taught vegetable alchemy. He turns the simple local produce—onions, potatoes, bitter greens—into dishes like his famous gargouillou: a tongue-twisting mélange of up to forty seasonal greens served with a thin slice of Aubrac ham and topped with a frenzy of edible flowers. Michel does in fact recognize the bees' formative work in his cuisine, stamping all of his signature Laguiole knives with the winged creature. But equally important are the plants themselves: "I nurture my plants from the time they are seeds to the first sprouting, until they are fully formed and ready to give the gift of themselves to me." Michel makes it plain: "This responsibility also fuels my passion."

His drive to alloy passion with responsibility—not only for his plants but also for his staff, his customers, his region, and most of all his family—has turned Michel into one of the world's most influential chefs. It has also made him somewhat of a culinary curiosity. Lithe despite being well into his sixties and dressed in all white, from his coat down to his clogs, he is often described as intensely serious, ascetic, monkish even. Some go so far as to peg Michel as a majestic recluse, sequestering himself in a restaurant that cantilevers over the valley below like a crash-landed spaceship. Then we watch him hang pairs of ruby-red cherries around his granddaughter's ears, button up an enormous chef's jacket around her younger brother's tiny frame, and effervescent is the adjective that comes to mind, jubilant even. Michel may be profoundly sober about his craft, but as the staff meal approaches—his own family trickling in to greet him including his wife, Ginette, and his co-chef son, Sébastien—it becomes clear that a self-satisfied joy, not solemnity, is his fount of inspiration.

"Our family has always gathered at the table together during staff meal," says Michel. "It is the one time during the day for us all to be together, and it has always been like this." He explains that the practice of bringing family into the staff-meal fold started when his mother first opened the restaurant in the 1950s—a venture to subsidize her husband's unpredictable blacksmithing salary—in its original Laguiole township location. She was, and is, his biggest inspiration. "One of my favorite memories as a child was a simple dish my mother prepared for me of bread covered in milk skin," he says, explaining that she would add a liberal sprinkling of cocoa powder on top. He has staked his career on translating these types of

humble dishes for well-heeled diners. "The mothers of this region have learned to transform the simplest things into the most extraordinary flavors," explains Michel. "These simple dishes shaped who I am as a chef, how I cook, what is important to me."

So while high-paying guests appreciate Michel's philosophy of niac—as Michel explains, the artistic part of the dish "that surprises," such as a lightly sweet powder made with lemon zest and ginger—staff meal always sets about to gratify without the bells and whistles. And today's buffet of dishes does just that. Thin disks of braised potatoes, slowly roasted pork, and sprightly tomato salad tossed with chicken gizzards and hearts are laid out for all to enjoy. Michel exclusively oversees

the restaurant's complex menu, so the duty of managing the staff meal falls to Régis Saint-Geniez, Michel's sous chef for twenty-eight years. When Régis is pressed for his favorite dishes, he is diplomatic: "I have no particular favorite. Even humble things can be the best you've ever eaten if they are shown in their best light." It is the same lesson Michel leaves us with, one he credits his mother with imparting to him: "The staff meal is not about complication. It is a matter of trusting each other to make the best meal we can. Simple food leads to the most enjoyable time together. It creates a spirit of fellowship, of obligation to each other. It creates love." An emotion Michel Bras reverberates— stridently as a thousand bees—and the very thing that anchors him to his home.

Your laserlike focus on growing, prepping, and cooking vegetables from your region is legendary. Does the staff meal benefit from this?

Vegetables for me offer an ever-changing fire of color and life. They speak to me and I respect them ultimately. They are simple and yet the most complex. Today we have forty-six vegetables that we are using on our menu from my garden and from the market this morning. What is left over will be used for the staff meal. We use everything we have. Even our vegetable peelings we use for our compost for our gardens. It is a continuous circle. It is life giving life.

Your restaurant has helped to set the standard for modern cuisine, yet you yourself are not classically trained. How did you set about creating your own culinary education?

I am not classically trained. I never worked anywhere else. I learned from observing and from trial and error and from listening to my heart. The land taught me things. My gardens. Photography. My staff and my family. I learn from everything and then I translate this to the plate.

Your family always shares in the staff meal each evening, a tradition stretching back to your boyhood. What lessons have you learned while sitting at the table?

From my mama I learned about the good and the beautiful things in life. What was beautiful to the customer and to the spirit. From my papa I learned about organization and about how being strict and disciplined with yourself will lead to a rewarding life. They are the rules I live by. Goodness, beauty, discipline, organization. This makes for a happy life.

Did you always know you wanted to follow in your mother's footsteps, taking over as head chef in the family restaurant?

I did not want to be a chef in the beginning. I loved mathematics. I wanted to be an engineer, to spend a life learning how things worked, how to break them apart. I did not do this job at first because I loved it. I did it because I was the oldest son and it was my responsibility to my family. The oldest son would be the sacrifice in my family. I was the sacrifice for them.

From your sacrifice also comes your success. How did you shift your mindset to make this happen?

In the year 1960 I decided that this is what I would do. I found my passion by bringing all of the things that I love in my life together. It's not a job anymore. It is everything that I am, and because of this, I am fulfilled. You have to take your time to appreciate things. You cannot be in a hurry. You have to listen to the land, to your inner spirit. You have to be aware of your surroundings and sometimes surround yourself with nothing but silence. It is only then that you can find your passion.

So many of the restaurants we have visited credit you as their ultimate inspiration, even going so far as to say they would want you to join their own staff meals. Where do you continue to draw your own inspiration from?

For me the Aubrac is very rich in natural ingredients, but some might look at it and say that there is very little here. This fuels me to turn something simple, something that might not at first appear to have much to it, and to transform it into everything. To take nothing and turn it into everything. This is very motivating for me.

Why is the staff meal important to you, your staff, and your family?

Love has been the most important word in my work and my life. It is my driving force. I give this love to my staff, to my family. I love them all. They are of utmost importance to me. Our staff meal helps create this feeling of devotion.

What is your best piece of staff meal advice for those tasked with making it for their peers?

Humble ingredients, such as bread or potatoes, can be transformed by a person who really cares for it.

FRESH TOMATO and CAPER SALAD
with CONFIT of CHICKEN HEARTS and GIZZARDS

This recipe sits squarely in the shaded overlap between Michel Bras's dedicated seasonality and staff meal's inherent thriftiness. After Michel scored a basket of ripe-to-bursting tomatoes during his 4 a.m. trawl of the nearby Rodez farmers' market, it was left to the chef de partie, Mickaël Ciré, to turn the red beauties into the staff meal. Also left with chicken hearts and gizzards (the remaining meat was reserved for the menu that evening), the Frenchman delighted in the challenge of bringing the two together. "At Michel Bras we do everything with nothing," said Mickaël. "You can do something with a luxurious ingredient, of course, but to do something with nothing, that is the test of a real chef."

Serves 6

CONFIT

8 OUNCES (227 GRAMS) CHICKEN HEARTS (SEE NOTE)

8 OUNCES (227 GRAMS) CHICKEN GIZZARDS (SEE NOTE)

4 THYME SPRIGS

1 HEAD GARLIC, CUT IN HALF

3¼ CUPS (770 MILLILITERS) RENDERED CHICKEN FAT, DUCK FAT, OR CANOLA OIL

KOSHER SALT AND FRESHLY GROUND BLACK PEPPER TO TASTE

TOMATOES

8 VERY RIPE LARGE TOMATOES, COARSELY CHOPPED

½ CUP (16 GRAMS) BASIL LEAVES, TORN INTO BITE-SIZED PIECES

2 TABLESPOONS (17 GRAMS) CAPERS, DRAINED

2 TABLESPOONS (30 MILLILITERS) OLIVE OIL

1 TABLESPOON (15 MILLILITERS) FRESHLY SQUEEZED LEMON JUICE

FOR SERVING

1 SLICED BAGUETTE

For the confit: Preheat the oven to 350°F (177°C). Rinse the hearts and gizzards under cold running water to remove excess blood. Season well with salt. In a small baking dish, combine the hearts and gizzards with the thyme and garlic halves. Pour in chicken fat until the gizzards and hearts are fully submerged, adding more fat or olive oil if necessary. Bake for 30 minutes, or until small bubbles begin to actively rise to the surface.

Reduce the temperature to 325°F (165°C), and continue to bake, maintaining a lazy bubbling, for 2 hours, or until the gizzards give no resistance when pierced with a sharp knife. Remove from the oven and set aside to cool to room temperature.

Using a slotted spoon, carefully remove the hearts and gizzards. Drain on paper towels. Thinly slice and season with salt and pepper. Set aside. The drained fat can be saved and used again for sautéing.

For the tomatoes: In a bowl, toss together the tomatoes, basil, capers, olive oil, and lemon juice. Add the hearts and gizzards, season with salt and pepper, and toss again. Serve immediately with baguette slices.

Note

Found in all birds, the gizzard—in a chicken it is about the size of a small button mushroom—is a specialized secondary stomach with thick muscular walls. As with any hardworking muscle, slow cooking via the confit technique tenderizes a gizzard. Similar in texture to braised squid but with a distinct chicken flavor, gizzards (as well as the more neutral-tasting hearts) will make you think twice about throwing out that white bag of "giblets" tucked into the chicken's dank cavity. In fact, save the gizzards and heart each time you roast a chicken, wrapping them tightly in plastic wrap and storing in your freezer (store the livers separately). Eventually you will acquire enough to thaw and make this dish. There's no need to stockpile, however, if your butcher agrees to save them on your behalf.

POTATOES BRAISED in VEGETABLE BROTH

Leave it to Michel Bras and his team to create a potato dish that tastes as light and vibrant as a summer salad. The key is the restaurant's vegetable-rich broth. Light-years beyond what can be found on store shelves, Bras stock is made from seasonally appropriate produce all in pristine condition—no bruised carrots and hacked onion tops here. Slowly simmered, strained, and reduced slightly, it is the green-tasting essence of everything alive and prospering in the Aubrac region.

This recipe is a foundation upon which you can build your own broth. We recommend experimenting with various herbs, citrus zests, whole spices such as coriander, and excess from your garden (green tomatoes add a clear-eyed vibrancy and chive flowers a peppery punch). It goes without saying that you absolutely must save any leftover broth for use in soups or stews or for plumping whole grains and legumes. If short on time, use the highest quality store-bought vegetable stock you can find to make this cream-less spin on the classic French gratin.

Serves 6

2 LARGE WHITE ONIONS, 1 HALVED AND 1 COARSELY CHOPPED

2 TABLESPOONS (30 MILLILITERS) OLIVE OIL

1 LEEK, GREEN AND WHITE PORTIONS, COARSELY CHOPPED

1 MEDIUM FENNEL BULB AND FRONDS, COARSELY CHOPPED

3 MEDIUM CARROTS, COARSELY CHOPPED

2 SMALL PARSNIPS, COARSELY CHOPPED

2 RIBS CELERY, COARSELY CHOPPED

4 SPRIGS EACH THYME AND TARRAGON

4 LEAVES OF SORREL

ZEST OF 1 LEMON

12 BLACK PEPPERCORNS

6 MEDIUM RUSSET POTATOES, SCRUBBED

KOSHER SALT AND FRESHLY GROUND SARAWAK PEPPER TO TASTE (SEE NOTES)

Preheat oven to 450°F (232°C).

Heat a cast-iron skillet over high heat until a drop of water flicked on the surface sizzles. Using tongs, carefully place the onion halves, cut-side down, into the skillet and sear until the surfaces are charred black, about 4 minutes. Remove from the pan; set aside.

In a stockpot, heat the oil over medium-high heat and sauté the chopped onion, leeks, fennel, carrots, parsnips, and celery until barely softened, about 10 minutes.

Add the blackened onion and enough water to cover the vegetables by an excess inch (2.5 centimeters), about 2½ quarts (2.4 liters). Bring to a boil, then reduce the heat and simmer, uncovered, for 20 minutes, skimming the surface of fat and scum as necessary. Add the herbs and zest; continue to simmer, uncovered, for another 15 minutes.

Season the finished stock with salt to taste. Strain the seasoned stock through a fine-mesh sieve, pressing on the solids to extract the trapped but flavorful liquid. Discard the spent solids. Yields about 1½ quarts stock (1.2 liters); will keep frozen for several months or covered in the refrigerator for up to 1 week.

Peel the potatoes and slice about ⅛-inch (3 millimeters) thick; season with salt and Sarawak pepper. In a ceramic 9 x 11-inch (23 x 28 centimeter) baking dish, arrange the potatoes in a single layer, "gratin-style" by overlapping almost completely; repeat with a second layer.

Pour enough hot stock to come three-quarters of the way up the potatoes in their baking dish, about 1 quart (960 milliliters).

Bake until the potatoes are easily pierced with a fork and lighly brown, about 40 minutes. Let cool for 5 minutes to set, then slice and serve from the baking dish.

Notes

The kitchen at Michel et Sébastien Bras uses only white Malaysian Sarawak pepper from the island of Borneo. Adding a distinctly floral, almost wine-like, flavor Sarawak pepper also imparts a pointed spicy heat. It is an artisanal product and expensive to buy, but can be found online, or replaced with regular white pepper, preferably freshly ground.

Extra-cooked potatoes make an excellent foundation for a German potato salad.

BRINED PORK LOIN
with CARAMELIZED VEGETABLES

Michel et Sébastien Bras sits high above the volcanic and granite plateau of the Massif Central in southern France. It is a severe but fertile landscape known throughout the country for its Aubrac cattle (a breed once raised for milk but now mostly bred for beef), although we found that pork is the overlooked hero of the region. "It's some of the best in the world," says Michel Bras. A quick trip down the hill to the township of Laguiole will confirm this regional pork pride. Its small shops supply tourists and locals with myriad pig products and the tools to slice them up, Laguiole also being synonymous with world-class kitchen knives.

Unlike pork shoulder (see the whey and brine braised shoulder on page 269), which can be cooked until it literally falls off the bone, pork loin has a more delicate disposition. To prevent the meat from turning dry and characterless, sous chef Régis Saint-Geniez brines the loin overnight, locking both moisture and seasoning deep inside. The vegetables placed underneath the roasting loin change according to the leftovers on hand but are carefully prepared, even when being served to the staff. "It's all about the produce," says pastry chef Rafael Falconi. "This is the prize on the plate. It's not about the chic ingredients. It's about the vegetable. The humble vegetable that is made into something very beautiful." Bathed in the pork-salted juices of the loin above, the vegetables used here do in fact become dazzlers, turned into a kind of softened condiment for topping the sliced pork.

Serves 6

1½ CUPS (438 GRAMS) KOSHER SALT, PLUS MORE FOR SEASONING

ONE (3-POUND/1.4 KILOGRAM) BONELESS PORK LOIN (SEE NOTE)

2 TABLESPOONS (30 MILLILITERS) OLIVE OIL

FRESHLY GROUND BLACK PEPPER, TO TASTE

4 ROMA TOMATOES, QUARTERED

3 RIBS CELERY, THICKLY SLICED

3 LARGE CARROTS, THICKLY SLICED

1 LARGE ONION, HALVED AND THINLY SLICED

4 THYME SPRIGS

2 BAY LEAVES

2 ROSEMARY SPRIGS

Note

When purchasing your loin, ask your butcher to go easy on trimming the "fat cap" or outer layer of fat running its length. Leaving on a little extra helps create that golden, crispy top layer just begging to be pinched off—and snacked upon—while the loin rests.

In a nonreactive container large enough to hold the loin, combine 1 gallon (3.8 liters) water and the salt, stirring until dissolved. Add the loin, cover, and refrigerate for at least 8 hours but no longer than 12.

Drain the loin. Fill a large container with fresh cold water and submerge the loin, soaking under running water for 5 minutes. Drain well. The pork can now be wrapped and stored in the refrigerator, up to a full day, before roasting.

Preheat the oven to 400°F (204°C), placing a roasting pan large enough to hold the loin inside.

On a clean work surface, brush the loin with 1 tablespoon (15 milliliters) of the oil and season generously with pepper; additional salt is not required. Truss the loin evenly with kitchen twine if desired (this will help it keep its shape while cooking). Carefully place the loin, fat side down, in the preheated pan and roast for 30 minutes; this helps create a crispy fat layer.

Combine the tomatoes, celery, carrots, onion, thyme, bay leaves, and rosemary with the remaining olive oil. Season with pepper and mix well.

Reduce the heat to 350°F (177°C). Carefully lift the loin, spread the vegetables evenly in the pan, and then top with the loin, fat side up. Roast until the internal temperature reaches 150°F (66°C), about 45 minutes.

Remove from oven and transfer the loin to a cutting board to rest for at least 25 minutes.

As the loin rests, continue roasting the vegetables until they are lightly caramelized, about 15 minutes. Taste for salt (they may not need any) and season accordingly before serving.

If trussed, snip and remove the twine and cut the loin into thin slices. Arrange on a serving platter and spoon the vegetable and roasting juices over top.

It is best to store extra pork in loin form, slicing off as much as you need for a sandwich the next day, and returning the rest, covered, to the refrigerator.

MORIMOTO

PHILADELPHIA, PENNSYLVANIA

CRISPY OCTOPUS SUCKERS

FISH BONE SOUP WITH
JALAPEÑO OIL

BROILED FISH COLLARS WITH
GOBO AND GINGKO NUT RICE

JAPANESE BEEF CURRY

CHICKEN PASTA CAESAR SALAD

t is a still and sunny morning in downtown Philadelphia, but the kitchen at Morimoto is in full swing. Cooks shuck milky white scallops, slice whole lobes of glistening foie gras, and poach two-pound lobsters at a relentless pace. So while touring the busy basement prep kitchen of the restaurant—the perennially popular Japanese-fusion collaboration between Iron Chef Masaharu Morimoto and Philadelphia restaurateur Stephen Starr—we ask the restaurant's chef de cuisine, Chris Greway, about his staff meal game plan to feed his hardworking crew of nearly thirty. Before he has a beat to answer, we hear a shout from deep inside the restaurant's dry-storage pantry. "Double starch on Saturdays!" barks Joe Monnigh, a baby-faced sous chef with over twelve years of experience. "For the busiest nights of the week, you need a good foundation in your stomach." Chris nods in agreement, and Joe roots around the stockpile of Asian ingredients—jarred gingko nuts, dried Japanese peppers—for the secret stash of Italian farfalle pasta: starch number one.

As one would expect from a restaurant with a large Japanese staff, rice nearly always graces the family meal table: enter starch number two. Returning to the main kitchen upstairs, we find Hiroki Fujiyama, the restaurant's head sushi chef, working on a Japanese beef curry to be served over the restaurant's signature "new crop" California medium-grain variety. "We only have one

hour to make a dish," says Hiroki, browning a small mountain of ground beef in an oversized rondeau, "and that time goes fast." Hiroki's unhurried efficiency, however, comes from a childhood of happy curry memories cobbled together to create a recipe of his own, a combination of his mother's home-cooked version and the one his father served at his restaurant in Japan. Hiroki's long black hair, clearly growing out of a recent blond phase, gives him that confident, punk-rock edge, so only his quick glance up at the clock makes us think he may be sweating the 3 p.m. deadline.

"You know, it's kind of like a marathon runner the night before the run," says Joe, who is now working on his salad dressing at the station over from Hiroki. "They eat a big pasta dinner. It's the same thing for a restaurant staff." So he takes it upon himself to create a dish that practically defines carbo-loading: chicken and pasta Caesar salad tossed with garlicky homemade croutons. Joe

assures us that the salad is not a family recipe, just a by-product of his ongoing obsession to get the dressing as close as possible to Hidden Valley Ranch. "I know if I make it up to Hidden Valley standards, the staff will love it," he says, a nod to many a cook's subversive kinship with mass-produced comfort foods.

Laid out by 3 p.m. sharp in the front of the kitchen, this staff meal is an eclectic mix: Hiroki's turmeric-colored beef curry, repurposed odds and ends as personified by fried octopus suckers, and Joe's American crowd pleaser. After the meal we ask two of the restaurant's "black shirts" (the nickname for the Morimoto servers) if they mind the mash-up of cuisines. They look up from their napkin folding and cast a deliberate glance at their empty plates. Point taken. Just then, server Ali Lynch chimes, "I'm a teacher here in Philadelphia. As soon as the final bell rings, I run out the door." Joe and Hiroki would both appreciate her personal finish line: The Morimoto staff meal.

Come In, We're Closed

A Conversation with Chef and Owner MASAHARU MORIMOTO

What was the first family meal you served at Morimoto?

For the opening of Morimoto Philadelphia, I ordered special long nori seaweed and large sushi mats. I placed them end to end from the entrance to the edge of our sushi bar [a distance of over 150 feet long]. Then all of our employees made a single long sushi roll together. It was a ceremonial activity, which in Japan is often done to wish long life and long business.

Can you explain the Japanese tradition of makani?

In Japan *makani* [staff meal] is provided to employees as a benefit. It is also a way for young beginner chefs to hone their culinary skills. In Japan young cooks do not have a chance to cook at all. They clean the kitchen or at best do some prep work. So making *makani* is a great opportunity for them to make something and get comments from the older chefs.

Why is the family meal important to you both at home and the restaurant?

Eating a meal with family members is important just like *makani* at the restaurants. It creates time for communication.

What are your personal staff meal favorites?

Japanese curry rice, spicy cod roe pasta, grilled samma.

If you had to make a staff meal using only four ingredients from the Morimoto kitchen, what would you create?

Rice and eggs to make fried rice. Miso and tofu to make a miso soup.

What is one ingredient that no home cook should be without? One tool?

Definitely soy sauce, and a Japanese aluminum grater to grate ginger and daikon.

What is one food scrap that is always repurposed for staff meal?

The skin of daikon [radish], which has a nice crunchy texture. You can cook it with other vegetables.

What was your most memorable staff meal?

About twenty years ago I did a two-week fast. After the fast, a fellow sushi chef made a rice congee for me, thinking that I could not eat anything solid. Then he thought even rice would be too much, skimmed the liquid off of the top of the congee, and gave it to me. When I ate it, I was truly delighted.

CRISPY OCTOPUS SUCKERS

Head sushi chef Hiroki Fujiyama was inspired to add this dish to the menu at the last minute, explaining that the suckers are a common snack food in Japanese kitchens where almost every part of a pricey whole octopus is eaten. Once fried, these popcorn-sized nuggets have a pleasant chew and a lot of flavor. Or as Chris Greway aptly describes, "They taste like croutons!"

Serves 4

1 POUND (454 GRAMS) FRESH OCTOPUS SUCKERS, AT LEAST ¾ INCH (2 CENTIMETERS) IN DIAMETER (SEE NOTE)

2 TABLESPOONS (30 MILLILITERS) SOY SAUCE

1 TABLESPOON (15 MILLILITERS) MIRIN

1 TABLESPOON (15 MILLILITERS) TOASTED SESAME OIL

1 TEASPOON (4 GRAMS) GRANULATED SUGAR

1 GARLIC CLOVE, MINCED

1 TEASPOON (3 GRAMS) PEELED AND FINELY GRATED GINGER

1 TEASPOON (6 GRAMS) KOSHER SALT

1½ QUARTS (1.4 LITERS) CANOLA OIL, FOR FRYING

¼ CUP (32 GRAMS) CORNSTARCH

Bring a large pot of water to a boil and prepare an ice bath in a large bowl.

Blanch the suckers in boiling water for 15 seconds, then drain them and plunge them into the ice bath.

Once cool, clean each sucker under cold running water to remove any sand trapped inside. Drain well on paper towels.

In a bowl, combine the soy sauce, mirin, sesame oil, sugar, garlic, ginger, and salt. Add the suckers. Cover and marinate in the refrigerator for 1 hour, or up to 3.

In a large pot, heat the canola oil to 350°F (177°C).

Drain the suckers, shaking to remove any excess marinade. Discard the marinade. Dredge the suckers in the cornstarch. Fry them until golden-brown and crispy, 2 to 3 minutes. Remove from the oil with a slotted spoon and place on paper towels to drain. Season with salt and serve while hot.

NOTE

Sourcing octopus suckers can be a challenge. We do not suggest splurging for a whole fresh octopus just to extract its suckers, but if octopus happens to be the main event of your meal, you should look to buy one with suckers that are at least nickel-sized. Remove the suckers from the octopus by slicing them off as close to the tentacle as possible. Just use a very sharp knife and cut between the base of the sucker and the meaty tentacle. You'll leave behind a small divot where the sucker once protruded. If you are unable to source suckers from your fishmonger, fresh squid cut into 1/4-inch (6 millimeter) rings is a reliable substitute; just forgo blanching before frying.

FISH BONE SOUP with JALAPEÑO OIL

The cooks at Morimoto butcher a staggering amount of fresh fish every day for their sushi bar, so fish skeletons quickly become the detritus du jour. The bones are saved and used to make a fast and flavorful fish stock that is then spun into a variety of simple family meal soups. This one gets a hit of heat from a spicy jalapeño oil that swirls luminescent in the bowl, and is a wonderful condiment on its own for rice dishes like the Gobo and Gingko Nut Rice (page 203).

Serves 4

FISH STOCK

3 WHOLE SMALL FISH SKELETONS FROM A MILD, WHITE FISH LIKE FLOUNDER, SOLE, OR TILAPIA WITH HEADS ON AND GILLS REMOVED

1 MEDIUM YELLOW ONION, QUARTERED

1 RIB CELERY, QUARTERED

2 GARLIC CLOVES

JALAPEÑO OIL

3 JALAPEÑOS, STEMMED BUT NOT DESEEDED AND THINLY SLICED

1 CUP (237 MILLILITERS) CANOLA OIL

SOUP

1 QUART (946 MILLILITERS) FISH STOCK

1 TEASPOON (6 GRAMS) KOSHER SALT

2 TEASPOONS (8 GRAMS) GRANULATED SUGAR

1 TABLESPOON (15 MILLILITERS) SOY SAUCE

6 BABY BOK CHOY, SEPARATED INTO INDI-VIDUAL LEAVES

1 BUNCH ENOKI MUSHROOMS, TRIMMED (ABOUT 2½ OUNCES/75 GRAMS)

5 OUNCES (141 GRAMS) FIRM TOFU, DICED

For the fish stock: Using a heavy knife or kitchen shears, cut the fish skeletons into small pieces. Rinse the skeletons and heads under cold running water until the water runs clear.

In a large pot, combine the bones, onion, celery, and garlic and cover with 2 quarts (1.9 liters) cold water. Simmer for 1 hour, skimming away fat and impurities that rise to the surface.

Strain through a fine-mesh sieve into a storage container and cool to room temperature. Yields about 1½ quarts (1.4 liters). Once cooled, the stock can be frozen in a sealed container for up to 3 months.

For the jalapeño oil: In a saucepan, combine the jalapeños and oil and bring to a boil. Lower the heat and simmer for 10 minutes. Remove from the burner and set aside at room temperature to infuse for 20 minutes, then strain out and discard the peppers and seeds, reserving the oil. Yields 1 cup (237 milliliters). Extra oil can be stored in the refrigerator for up to 3 weeks and can be used in any recipe requiring both oil and a spicy kick.

For the soup: In a large pot, bring 1 quart (946 milliliters) of stock to a simmer. Add the salt, sugar, soy sauce, bok choy, mushrooms, and tofu, lower heat to medium, and simmer until the mushrooms are tender, 6 to 8 minutes. Drizzle 1 tablespoon (15 milliliters) of jalapeño oil into the pot and stir to incorporate. Serve with warm jalapeño oil on the side for those who want an extra hit of heat.

BROILED FISH COLLARS WITH GOBO and GINGKO NUT RICE

"The sushi chefs here have 101 ways to prepare fish collars, like French chefs have ways to prepare an egg," says chef Chris Greway. He's seen them steamed, broiled, doused with hot oil, ginger, and soy sauce, and even turned into a Japanese take on the French pot-au-feu: a combination of collars, bacon, and onions slowly cooked in fish stock.

Referred to generically as *kama* in Japan, fish collars (anatomically speaking, the neck of the animal) are a triangular wedge of bone that yield succulent sweet nuggets of dark meat. "Delicious. Really good stuff," promises Chris. If you ask a fishmonger to reserve the heads for you, chances are he or she will be more than happy to cut off the two collars—like cheeks, there is one on each side of the head at its base—or at least show you how to butcher them yourself. Here, the collars are simply broiled and served alongside a flavorful rice dish that line cook Tomoyuki Takasu made directly in an industrial-size rice cooker. We have given stovetop instructions for those without a rice cooker at home but for those with this kitchen appliance, feel free to experiment.

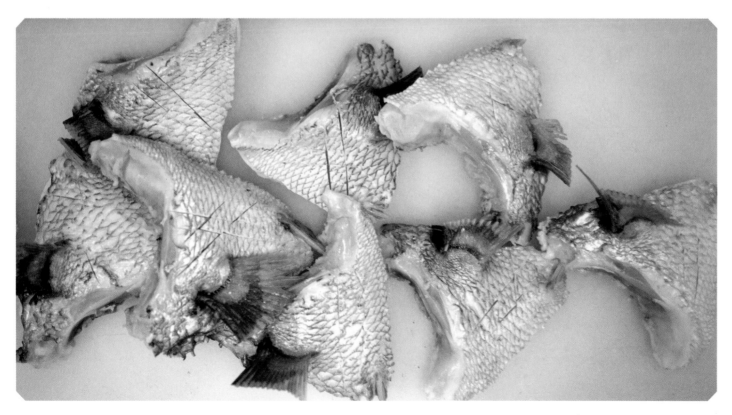

continues on next page

Serves 4 to 6

GOBO AND GINGKO NUT RICE

2 CUPS (380 GRAMS) SHORT-GRAIN BROWN RICE

1 QUART (946 MILLILITERS) FISH STOCK (SEE FISH BONE SOUP WITH JALAPEÑO OIL, PAGE 202)

3 TABLESPOONS (45 MILLILITERS) SOY SAUCE

2 TABLESPOONS (30 MILLILITERS) MIRIN

2 TABLESPOONS (30 MILLILITERS) SAKE

1 TEASPOON (6 GRAMS) KOSHER SALT

6 SHIITAKE MUSHROOM CAPS, CUT INTO ¼-INCH (6 MILLIMETER) SLICES

2 MEDIUM CARROTS, THINLY SLICED

2 PIECES GOBO (6 INCHES/15 CENTIMETERS IN LENGTH), PEELED AND THINLY SLICED (ABOUT 5 OUNCES/142 GRAMS; SEE NOTE)

¾ CUP (180 GRAMS) JARRED GINKGO NUTS, DRAINED (SEE NOTE)

BROILED FISH COLLARS

8 SMALL FISH COLLARS, PREFERABLY SEA BREAM (SEE RECIPE HEADER)

2 TABLESPOONS (30 MILLILITERS) CANOLA OIL

KOSHER SALT AND FRESHLY GROUND BLACK PEPPER TO TASTE

Rinse the rice under cold running water until the water runs clear.

Place the rice in a pot along with the fish broth, soy sauce, mirin, sake, and salt and bring to a boil. Reduce the heat to medium-low, cover the pot, and cook for 30 minutes.

Remove the lid and arrange the mushrooms, carrots, gobo, and ginkgo nuts on top of the rice. Re-cover the pot and cook until the rice and vegetables are tender and the broth has been completely absorbed, about 15 minutes.

Toss to combine all the ingredients. Set aside, keeping warm.

For the fish collars: Place an oven rack at the highest level and preheat the broiler to high. Line a sheet tray with aluminum foil.

Using a knife, scrape any stray scales from the collars. Rinse them under cold running water and remove any excess blood or organs clinging to the flesh and bone inside. Pat dry with paper towels.

Liberally brush the collars with oil and season on all sides with salt and pepper. Place the collars, skin-side up, on the sheet tray. Broil on the upper rack of the oven, allowing the collars to cook until the skin is golden brown and lightly crispy, about 9 minutes.

Arrange in a serving bowl with the rice on the bottom and fish collars on top, and serve immediately.

Note

Line cook Tomoyuki Takasu employs two little-known nutrient power-houses—gobo and ginkgo nuts—to create this one-pot rice dish. Burdock (known as gobo in Japan) is a long, skinny brown taproot that is sweeter than a carrot and slightly stringier than a parsnip. Gobo browns when exposed to air, so after slicing or peeling be sure to immerse it in water to avoid oxidation. If it is not available in your area, substitute with parsnip or celeriac. Ginkgo nuts are high in fiber as well as vitamins A and C but are hard to find fresh or jarred. If you cannot obtain ginkgo nuts—or know of a nearby tree to harvest them yourself—substitute an equal amount of shelled edamame, either freshly steamed or frozen and defrosted.

JAPANESE BEEF CURRY

Beef curry is like the "spaghetti and tomato sauce" of Tokyo. It makes an easy weeknight meal for busy Japanese families since the ingredients are always on hand, including the all-important and conveniently pre-packaged S&B Golden Curry sauce—available Stateside in Asian specialty shops. Hiroki Fujiyama uses this family recipe as his go-to staff meal dish because of its flexibility. "You can use whatever is left over. . . beef, pork, shellfish, or a combination," he says. When asked what besides rice this dish can be served over, Hiroki suggests spooning it on Indian naan bread or buttery mashed potatoes. And just like a good tomato sauce, this dish is perfect to make ahead—a few hours or up to two days—before reheating and serving.

Serves 6

STOCK

1 LARGE YELLOW ONION, COARSELY CHOPPED

2 LARGE CARROTS, COARSELY CHOPPED

2 RIBS CELERY, COARSELY CHOPPED

¾ CUP (177 MILLILITERS) DRY RED WINE

⅓ CUP (87 GRAMS) TOMATO PASTE

2 TABLESPOONS (30 MILLILITERS) WORCESTERSHIRE SAUCE

1 TABLESPOON (15 MILLILITERS) CHICKEN BOUILLON CONCENTRATE

CURRY

2 TABLESPOONS (30 MILLILITERS) CANOLA OIL

2 POUNDS (907 GRAMS) GROUND BEEF CHUCK (80% LEAN)

2 TABLESPOONS (13 GRAMS) MILD YELLOW CURRY POWDER

ONE (3½-OUNCE/100 GRAM) PACKAGE JAPANESE CURRY SAUCE CONCENTRATED CUBES (PREFERABLY S&B GOLDEN CURRY)

KOSHER SALT TO TASTE

FOR SERVING

COOKED RICE, NAAN BREAD, MASHED POTATOES, OR HASH BROWNS

For the stock: In a large saucepan, combine the onion, carrot, celery, red wine, tomato paste, Worcestershire, and chicken bouillon. Add 1½ quarts (1.4 liters) of water and bring to a boil. Reduce the heat to medium to maintain a brisk simmer for 45 minutes, until the vegetables are tender and the liquid has reduced slightly.

For the curry: In a large sauté pan over medium-high heat, pour half the oil and heat until hot but not smoking. Add half the beef, stirring to break up any big clumps, and sauté until the meat is browned and has given up much of its fat, about 6 minutes. Add half the curry powder and cook until aromatic, about 4 minutes. Remove from the heat, tilt the pan to drain out excess fat, and reserve the cooked beef on a plate. Repeat the browning process with the remainder of the oil, beef, and curry powder, this time not draining the fat.

Add all of the cooked beef to the vegetables and stock, including the fat: "Fat equals flavor," according to Hiroki. Whisk the curry sauce mix into the liquid (it will dissolve quickly). Bring the curry to a boil to activate the thickening properties of the curry paste and cook until the liquid has reached the consistency of thick gravy, 12 to 15 minutes.

Serve immediately over the starch of your choice.

CHICKEN PASTA CAESAR SALAD

With a 50/50 mix of Japanese and non-Japanese on staff, sous chef Joe Monnigh is vigilant about providing a variety of comfort foods. "You have to adapt and evolve to try to please everyone," he says, which is why this crunchy creamy salad was the perfect staff meal addition to the otherwise Asian lineup.

This recipe is time consuming from start to finish but can be streamlined with shortcuts—bottled dressing, unmarinated chicken, store-bought croutons, leftover pasta—all of which are justifiable in the flood of weekday to-dos.

Serves 8

MARINATED CHICKEN

1 POUND (454 GRAMS) BONELESS, SKINLESS CHICKEN THIGHS

5 GARLIC CLOVES

1 TEASPOON (2 GRAMS) DRIED THYME

1 TEASPOON (2 GRAMS) DRIED PARSLEY

½ CUP (118 MILLILITERS) OLIVE OIL

1 TEASPOON (6 GRAMS) KOSHER SALT

1 TEASPOON (2 GRAMS) FRESHLY GROUND BLACK PEPPER

CROUTONS

4 TABLESPOONS (56 GRAMS) UNSALTED BUTTER

2 GARLIC CLOVES, MINCED

1 TEASPOON (2 GRAMS) CRUSHED RED PEPPER FLAKES

2 TEASPOONS (4 GRAMS) DRIED OREGANO

1 TEASPOON (6 GRAMS) KOSHER SALT

½ BAGUETTE, CUT INTO ½-INCH (13 MILLIMETER) CUBES

DRESSING

3 LARGE EGG YOLKS (PREFERABLY PASTEURIZED)

6 OIL-PACKED ANCHOVY FILLETS

2 TABLESPOONS (30 MILLILITERS) DIJON MUSTARD

JUICE OF 2 LEMONS

2 GARLIC CLOVES, MINCED

2 TEASPOONS (10 MILLILITERS) WORCESTERSHIRE SAUCE

1 TEASPOON (5 MILLILITERS) TABASCO SAUCE

3 CUPS (710 MILLILITERS) CANOLA OIL

KOSHER SALT AND FRESHLY GROUND BLACK PEPPER TO TASTE

SALAD

16 OUNCES (450 GRAMS) FARFALLE (BOW TIE) PASTA

2 ROMAINE HEARTS, COARSELY CHOPPED

¼ LARGE RED ONION, THINLY SLICED

1 CUP (100 GRAMS) FINELY GRATED PARMESAN CHEESE

KOSHER SALT AND FRESHLY GROUND BLACK PEPPER TO TASTE

For the marinated chicken: Place the chicken in a large resealable plastic freezer bag. In a food processor or blender, purée all the remaining ingredients. Pour the marinade into the bag, press out as much air as possible, and seal. Refrigerate for a minimum of 1 hour, or up to a full day.

When ready to cook, preheat the oven to 450°F (232°C). Line a sheet tray with parchment paper.

Remove the chicken from the bag, shaking off and discarding marinade, and arrange in a single layer on the sheet tray. Bake until the chicken reaches an internal temperature of 165°F (74°C), 18 to 20 minutes.

Cool to room temperature, then coarsely chop the chicken into bite-sized pieces. Refrigerate until chilled.

For the croutons: Preheat the oven to 400°F (204°F). Line a sheet tray with parchment paper.

Melt the butter in a large pot over medium heat. When the foam subsides, stir in the garlic, red pepper flakes, and oregano and cook for 2 to 3 minutes. Remove from the heat, add the bread cubes, and toss to coat. Place the buttered cubes in a single layer on the sheet tray. Bake until golden brown and crispy, about 12 minutes. Cool to room temperature. (Extra croutons can be stored at room temperature in a tightly sealed plastic bag for up to 1 week. Before using, arrange on a sheet tray and crisp them in a 300°F (149°C) oven.)

For the dressing: Combine the egg yolks, anchovies, mustard, lemon juice, garlic, Worcestershire, and Tabasco in a blender and pulse until combined. Set the speed to high and add oil in a slow, steady stream until the dressing begins to thicken, about 45 seconds. At this stage, loosen it just a bit by adding 2 tablespoons (30 milliliters) water, then continue incorporating the oil. Season with salt and pepper. This dressing is thick, somewhere between a mayonnaise and a typical Ranch dressing, and yields about 3 cups/710 milliliters. It can be made several days in advance and stored in a covered container in the refrigerator.

For the salad: Cook the pasta according to the package directions. Drain, cool under cold running water, and drain again.

In a large serving bowl toss together the pasta, lettuce, onion, cheese, two generous handfuls of croutons, and all of the cooked chicken. Add 1 cup (237 milliliters) dressing and mix well to coat. Serve immediately with extra dressing on the side.

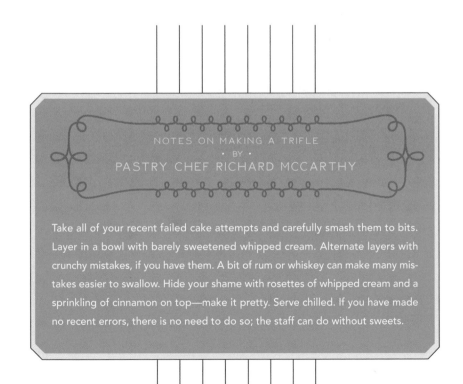

NOTES ON MAKING A TRIFLE
· BY ·
PASTRY CHEF RICHARD MCCARTHY

Take all of your recent failed cake attempts and carefully smash them to bits. Layer in a bowl with barely sweetened whipped cream. Alternate layers with crunchy mistakes, if you have them. A bit of rum or whiskey can make many mistakes easier to swallow. Hide your shame with rosettes of whipped cream and a sprinkling of cinnamon on top—make it pretty. Serve chilled. If you have made no recent errors, there is no need to do so; the staff can do without sweets.

MUGARITZ

ERRENTERIA, SPAIN

MARMITAKO DE BONITO
(BASQUE TUNA STEW)

GARLIC-BAKED CHICKEN THIGHS
WITH FOIL-ROASTED VEGETABLES

CROSSHATCHED POTATOES
AND PARSLEY SAUCE

ARROZ CON LECHE PARA LA FAMILIA
(RICE PUDDING FOR THE FAMILY)

"The hardest time I have had here at Mugaritz," says chef and owner Andoni Aduriz, "is showing new cooks from other restaurants that family meal is a station. Just like fish, or meat, or pastry." So before kitchen interns wind their way from San Sebastián, Spain, to the restaurant's agrarian hilltop home, they are given a written overview of the Mugaritz staff meal responsibilities. The document sets the tone with an italicized, all-caps precedent, "Family Meal Station: THE MOST IMPORTANT STATION," and continues with the first of thirteen provisos: the most important thing is to cook with soul and health.

And so they do. Every intern who works at Mugaritz rotates through the station four times during their eight-month stay. They shop at the local market for ingredients, cook from preplanned ten-day menus collated in a large black binder of traditional Basque recipes—each one neatly typed and reviewed by a partnering nutritionist—and once the meal is made, the cook responsible serves it personally to the entire staff. It's a lot of moving parts for the new cooks, but a seasoned chef de partie is assigned to guide them through the basics, including their first crack at making authentic paella, a dish served faithfully every Sunday. Combined, this minute attention to staff meal detail makes others, in contrast, look like slapdash afterthoughts, even if they are equally tasty.

So as we shadow Rafa Costa E Silva, a youthful sous chef from Brazil who is

something of the kitchen jester, our appetites and expectations build. He guides us through the restaurant's collection of modern buildings—from the kitchen to the culinary lab to the bunkhouse out back for the interns—stopping momentarily to wave to the former Basque revolutionary gardening next door. Before we duck back inside, he points out a giant oak tree, its winter branches bare and gnarled and nearly spanning the dining courtyard. He explains that *haritz* means "oak" in Basque, and *muga* means "border." The tree marks the imaginary line where the restaurant straddles two townships. Thus the name Mugaritz was forged.

Nearly ravenous after the tour, we finally line up at 1 p.m. with several dozen off-season staffers who stay on while the restaurant closes for the winter months. (The break allows Andoni and his team to plan their experimental multicourse tasting menus and play with new cooking techniques. When the restaurant reopens in the late spring, the number of staff swells accordingly.) The meal today is made by Adur Arieta, a towering San Sebastián native whose parents were both cooks before him. Everyone eats heartily of the tuna and potato stew, the roasted chicken with crispy, garlic-scented skin, and most especially, the cinnamon-spiked rice pudding so wonderfully thick that a spoon stuck into it stands straight. The food is faultless. Basque to the core, it is healthily balanced yet worthy of a second helping. Despite this, the dining room

itself has all the charm of a subterranean bunker. Although everyone from Andoni was forged down agrees—this is the most important room in the entire restaurant. The place that brought them back together, despite everything falling apart.

When Rafa talks about the electrical fire that ravaged the restaurant's kitchen on February 15, 2010, there is still a lingering sense of shock. "Seven o'clock Monday morning, Andoni called us: 'Come to Mugaritz. A fire happened here.'" When he opened the kitchen door, it was a moon-scape of char and soot. "You would just cry," he says. It was the fire heard round the culinary world. "Every single cook in Spain, in the United States, in Brazil, they all called," says Rafa. With help from funders both close to home and as far-flung as the United States and Japan, Andoni and his team of cooks and construction workers set about rebuilding their kitchen, this time using the blueprints of their dreams.

On June 15, just a mere four months after the fire, Mugaritz reopened. It is now the fantasy kitchen Andoni envi-sioned: sleek, cool, bright, and cutting-edge modern. But we are most impressed by the dedicated family meal station, a completely separate slice of the kitchen where the twice-daily staff meals are made. We ask Rafa if anything about the staff meal has changed since the fire. "No, no, no. It's the same! The characters change, but the feeling? The feeling is definitely the same." With that, he dashes upstairs to the office and returns wearing an enormous papier-mâché bear head, an absurd relic from a slightly haywire cook-ing demonstration by the Mugaritz team. Everyone cracks up, including Andoni, and despite everything that could make you cry, for the staff at Mugaritz, the future is smiling down upon them.

It's a long, winding, steep road to get to Mugaritz. What was here before you turned it into a restaurant?

Mugaritz was—as incredible as it sounds—a bar. Even though this road is remote, there were a lot of people passing by. This was the main road that takes you to the town.

Why did you decide to put a restaurant here, on top of a hill, in a fairly remote part of northern Spain?

Thirteen years ago, when I was looking for a place to open in San Sebastián, everything was so expensive. I just didn't have the money to rent. This place was abandoned—there was nobody here—so there was the possibility to actually pay the rent.

We know the oak tree out back is an important piece of symbolism for the restaurant. Can you explain why?

We are in Errenteria and if you cross a minute that way, you are in Astigarraga. The house, the *casita*, is in Astigarraga and the restaurant is in Errenteria. The oak tree marks the border. That you are in between two sides works to define Mugaritz also. Here it is a group experience, but also it is an individual experience. It is modern food, but also a very traditional environment with very traditional products. So we can define ourselves in different ways at the same time.

Why is the staff meal important here?

I worked in fourteen restaurants before I opened Mugaritz, and all of the family meals were very bad. We would eat fast and not pay attention to the food. During those years that I worked, I realized that what makes the difference between the good and the exceptional are the details.

How so?

There is a big difference between what you say and what you do. For me, it was very important to build up the concept of staff meal. I know that other people realize that something is important when you yourself pay attention to all the details. When cooks from the outside would come here, they had this idea of the family meal: doing it any way, no matter how and not putting in the time. So when the cooks came in here, I had to explain all of the aspects of the staff meal. All day, from morning to night, no matter if you are doing the fish station, the meat station, everything has to be perfect. And that includes family meal.

It is incredible that after so little time, you have emerged better than ever after a fire that left you kitchen-less. Can you remember the first staff meal you made when things were not so certain?

I remember the first thing that we made here for family meal right after the fire was just one single plate, a soup with lentils or chickpeas. Honestly, I can barely remember. It was in the middle of the cleaning and all the craziness. It was a chance for everyone to be on their own, thinking about their own things.

We know that you have a nutritionist work with your team to build better, more healthful staff meals. What was one change in your approach that really stands out after going through this process?

Before, we put everything on the table and everyone would just serve himself or herself. There would be meat, so some people would just eat meat. She said that if we made a complete plate for everyone, we would be able to serve a more balanced meal, with the cost being almost the same.

Has the staff meal evolved over time?

When we began Mugaritz, there were eight people in the kitchen and now we have thirty-five. When we got to a point where we asked ourselves "How many stagiaires [cooking interns] do we want?" we immediately said that we wanted two people just for family meal. It's now about attention to detail.

MARMITAKO DE BONITO (Basque Tuna Stew)

Many of Spain's greatest dishes have come from the humblest origins, and this one is no exception. Created by local fishermen, *marmitako* roughly translates to "from the pot," which is how this stew was served during long fishing voyages in the North Atlantic waters. Slightly spicy and very hearty, it makes good use of the local bonito—a type of small tuna—utilizing the meat for the stew but also the bones for the stock. So while tuna bones are elsewhere considered too "fishy" for broth making, in Basque Country the local catch is used with superb results. The key is to thoroughly clean the bones under running water to remove any blood and guts. Unless you have caught your own tuna or know a local fishmonger, very fresh tuna bones can be hard to come by. Substitute with bones from any whole fish or, in a pinch, use shrimp shells. Of course, premade fish stock is the fastest and most reliable alternative.

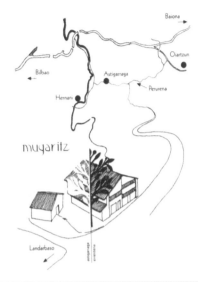

continues on next page

Serves 6

FISH STOCK

2 TABLESPOONS (30 MILLILITERS) EXTRA-VIRGIN OLIVE OIL

2 POUNDS (908 GRAMS) TUNA BONES, RINSED THOROUGHLY (SEE RECIPE HEADER)

2 MEDIUM CARROTS, COARSELY CHOPPED

1 GARLIC CLOVE, SLICED

1 MEDIUM YELLOW ONION, COARSELY CHOPPED

1 LEEK, COARSELY CHOPPED (WHITE AND LIGHT GREEN PARTS ONLY)

STEW

5 TABLESPOONS (74 MILLILITERS) EXTRA-VIRGIN OLIVE OIL

1 LARGE GREEN BELL PEPPER, FINELY CHOPPED

½ LARGE RED BELL PEPPER, FINELY CHOPPED

1 ROASTED RED PEPPER, DRAINED AND FINELY CHOPPED

½ LARGE YELLOW ONION, FINELY CHOPPED

1 GARLIC CLOVE, MINCED

1 WHOLE SMALL GUINDILLA CHILE PEPPER, SEEDED AND COARSELY CHOPPED (OPTIONAL OR SUBSTITUTE YOUR FAVORITE SMALL FRESH CHILE)

1 TEASPOON (2 GRAMS) PIMENTÓN (SPANISH SMOKED PAPRIKA)

4 SMALL RUSSET POTATOES, PEELED AND CUT INTO 1-INCH (2.5 CENTIMETER) CUBES

½ CUP (118 MILLILITERS) TOMATO PURÉE

1¼ POUNDS (568 GRAMS) BONELESS, SKINLESS YELLOWFIN TUNA STEAK, AT LEAST 1 INCH (2.5 CENTIMETER) THICK AND CUT INTO 1-INCH (2.5 CENTIMETER) CUBES (SEE NOTE)

KOSHER SALT AND FRESHLY GROUND BLACK PEPPER TO TASTE

FINELY CHOPPED FLAT-LEAF PARSLEY FOR SERVING

For the stock: In a large stockpot, heat the oil over high heat until shimmering. Add the bones and sauté until any clinging meat turns opaque, about 2 minutes. Add the carrots, garlic, onion, and leek, and sauté until the vegetables are tender, about 5 minutes. Cover with 1¾ quarts (1.7 liters) of water, lower the heat, and simmer, uncovered, for 30 minutes. Strain into a clean container and discard the solids. Yields 1½ quarts (1.4 liters). Extra stock can store for several months in the freezer.

For the stew: Rinse out and dry the stockpot. Heat the oil over medium-high heat and when hot, add the peppers and onion. Sauté until the onion is translucent, about 6 minutes. Add the garlic, chile pepper, and pimentón and sauté until aromatic, about 1 minute. Add the potatoes and tomato purée and cook until the liquid is slightly reduced, stirring to prevent scorching, about 2 minutes. Add all of the stock, cover the pot, lower the heat, and simmer until the potatoes are tender, 10 to 12 minutes.

Season the tuna pieces generously with salt and pepper. Heat a large sauté pan until smoking. Add the oil, then immediately sear the tuna pieces quickly on all sides to achieve a light brown crust, about 3 minutes total cooking time. (Err on the side of underdone, since the tuna will continue to cook in the next step.) Transfer the tuna to the simmering stew, garnish with parsley, and serve straightaway. Don't delay! The longer the tuna stays in the hot liquid, the more it will continue to cook, and possibly dry out.

Note

When North American bonito is not in season, Mugaritz substitutes fresh salmon steaks and uses fish stock from their freezer. Mackerel would also work well.

GARLIC-BAKED CHICKEN THIGHS
with FOIL-ROASTED VEGETABLES

For a restaurant that serves fewer than a hundred customers per day, Mugaritz maintains stunning staff diversity. At any given time, a dozen different countries are represented in the kitchen. During our visit, locals worked alongside cooks from Pittsburgh, Brazil, Japan, and Paris. Although the cook from Mexico City was the easiest to spot. His giveaway? A gigantic jar of wickedly hot cayenne rama peppers next to his plate. So the purpose of this unadorned dish is to provide a healthful option—a lean protein and fresh vegetables—that will please a variety of palates. "We try not to put too many condiments on food," says sous chef Rafa Costa E Silva, "and try not to make it too heavy or too spicy." For that, one simply needs to befriend the cook from Mexico.

The cleverest part of this dish is the technique for whole roasting the vegetables. Wrapped in foil, skin and all, they take no time to get in the oven, since peeling, seeding, and chopping are saved until the vegetables are cooked and easier to tackle.

Serves 6

VEGETABLES

2 TABLESPOONS (30 MILLILITERS) OLIVE OIL, PLUS MORE FOR SERVING

2 LARGE YELLOW ONIONS

1 LARGE EGGPLANT

2 LARGE GREEN BELL PEPPERS

2 LARGE RED BELL PEPPERS

KOSHER SALT AND FRESHLY GROUND BLACK PEPPER TO TASTE

CHICKEN

6 SKIN-ON, BONE-IN CHICKEN THIGHS

2 TABLESPOONS (30 MILLILITERS) OLIVE OIL, PLUS MORE FOR SERVING

KOSHER SALT

6 GARLIC CLOVES, THINLY SLICED

For the vegetables: Preheat the oven to 425°F (204°C). Lightly slick the onions, eggplant, and peppers with oil and season with salt and pepper. Wrap each vegetable individually in aluminum foil and arrange in a single layer on a sheet tray. Bake until tender, about 1 hour. (Depending on size, onions may take up to 30 minutes longer. Use a skewer to test for doneness: if it pierces with just slight resistance, they are done.) Remove from the oven and set aside until cool enough to handle, about 20 minutes.

While the vegetables are cooling, brush the chicken with oil and season generously with salt. Place the chicken in a baking dish, skin-side up, sprinkling the garlic evenly over the pieces. Bake for 15 minutes, then lower the heat to 350°F (177°C) and continue to bake until the chicken is cooked through, about 30 minutes, or the internal temperature reaches 165°F (74°C).

While the chicken is roasting, remove the foil from the vegetables. Peel the eggplant, stem and seed the peppers, and remove the skin and tough outer layers of the onions. Cut all the vegetables in uniform strips and arrange on an oven-safe platter. Cover with foil and place in the oven to reheat for the last 10 minutes of the chicken's roasting time.

Finally, to crisp and color the chicken skin before serving, place the baking dish under a hot broiler for about 5 minutes. Serve immediately alongside the warmed vegetables. Both components taste great with the Parsley Sauce on page 216.

CROSSHATCHED POTATOES and PARSLEY SAUCE

At first glance these potatoes may seem plain, but they boast two notable distinctions. First, the cross-hatching deep into the halves transforms them during roasting into tiny potato hedgehogs both softly spiky and slightly crispy at the edges. Second, the accompanying parsley sauce is a recipe workhorse. Easy to prepare, it lends an acidic pop to potatoes, chicken, or roasted vegetables. It can also serve double duty as a salad dressing or a sauce for grilled meats, especially lamb.

Serves 6

POTATOES

6 MEDIUM RUSSET POTATOES (ABOUT 2½ POUNDS/1 KILOGRAM)

2 TABLESPOONS (30 MILLILITERS) OLIVE OIL

KOSHER SALT AND FRESHLY GROUND BLACK PEPPER TO TASTE

PARSLEY SAUCE

1 GARLIC CLOVE

1 SMALL BUNCH FLAT-LEAF PARSLEY (LEAVES ONLY)

1 CUP (237 MILLILITERS) OLIVE OIL

1 TABLESPOON (15 MILLILITERS) WHITE VINEGAR, PLUS MORE AS NEEDED

KOSHER SALT AND FRESHLY GROUND BLACK PEPPER TO TASTE

For the potatoes: Preheat the oven to 375°F (191°C). Scrub the potatoes well, then cut each in half lengthwise. With a sharp paring knife, cross-hatch three-quarters of the way through the potato flesh to create a grid of ⅓-inch (8 millimeter) squares; it will look a little like grill marks without the char. (Do not cut all the way to the skin or the potato will fall apart when served.) Brush the potatoes with oil, season generously with salt and pepper, and arrange in a single layer, skin-side down, on a sheet tray. Bake until the potatoes are tender and slightly crispy, about 1 hour. Keep warm until serving.

For the parsley sauce: In a blender, combine the garlic, parsley, oil, and vinegar and blend on high speed until the liquid is smooth and bright green, about 1 minute. Season with salt and pepper, and extra vinegar to taste, blending to incorporate. Serve at room temperature with the warm potatoes.

This sauce will separate as it sits. A brisk stir with a fork or shake in a jar will bring it back together.

ARROZ CON LECHE PARA LA FAMILIA

(Rice Pudding for the Family)

Mugaritz plans all their staff meals on a ten-day calendar-style menu. Each date lists a three-course meal that always ends with something sweet. Following their nutritionist's sensible advice, platters of fresh fruit and yogurt appear nine out of the ten days. For one day, and one day only, a *postre* (dessert as we all hope it to be) is served. This arroz con leche is the Basque version of rice pudding, but without eggs or vanilla. It is easy to make in large batches, but at Mugaritz, the staff is served very small portions of this intensely creamy dessert to avoid a sugar crash midway through the night. If you are after larger servings (more than ½ cup/118 milliliters per person), we suggest you at least double this recipe.

Serves 4

1 QUART (946 MILLILITERS) WHOLE MILK

1 CINNAMON STICK

⅓ CUP (80 GRAMS) SHORT-GRAIN WHITE RICE SUCH AS BOMBA (SEE PAGE 46) OR ARBORIO

SCANT ½ CUP (100 GRAMS) GRANULATED SUGAR

In a heavy-bottomed pot over medium-high heat, bring the milk to just under a boil. Remove from the heat, add the cinnamon, and infuse for 10 minutes.

Return the pot to the heat, again bring the milk to just under a boil, and add the rice. Lower the heat to a simmer and cook for 15 minutes, stirring from time to time to release the starch from the rice. Add the sugar and stir until dissolved. Adjust the pot so it is just barely on the burner, allowing for enough heat to maintain a very gentle, molten lava bubbling. Stir gently throughout the cooking process to avoid scorching the bottom. Cook until the liquid is reduced to a thick and creamy porridge and the rice is plumped and completely soft, about 75 minutes. Remove the cinnamon stick and serve immediately.

Alternatively, cover the surface of the rice with plastic wrap and refrigerate until chilled, then serve with a dollop of whipped cream on top.

OLEANA

CAMBRIDGE, MASSACHUSETTS

Ileana does not serve a staff meal. Instead, the Eastern Mediterranean restaurant in Cambridge's Inman Square serves a superlative one. Set out in the open kitchen, just beyond a bar stacked with copies of the restaurant's own paean to Middle Eastern spices aptly entitled *Spice*, it is beautiful daily buffet. Dishes are created from organic produce from nearby Siena Farms, an expanding experiment in community supported agriculture co-owned by the restaurant's chef and owner, Ana Sortun, and run by her husband, Chris Kurth. After the staff serves themselves from the selection of healthful dishes, they settle beside the dining room's open fire, eating and chatting mirthfully as Turkish hanging lamps transform the afternoon sun into lambent flecks of light. It is the picture of staff meal perfection. But just because things are idyllic at Oleana does not mean its cooks are free from past staff meal grievances, memories that cling to their culinary careers like lint on Velcro.

As word spreads that "staff meal experts" are in the kitchen, we find ourselves becoming de facto therapists for cooks with traumatic staff meal stories. "There was a place where I worked at that only served us pasta," says a line cook (name redacted), whose disappointment quickly turns into a devilish grin. "Well, except for on Sundays." As it happens, the chef de cuisine was off that day, so the staff would raid the pantries as well as the restaurant's prized truffle stash. "We'd just go nuts," he admits. Another line cook ups the ante with his tale of eating pig's blood every day, explaining that because blood sausages were made daily, any leftover blood was used in the staff meal, lest it coagulate. "You start to not love blood pasta anymore," he says. We feel his pain.

Fortunately, these two cooks are now in good hands. An all-female dream team—made up of Ana as well as chef de cuisine Cassie Piuma and sous chef Cara Chigazola Tobin—shares the Oleana staff meal duty. "We all kind of have our own specialties," says Cara, explaining that as a native Californian, she tends to lean heavily on Mexican staples like her lauded pork carnitas, while Ana cooks more traditional Middle Eastern offerings, albeit healthful ones. "I always notice that if I make something a little heavier, the staff moves a little slower," says Ana. So although the trio is

THE MAGIC IS IN THE HANDS

tasked with using leftovers and off-cuts, the meal must also be good for them. "We try to put up a balanced meal," Ana insists, "not just one thing."

Today's staff meal embodies this simple philosophy: to create great-tasting food that doubles as nutritious fuel. The bright red pepper soup, sumac-flecked fattoush salad, spiced chicken schwarma wrapped in a warm pide, (a large, thin, pocketless pita), and smoothie-like ayran make an energizing lineup. It's the kind of balanced meal you would feel good serving to your own growing brood. Which is, in fact, the way these three women view it. "It's literally like cooking for your family," Cara tells us. Cassie makes the same point. "The fact that you're doing a family meal book," she says, "it's so perfect here because this place is like a little family."

The meal over, we reflect on the staff meal horror stories we heard earlier in the day—and from time to time throughout the writing of this book—to decode the message this stellar staff meal sends to those burned by the bad ones. Really, it all boils down to keeping the faith. That somewhere along the line there's a good staff meal with your name on it. And if all else fails, follow Ana's lead. She says she has never had a bad staff meal her entire career, and the reason is simple: "Usually, I was the one that was making it."

What are your go-to ingredients to pull together a good, fast, fresh staff meal?

Yogurt. Good, thick yogurt. Olive oil. These are the two things that we go through the most here. And then something like dried mint. We also use a lot of dried chiles and red pepper flakes but none of the food is spicy. We use it like black pepper, to lift up the dish. And lamb would obviously be a no-brainer.

What first drew you to Eastern Mediterranean cuisine?

I was cooking at Casablanca [in Harvard Square] and these two ladies invited me to go to Turkey. I said, "I'm gonna go!" so I took a trip to Turkey about twelve years ago. When I got there, they took me by the hand and became sort of mentors/ teachers. These ladies really inspired me. By the end of the trip, I was just like, "Wow, this stuff is cool."

Can you talk about the fundamentals of Eastern Mediterranean cooking? And perhaps share some cookbooks you would recommend as resources?

I find a lot of Ottoman roots in Eastern Mediterranean cooking so it is definitely set apart from the rest of the Mediter-ranean by its use of spices. They are used differently there than they are in India, Thailand, or in other countries where spices are used. If someone is just trying to get a sense of the cuisine, author Clau-dia Roden has this beautiful balance of getting you to really understand the fla-vors and the guts of a dish by doing some-thing simple but complex tasting.

What does the Eastern Mediterranean spice cabinet hold?

Sumac, chiles like Urfa and Aleppo, cin-namon, cumin. Allspice is huge, especially in Lebanon. Then there's also ginger and coriander and spices that are used in India as well. Also dried herbs like spearmint, oregano, za'atar, which is a combination of wild thyme, sesame seeds, and sumac— Eric Ripert is using that now. [Smiling] I think it's going to be on Doritos soon.

As the author of a cookbook titled Spice, do you find that there is one spice every cook probably has in their pantry but is probably underutilizing?

People always think of allspice as some-thing that is only "wintery" or "squashy." But if you take whole allspice and put it in a peppermill and just grind it over summer sliced tomatoes with some black pepper— you need to use them in unison—it's really amazing.

Allspice is in the spice blend for the chicken schwarma. Is this dish a staff meal favorite?

I think everyone has his or her own favorite thing. It depends on the season. In the winter there's an oxtail soup or a rice dish or some kind of protein. But we always have a big salad. In summer we do gazpa-chos, vegetable smoothies, that kind of thing. Today, because we're heading into spring, we're going to do a yogurt drink and a red pepper–bulgur soup, which is quintessential Turkish flavor. The bulgur is a whole grain, so it's full of energy. And it is super easy to make. It's the perfect staff meal.

Why do you think some restaurants don't serve a very good staff meal?

If it's not that great, it doesn't really come down to the economics of it, it comes down to the time aspect of it. Just having enough time to make it good. Quickly.

What is your staff meal philosophy?

I always believed that the only perk that anybody gets in a restaurant is some food and some good wine. We need good energy food. When staff meals are heavy, like mac and cheese, I swear to God, when I do that, the staff . . . well, let's just say it's not the best night.

CUCUMBER AYRAN (Yogurt Soda)

Black tea may be Turkey's favorite hot beverage, but ayran takes the crown for favorite cold drink. In Ankara, the country's capital, it's even on the McDonald's menu, right next to the Coca-Cola. Ayran is a simple combination of thick yogurt (called labneh) blended with water and a pinch of salt, for both flavor and electrolyte balance in the sweat-inducing weather. At Oleana they also add something normally destined for the trash, piles of cucumber peelings, to add flavor and brightness to the drink. An equal amount of thinly sliced unpeeled cucumber works too, as we have done below. "People need something that will carry them through the night," she says, and like its American subspecies, the "smoothie," this drink does just that.

NOTE

Part yogurt, part fresh cheese, labneh is reminiscent of sour cream in taste but with a firmer consistency. Made by straining yogurt to the nth degree, it can be bought by the plastic container in Middle Eastern specialty stores and is also finding shelf space in mainstream markets. Store-bought labneh can be salted or unsalted, so make sure you check its ingredient list before adding salt. It can be replaced with thick Greek-style yogurt.

Serves 4

1 CUP (245 GRAMS) LABNEH, CHILLED (SEE NOTE)

½ LARGE SEEDLESS CUCUMBER, UNPEELED AND THINLY SLICED

2 CUPS (473 MILLILITERS) SPARKLING WATER, CHILLED

PINCH OF KOSHER SALT

ICE AS NEEDED

In a blender, combine the labneh, cucumber, sparkling water, and salt. Add enough ice to chill the liquid, but avoid blender overflow (about a handful). Blend on high speed for 1 to 2 minutes, until the mixture is light green, frothy, and the consistency of whole milk. Pour into short tumblers and serve on a hot summer night.

TURKISH RED PEPPER and BULGUR SOUP

This is a soup that Turkish children grow up with, explains chef de cuisine Cassie Piuma: "For me, it's like orzo with butter and cheese." It is also nutrient-dense—packed with hearty whole-grain bulgur that cooks to tender quickly—and bursting with flavor, thanks to Cassie's heavy hand with a Turkish red pepper paste Oleana keeps in stock. The paste can be difficult for the home cook to source but is easily replaced with roasted red bell peppers that have been drained and puréed, as we have done here. When topped with pan-fried cubes of halloumi cheese, this soup's a meal in itself, and a beautiful one at that. "Oh, it's really pretty when it's done," Cassie agrees. "It's kind of glistening and nice and red and shiny."

Serves 6 to 8

1 CUP (160 GRAMS) FINE (#1) BULGUR WHEAT (SEE NOTES)

2 TABLESPOONS (30 MILLILITERS) EXTRA-VIRGIN OLIVE OIL

2 LARGE RED BELL PEPPERS, FINELY CHOPPED

1 LARGE YELLOW ONION, FINELY CHOPPED

2 QUARTS (1.9 LITERS) CHICKEN STOCK

1 CUP (240 GRAMS) CANNED CHOPPED TOMATOES, JUICE RESERVED

1 CUP (237 MILLILITERS) ROASTED RED BELL PEPPER PURÉE (SEE RECIPE HEADER)

1 TABLESPOON (2 GRAMS) DRIED MINT

8 OUNCES (227 GRAMS) HALLOUMI CHEESE, CUT INTO SMALL CUBES

KOSHER SALT AND FRESHLY GROUND BLACK PEPPER TO TASTE

GROUND URFA BIBER (OPTIONAL; SEE NOTE)

NOTE

In Middle Eastern specialty shops, bulgur wheat is sold according to size: the sand-like #1 being the finest, the gravel-like #4 the coarsest. The smaller the grind, the quicker the cooking time. Most grocery stores now carry at least one "quick-cooking" variety, but if a substitution is necessary, quinoa comes closest. The same shop may carry Urfa biber (which translates roughly as "peppers from the town of Salinurfa"), a ground chile that looks a lot like dark purple soil and has a unique raisin-like fruitiness similar to the dried ancho chile—its most reliable substitute.

In a bowl, soak the bulgur in 1 quart (946 milliliters) of very warm water for 1 hour. Drain well and set aside. (The soaking prevents the finished soup from becoming sludgy.)

Meanwhile, heat the oil in a large pot over medium-high heat. When hot, sweat the fresh peppers and onions until soft, about 8 minutes. Add the stock, tomatoes, pepper purée, and mint. Bring to a boil, then lower heat and simmer for 20 minutes, or until the tomatoes are tender.

Stir in the drained bulgur. Simmer gently for 5 to 10 minutes to allow the bulgur to swell and soften completely, thickening the soup.

Meanwhile, heat a cast-iron or nonstick skillet over high heat, without oil. When hot, add the halloumi cubes and sear quickly until golden brown and soft, about 2 minutes total.

Season the soup with salt and pepper, and ladle into bowls. Garnish with softened cubes of halloumi and a sprinkle of Urfa pepper, if desired. Serve immediately.

CHICKEN SCHWARMA with GARLIC TOUM

There was a surplus of chicken thighs in just about every restaurant kitchen we visited. While the white meat is reserved for the customer's plate, the dark meat typically ends up on the staff meal table. This suits everyone at Oleana just fine, especially if it means schwarma for supper, a sandwich-like pita wrap that is the Middle East's version of fast food. To get the chicken ready for the wrap, Ana Sortun first rubs the thighs with garlic and warming "schwarma spice," then braises the lot in white wine.

Toum, a Lebanese garlic sauce, is used as both a schmear inside the pita and as a dipping sauce on the side. "Essentially, it's whipped garlic," explains Ana, who stirs in a little yogurt to mellow its raw garlic flavor. Since toum packs a garlic punch, Ana recommends using it as you would butter: liberally but sensibly. Extra toum at Oleana is stirred into sautéed greens from Siena Farms, including baby kale, spinach, fava bean greens, purple radish greens, and tatsoi. Says Ana: "It's like having garlic butter, but there's no butter."

Serves 6 to 8

CHICKEN

3 TABLESPOONS (21 GRAMS) SCHWARMA SPICE (SEE NOTES)

2 TABLESPOONS (30 MILLILITERS) OLIVE OIL

2 GARLIC CLOVES, MINCED

3 POUNDS (1.4 KILOGRAMS) SKIN-ON, BONE-IN CHICKEN THIGHS

1 TABLESPOON (18 GRAMS) KOSHER SALT

1 CUP (237 MILLILITERS) DRY WHITE WINE

TOUM

2 SMALL GARLIC CLOVES

1 TABLESPOON (15 MILLILITERS) FRESHLY SQUEEZED LEMON JUICE

½ TEASPOON (3 GRAMS) KOSHER SALT

¾ CUP (178 MILLILITERS) CANOLA OIL

½ CUP (125 GRAMS) LABNEH (SEE NOTE, PAGE 224)

TO SERVE

6 TO 8 VERY LARGE (12-INCH/30.5 CENTIMETER DIAMETER) PIDE (POCKETLESS PITA BREADS; SEE NOTES)

1 ROMAINE HEART, COARSELY CHOPPED

THINLY SLICED DILL PICKLES, SEVERAL PER SANDWICH

For the chicken: Preheat the oven to 400°F (204°C). Combine the schwarma spice, olive oil, and garlic to form a thick paste. Coat the thighs with the paste and season with salt. Arrange the pieces in a single layer in a high-sided baking pan. Pour the wine into the bottom of the pan and add enough water to cover the chicken by three-quarters. Roast, uncovered, for 1 hour, or until the chicken is falling-off-the-bone tender and most of the liquid in the pan has evaporated. Set aside until cool enough to handle, then remove and discard the bones. Roughly chop the meat and skin and set aside.

For the toum: Place the garlic, lemon juice, and salt in a blender and purée on high speed until smooth, about 30 seconds. With the blender still on high, add the oil in a slow, steady stream. Once incorporated, add the yogurt and blend until combined. Add a small amount of water if the toum is too thick to pour easily.

To serve: Wrap the pitas in foil and heat in a low oven until warm but not brittle (you'll need flexibility to wrap). Spread a thin layer of toum onto one side of every warm pita, then add a handful of the chicken in the center. Top the chicken with chopped Romaine and pickles. Roll up the pita, folding in the sides burrito-style. They can be eaten immediately, or heated until crispy in a hot cast-iron pan; no oil is necessary. Serve with extra toum on the side for dipping or drizzling.

NOTES

A blend of warming ground spices—including cumin, coriander, paprika, and cinnamon—preblended and packaged schwarma can be found in the spice section at Middle Eastern markets, or online.

If you cannot find large, thin, pocketless pita (also known as pide), lavash flatbread or large tortillas can be substituted.

MEYER LEMON FATTOUSH SALAD

Even when pita goes slightly stale, it is still put to good use at Oleana. Cut into strips and deep-fried (or oven-baked, as we have done below), pita forms the foundation for this Middle Eastern chopped salad known generically as fattoush (pronounced fat-TOUSH), a member of the fattat family of dishes, all of which use stale unleavened bread. The pita, herbs, and escarole are tossed together with a dressing made both bright and sweet with seasonal Meyer lemons. If you are feeling adventurous, this salad can easily be fortified with feta, black olives, red cabbage, or jewel-like pomegranate seeds.

Serves 6 to 8

PITA

2 LARGE (ABOUT 12 INCHES/30.5 CENTIMETERS IN DIAMETER) OR 4 SMALL (ABOUT 6 INCHES/15 CENTIMETERS) PITA BREADS

¼ CUP (59 MILLILITERS) EXTRA-VIRGIN OLIVE OIL

KOSHER SALT TO TASTE

DRESSING

2 TABLESPOONS (30 MILLILITERS) SHERRY VINEGAR

1 TABLESPOON (15 MILLILITERS) FRESHLY SQUEEZED MEYER LEMON JUICE

¼ TEASPOON (4 GRAMS) GRANULATED SUGAR

1 TEASPOON (5 MILLILITERS) DIJON MUSTARD

1 SHALLOT, FINELY CHOPPED

½ CUP (118 MILLILITERS) EXTRA-VIRGIN OLIVE OIL

KOSHER SALT AND FRESHLY GROUND BLACK PEPPER TO TASTE

1 MEDIUM HEAD ESCAROLE, SHREDDED

½ LARGE SEEDLESS CUCUMBER, UNPEELED AND THINLY SLICED

¼ CUP (9 GRAMS) PACKED COARSELY CHOPPED MINT LEAVES

¼ CUP (9 GRAMS) PACKED COARSELY CHOPPED PARSLEY LEAVES

1 TABLESPOON (8 GRAMS) POWDERED SUMAC (SEE NOTE)

Preheat oven to 450°F (232°C). Cut the pitas into strips about 4 x ½-inches (10 x 1.25 centimeters). In a large bowl, toss the pita strips with olive oil and season liberally with salt. Place them on a sheet tray in a single layer and bake for 10 to 12 minutes, turning as necessary to brown both sides until golden and very crispy. Allow to cool completely. Yields about 2 cups (225 grams). Note that instead of baking, Oleana deep-fries their pita for extra crunchiness in a fraction of the time. Feel free to follow suit.

Whisk together vinegar, lemon juice, sugar, and mustard in a bowl until the sugar is dissolved. Add the shallot and let stand for 6 minutes. In a slow, steady stream, whisk in the olive oil until fully incorporated, then season with salt and pepper. Set aside.

Add the toasted pita and toss until the bread is completely coated with the dressing. Add the escarole, cucumber, mint, and parsley and toss. Season with salt and pepper and heap onto a serving platter. Dust the salad with sumac and serve immediately. Eat it all if you can; the pita crisps turn mushy overnight.

NOTE

The sumac plant is a relative of poison ivy, but fear not, its powdered spice is completely edible, with a pleasantly sour tang. Widely used in Middle Eastern cooking, chances are you've seen it dusted on a bowl of hummus. It can be found in any Middle Eastern grocery store, or online.

PICCOLO

MINNEAPOLIS, MINNESOTA

SLOW-COOKED RED BEANS
AND HAM HOCKS

CAST-IRON CORNBREAD WITH
MAPLE-BACON BUTTER

MR. PICKLES'S PULLED PORK

JOHNNY TWO SOCKS'S BBQ SAUCE

CELERY ROOT AND ALMOND SLAW

take it personally. I never cut corners. I try not to repeat it." This is the sacred covenant of the Piccolo staff meal, according to executive chef and owner Doug Flicker. Each day the Minnesota native prepares the sit-down spread for his small staff of twenty. Of the close to five hundred staff meals—from hearty lamb stew to pig heart chorizo tacos—he has made since Piccolo first opened in 2010, Doug has made it a point never to repeat a menu. So when 4 p.m. rolls around, he asks three things of all on staff: to stop, sit down, and eat. "This is the first time in my twenty years that I sit down every day for staff meal," says Doug, a stocky redhead with a charmingly offbeat sense of humor. "As opposed to standing at a counter and shoveling it in my mouth."

Today's meal began almost two days prior, when a whole pork shoulder, smothered in smoky chipotle paste and covered in Doug's signature spice blend, was refrigerated for a full day, the flavors left to penetrate deep within the flesh. Doug explains that Piccolo's modern American-tasting menu is ingredient-

heavy. "Each menu will produce a certain amount of waste that we need to use up for staff meal. So we've been eating a lot of pork lately," which, as Doug explains, is a by-product of their in-house butchering and why the shoulder made the staff meal menu today. But what he feeds his team does not solely depend upon leftovers. "Staff meal also kind of depends on my mood," admits Doug.

Today's blowout barbecue extravaganza—red beans slow cooked with ham hocks, crunchy slaw made surprisingly different with finely sliced celery root, and jalapeño-spiked cornbread served with a cloud of sweetened bacon butter—is clearly channeling a happy childhood memory buried deep in Doug's past. He reminisces about his home of Rochester in southern Minnesota, and tells the story of African American barbecue cook Thomas Hardy. He relocated from the South in the late 1960s and started serving his "radical" cuisine during a tense time of racial inequality. For Doug, after a childhood of Bologna Day Tuesdays (a tradition at his family-run bar, Flicker's Liquors, where a ring of bologna, a loaf of white bread, and

ketchup were turned into $2.00 sandwiches), Hardy's rebel barbecue joint struck a chord. "I was drawn to it," he says. "I still remember the smell of the wood."

It is not hard to connect the dots between Hardy's influence upon Doug's childhood and the renegade culinary verve the chef now deploys at Piccolo. The restaurant's motto, after all, is "Putting what is seasonal and creative over what is familiar," a not-so-subtle jab at the culinary rut to which some Minnesotans succumb. But while the food at the staff meal is always important, for Doug it goes beyond what is being served on any particular day. "The staff meal at Piccolo is more about the expe-

rience," says Doug. "It's one of those things that is really important to me to help keep everybody on the same page."

Doug's ultimate staff meal goal has always been to eliminate potential tension between the front of the house and the back of the house. It seems to be working. "Any gripes that we have are gripes that any family would have," says line cook Adam Johnson, "but at the end of the day everybody appreciates what everyone brings to the table." Then, perhaps without realizing it, Adam justifies Doug's ambitious crack at never repeating a staff meal twice: "This is probably the only job that I have ever looked forward to. Every day."

Why serve a staff meal every day?

It's a very important time of the day. It's ridiculous that we would dedicate our lives to feeding people and the community but not spend the time to feed ourselves. We've worked so hard. It is a way to say thank you and to give back. Plus, it's in my business partner's and my best interest that everyone stay happy.

What ingredients do you use to make the meals you serve to staff?

It's that balance of bringing stuff in versus using leftovers. For example, we have lamb ribs on the menu right now. We get the ribs in and on lamb portioning day we wind up with plenty of scraps. For the staff meal we'll do a stew with carrots and potatoes. I just try to make it taste as good as I would for the people who are paying for it.

If you could invite anybody to your staff meal, who would it be?

That's a really tough question. I would have to say my grandmother Flicker. She died before I really became good at cooking. Growing up with my grandparents' traditions, I didn't really see it as a type of cuisine. And now being away from it and looking back on it, it's amazing, all these humble dishes. I never really had that conversation with her; I would assume she could teach me a lot of things.

Are there any cookbooks an aspiring chef should check out?

I would say the Mikuni [*Food Fantasy of the Hotel De Mikuni* by Kiyomi Mikuni, 1987,1993], a really old book, beautiful. Also Marco Pierre White's *White Heat*. First edition. That book changed my life.

In what way?

He said all the things that were in my head. From the start of rock and roll to the beauty of lobster. Just amazing.

Any guilty pleasures that show up in the staff meal?

I love Velveeta. I will always love Velveeta because my mom made grilled-cheese sandwiches with it. So for me, it doesn't really matter what the product is. If you grew up with something, that's the way that it is. I think those are the things about food culture that matter most. Today we were all having a conversation about childhood desserts, and Polly [Nielson, chef de cuisine] said, "What's in a pistachio pudding?" and no one could really remember. So I was in the grocery store picking something up, and I walked past the Jell-O aisle, so we snuck in some packets of pistachio pudding. We had somebody make them when Polly wasn't looking.

Hunting is a popular pastime here in the middle of the country: ever bag your own staff meal?

No. I remember a year or two ago, reading the River Cottage books and becoming obsessed with hunting squirrel. We were going to make squirrel foie gras.

Did you do it?

No. It's still on my bucket list.

SLOW-COOKED RED BEANS with HAM HOCKS

While they taste and look a lot like baked beans from up North, these red beans are technically of the stovetop variety. No oven is necessary. At Piccolo, Doug Flicker likes to make them a day ahead of time, which means he has to start soaking the dried beans the day before that. The advance planning is worth it. The spicy, sweet, and smoky notes intensify if the dish is refrigerated and then warmed the next day.

Serves 10 to 12

2 TABLESPOONS (30 MILLILITERS) CANOLA OIL

1 MEDIUM YELLOW ONION, COARSELY CHOPPED

1 QUART (750 GRAMS) DRIED RED KIDNEY BEANS, SOAKED OVERNIGHT AND DRAINED

1 SMALL SMOKED HAM HOCK (ABOUT 1½ POUNDS/680 GRAMS)

2½ QUARTS (2.4 LITERS) CHICKEN STOCK

½ CUP (110 GRAMS) PACKED LIGHT BROWN SUGAR

¼ CUP (59 MILLILITERS) WHITE VINEGAR

¼ CUP (59 MILLILITERS) MOLASSES

1 JALAPEÑO, DESEEDED AND THINLY SLICED

1 TABLESPOON (6 GRAMS) CHILI POWDER

2 TEASPOONS (4 GRAMS) GROUND CUMIN

1 TEASPOON (2 GRAMS) CELERY SEED

3 TABLESPOONS (54 GRAMS) KOSHER SALT, PLUS MORE TO TASTE

In a large pot, heat the oil over medium-high heat, then sauté the onion until translucent. Add the beans, hock, and stock and bring to a boil. Lower the heat and simmer, uncovered, until the beans are three-quarters cooked, about 1 hour. Add the remaining ingredients and simmer gently, uncovered, until the beans and hock are completely tender and the liquid has reduced, 1 to 2 hours. (Piccolo likes their beans soupier, but the longer they simmer, the more they become a thicker baked-bean consistency.) Remove the hock; finely dice the meat and add it back to the pot, discarding any skin or bone.

Adjust the salt and serve immediately straight from the pot, or transfer to a baking dish and refrigerate, covered, overnight. Several hours before you are ready to serve, cover the beans with foil and heat slowly in a low oven, stirring in a tablespoon or two (15 to 30 milliliters) of water to help rehydrate if necessary.

CAST-IRON CORNBREAD with MAPLE-BACON BUTTER

There is a lone vegetarian on the Piccolo staff. While it took her a while to break this news to her meat-loving boss, once Doug Flicker got the message, he made sure she was taken care of. So while this stunning cornbread is sometimes made at Piccolo with bacon fat instead of butter and decked out with a handful of crumbled "billionaire's bacon" (strips that have been slow-cooked with sugar and molasses), it can just as easily be made without, as it was during the night of our visit. For those with a bacon itch, the addictive maple-bacon butter will adequately scratch it.

Serves 10 to 12

CORNBREAD

2 CUPS (250 GRAMS) CORNMEAL, PLUS 2 TABLESPOONS (16 GRAMS) FOR DUSTING

1 CUP (125 GRAMS) ALL-PURPOSE FLOUR

2 TEASPOONS (12 GRAMS) FINE SEA SALT

2 TEASPOONS (10 GRAMS) BAKING POWDER

1 TEASPOON (5 GRAMS) BAKING SODA

3 LARGE EGGS

2 CUPS (473 MILLILITERS) BUTTERMILK

4 OUNCES (1 STICK/112 GRAMS) UNSALTED BUTTER, MELTED

¼ CUP (57 GRAMS) FINELY CHOPPED DRAINED BREAD AND BUTTER JALAPEÑOS (PAGE 73) (OPTIONAL)

1 TABLESPOON (15 MILLILITERS) CANOLA OIL

MAPLE-BACON BUTTER

8 OUNCES (2 STICKS/224 GRAMS) UNSALTED BUTTER, AT ROOM TEMPERATURE

2 TABLESPOONS (30 MILLILITERS) MAPLE SYRUP, PLUS MORE TO TASTE

2 TABLESPOONS (30 MILLILITERS) SMOKED BACON FAT (SEE NOTE, PAGE 85)

1 TEASPOON (6 GRAMS) FINE SEA SALT

For the cornbread: Preheat oven to 400°F (204°C). Once hot, place a 12-inch (305 millimeter) cast-iron skillet in the oven 10 minutes before you are ready to bake the cornbread.

In a large mixing bowl, combine the cornmeal, flour, salt, baking powder, and baking soda. Lightly beat the eggs in a separate bowl. Whisk the buttermilk and butter into the eggs. Stir the wet ingredients into the dry until just incorporated, then quickly mix in the jalapeños, if desired.

Remove the skillet from the oven and carefully coat the pan with the canola oil (a heat-resistant silicone brush works best), then sprinkle with the remaining cornmeal. Pour the batter evenly into the skillet, return to the oven, and bake until puffed and golden brown, about 20 minutes.

Allow to rest for 10 minutes, slice in thick triangles, and serve straight from the skillet. Be sure to drape a kitchen towel over the handle to warn guests that it is still hot to the touch.

For the butter: While the cornbread is cooling, whip together the butter, maple syrup, bacon fat, and salt until combined, adding more maple syrup or salt to taste. Keep at room temperature until ready to serve. Extra butter stores well in the refrigerator, covered, for a week.

MR. PICKLES'S PULLED PORK

"BBQ is about simplicity—rub it down, let it go, forget about it," says chef Doug Flicker, aka Mr. Pickles on some days, Johnny Two Socks on others. (As we learned, these are two of his many goofy, offbeat alter egos who make their appearances when he wants to get a rise out of someone or just pass the time.) For twelve low and slow hours, this chipotle-slathered, spice-rubbed pork shoulder takes its sweet time in the oven.

Piccolo uses a bone-in pork shoulder roast (also known as picnic shoulder) for this recipe, a vaguely triangular cut from the lower front forelegs of the pig. It is not the same as a Boston butt (also known as blade roast, from the upper shoulder), which contains more fat and less connective tissue. Both can be used to make great pulled pork. The only drawback to using bone-in picnic shoulder is that it comes in one size: huge. A typical whole pork shoulder ranges anywhere from 8 pounds to 12 (3.6 to 5.4 kilograms) and beyond. If you would rather make less, use the desired amount of boneless shoulder, and reduce the cooking time accordingly. The time for the dry rub marinade remains the same.

Serves 10 to 12 generously

½ CUP (120 GRAMS) CHIPOTLE CHILES IN ADOBO

3 TABLESPOONS (45 MILLILITERS) LIQUID SMOKE (SEE NOTE)

ONE 8- TO 10-POUND (4 TO 5 KILOGRAM) BONE-IN PORK SHOULDER ROAST

½ CUP (110 GRAMS) PACKED LIGHT BROWN SUGAR

¼ CUP (72 GRAMS) KOSHER SALT

¼ CUP (28 GRAMS) SMOKED PAPRIKA

2 TABLESPOONS (16 GRAMS) COARSELY GROUND BLACK PEPPER

2 TABLESPOONS (15 GRAMS) CHILI POWDER

2 TABLESPOONS (14 GRAMS) ONION POWDER

1 TABLESPOON (7 GRAMS) POWDERED MUSTARD

3 CUPS (710 MILLILITERS) JOHNNY TWO SOCKS'S BBQ SAUCE (PAGE 240)

12 SMALL WHITE SANDWICH ROLLS, SPLIT

SLICED DILL PICKLES

CELERIAC AND ALMOND SLAW (PAGE 241)

In a blender, combine the chipotles and their adobo sauce with the liquid smoke and 3 tablespoons (45 milliliters) water; blend until a smooth, thick, paste is formed. Place the pork shoulder on a foil-lined sheet tray (for easier cleanup) and coat with the chipotle paste (there could be extra, depending on the size of the shoulder). Combine the brown sugar, salt, paprika, pepper, chili powder, onion powder, and mustard, mixing well. Sprinkle the entire shoulder with a thick layer of the spice blend. Refrigerate, uncovered, for 12 to 24 hours. Extra spice blend can be stored in the pantry for several months in a tightly sealed container.

The following day, preheat the oven to 225°F (107°C). Remove the pork from the refrigerator and wrap completely in aluminum foil. Prick the shoulder all over with a skewer about a dozen times to allow the roasting juices to drain. Place the wrapped shoulder in a roasting pan, then slow roast for 10 to 12 hours, or until the meat is meltingly tender, and registers between 200°F (93°C) and 225°F (107°C).

Remove the shoulder from the oven; rest for an hour at room temperature.

To serve: After the pork has rested, shred the meat with a fork or your hands and transfer it to a large bowl. Discard any large chunks of fat or gristle. Mix the shredded meat with a generous amount of barbecue sauce (a large ladleful or two) so that it is moist but not wet. Transfer to a baking dish, cover, and keep warm in a low oven until you are ready to serve.

Let guests assemble their own barbecue sandwiches by piling the buns with pork, pickles, and slaw and topping it all off with extra barbecue sauce.

Note

While Doug is well aware that authentic barbecue would be smoked over hardwood charcoal, he doesn't have the capacity to use an open flame at the restaurant. To get that smoky flavor without the smoke, he adds a very small amount of liquid smoke to the chipotle rub as well as his BBQ sauce. Some may call this cheating, but it is the easiest way to achieve authentic-tasting barbecue indoors without a stovetop smoker. Colgin Liquid Smoke can be found at most supermarkets, but a variety of brands can be found online.

JOHNNY TWO SOCKS'S BBQ SAUCE

Après-shredding, the pulled pork is mixed with Doug's own barbecue sauce recipe, a sort of Carolina–Kansas City smashup with a splash of Dr Pepper for those spicy, caramel notes. "Barbecue sauce shouldn't be fancy. It's meant to be humble," says Doug. So when it comes to using garlic powder instead of fresh, he believes in the powder. "Fresh just doesn't work the same," he says, "in my head, at least."

Yields about 2 quarts (1.9 liters)

8 OUNCES (227 GRAMS) SMOKED BACON, COARSELY CHOPPED

1 MEDIUM YELLOW ONION, COARSELY CHOPPED

3 CUPS (710 MILLILITERS) DR PEPPER

2 CUPS (500 GRAMS) TOMATO PASTE

1 CUP (220 GRAMS) PACKED LIGHT BROWN SUGAR

1 CUP (200 GRAMS) GRANULATED SUGAR

1 CUP (237 MILLILITERS) FRESHLY SQUEEZED LEMON JUICE

½ CUP (118 MILLILITERS) MOLASSES

½ CUP (118 MILLILITERS) WHITE VINEGAR

¼ CUP (28 GRAMS) SMOKED PAPRIKA

2 TABLESPOONS (30 MILLILITERS) SAMBAL OELEK (SEE NOTE, PAGE 105)

2 TABLESPOONS (14 GRAMS) ONION POWDER

1 TABLESPOON (8 GRAMS) COARSELY GROUND BLACK PEPPER

1 TABLESPOON (7 GRAMS) GARLIC POWDER

½ TEASPOON (2.5 MILLILITERS) LIQUID SMOKE, PLUS MORE TO TASTE

KOSHER SALT TO TASTE

Heat a heavy-bottomed pot over medium-high heat until hot. Add the bacon and cook until crispy, about 6 minutes. Add the onion and sauté until translucent, about 6 minutes. Add the Dr Pepper, tomato paste, sugars, lemon juice, molasses, vinegar, sambal, paprika, pepper, onion powder, garlic powder, liquid smoke, and 1½ cups (355 milliliters) water, whisking to incorporate. Lower the heat and simmer for about 30 minutes, stirring occasionally. Cook until the sauce is reduced to a thick but pourable consistency. (Piccolo prefers their sauce slightly runnier than most bottled supermarket varieties.)

Strain the sauce through a fine-mesh sieve, season with salt, and cool to room temperature, at which point it is ready to serve.

Extra sauce stores well in the refrigerator for several weeks (or in the freezer for several months), and makes an excellent gift for your departing guests.

CELERY ROOT and ALMOND SLAW

The beauty of this slaw is that it does not get soggy as it sits. This is thanks to celery root—the deeply furrowed green-brown root vegetable also known as celeriac or celery knob—whose dense off-white flesh stays crispy and full of vibrant celery-like flavor even if it sits for a day or two in the refrigerator.

Serves 10 to 12

2 LARGE EGG YOLKS, AT ROOM TEMPERATURE (SEE NOTES)

1 TABLESPOON (15 MILLILITERS) WHITE WINE VINEGAR, PLUS MORE TO TASTE

1 CUP (237 MILLILITERS) CANOLA OIL

CAYENNE PEPPER TO TASTE

KOSHER SALT TO TASTE

3 MEDIUM CELERIAC (ABOUT 1½ POUNDS/680 GRAMS)

6 MEDIUM CARROTS, PEELED AND COARSELY GRATED

¾ CUP (100 GRAMS) SKIN-ON TOASTED ALMONDS, COARSELY CHOPPED

Whisk the yolks and vinegar in a large bowl until combined. Pour the oil into the yolks in a slow, steady stream, whisking briskly to emulsify into a thick, creamy mayonnaise, about 2 minutes. Season with cayenne, salt, and additional vinegar to taste. Set aside, covered, in the refrigerator.

With a sturdy vegetable peeler, remove the celeriac's knobby outer layer. Cut the white flesh into thin matchsticks or julienne. See Notes for tips on making this job easier.

As you work, submerge both the whole and cut celeriac in ice water to prevent discoloration.

Drain the celeriac, drying it well on paper towels. Combine the celeriac with the mayonnaise, grated carrots, and almonds; toss together until well coated. Season with salt and additional vinegar, should it need some acidic balance.

Serve as a side salad or use it to top your pulled pork sandwiches. Unlike other slaws out there, this one stores well in the refrigerator for up to 3 days.

NOTES

Most professional kitchens use the Japanese mandoline made by Benriner to create perfect julienne. They are super-sharp, thus a bit dangerous, but OXO's julienne peeler can do the job too. Available online, the handheld tool peels in tiny strips instead of flat mats.

This recipe uses raw egg, and consequently there is a slight risk of salmonella or other food-borne illness. This risk is greatly reduced when you use the freshest, highest-quality eggs you can find—pasture-raised eggs from a trusted small farmer, for example. Do not use the eggs if their shells are cracked, and avoid touching the outside of the shells to the yolk or whites at any point. You can also skip making the fresh mayonnaise altogether and simply substitute with ½ cup (118 milliliters) jarred mayonnaise; our favorite brand is the Southern staple, Duke's.

Staff meal is greater than the sum of it's parts. if we can't sit together. share a meal and take the time to have a laugh and inquire about each others day... what kind of example are we setting for our guests?

THE SLANTED DOOR

SAN FRANCISCO, CALIFORNIA

PORK NECK SOUP WITH DATES AND BARLEY

STIR-FRIED BOK CHOY AND SHIITAKE MUSHROOMS

STEAMED CHICKEN WITH LILY BUDS

"Sit down. Sit down. Eat. Eat." These words warmly welcome us into The Slanted Door's off-site commissary kitchen, a cavernous space tucked deep in the dusty heart of San Francisco's Mission District. The voice belongs to Phai Pham, or "Mama" as she is affectionately known, an inky-haired quinquagenarian of extraordinary exuberance and the aunt of chef, owner, and local visionary Charles Phan—both Vietnamese expats who fled their native country as part of the exodus of 1975. Despite standing less than five feet tall, Mama is the kinetic engine that drives this state-of-the-art prep kitchen, and she has been feeding the staff since the original restaurant opened in 1995. The bustling army of cooks (many of them directly related to Mama and Charles) create hundreds of painstaking Vietnamese delicacies—hand-made chicken dumplings, delicate spring rolls, and shrimp-filled wontons—that are then delivered to Charles's venues around the city, including his first restaurant, The Slanted Door, a coolly modern flagship that has recently relocated from the Mission District to the city's culinary nerve center, The Ferry Building.

With no time to get either our coffee or our early-morning bearings, Mama hands us white porcelain soup spoons and chopsticks, then pats two chairs at the end of a long communal table. It is already packed shoulder to shoulder with a few dozen women, all Vietnamese or Chinese, and wearing the restaurant's signature black baseball caps. They dig into the steaming bowls of soup like a hungry

softball team. Mama, whose chef's jacket simply reads "Mama," sits down beside us. She starts slurping spoonfuls of rich pork broth and, with adamant fluttering of fingers, soundlessly orders us to eat. This is where the panic sets in. Did we just miss the creation of the entire meal?

"We didn't realize that family meal was so early," we say. Mama hears the nervous hedging and laughs. "Don't worry. This is our first family meal. We work very hard here and need lots of energy." With a staff that starts cooking at 6 a.m., this meal is their midmorning breakfast; the second staff meal will come later in the afternoon. Relieved (and impressed that such a large staff eats together not once, but twice, daily), we join the slurping and listen to the endless waves of laughter as Mama, equal parts matriarch and comedian, cracks jokes, the punch lines all in Vietnamese.

In a media-saturated food world where cooks are encouraged to perfect their sound bites, one can become slightly jaded to the "just add love" mantra. Spending a wild whirlwind of a day at Mama's side reminds us that there is truth, even power, to the catchphrase. Everything she does in the kitchen, she does with joy. Every encounter she has with a colleague is accompanied with a laugh, a hug, or a kind gesture. And every morsel of food she puts on the table is extraordinary, not because it is all perfection on the plate but because in Mama's

case "love" really is some sort of fourth-dimensional ingredient. "We work very hard here," Mama reiterates once again after catching us eavesdropping on her mirthful exchange with a cook named Peach, one of the few males on staff, "but there is no reason it can't be fun, too."

There's a large bronze bell near Mama's prep area. It is rung to let the staff working deep in the kitchen know when the family meal is ready. We anticipate its sharp clang as Mama adds a final flourish of oil to her enormous wok, its handle bandaged like a boxer's fist. But then a curious thing begins to happen. One by one the cooks are drawn into Mama's orbit; some by the aroma of steaming chicken and lily buds, some by an endearing word or two from Mama herself, and before we know it, the entire staff is back at the table, passing around the sriracha bottle and picking up on the joke-telling right where they left off. With a gravitational pull like Mama's, the bell is wholly unnecessary. You just sit down and eat.

A Conversation with Executive Chef and Owner CHARLES PHAN

Your employees refer to the staff meal as "Rice and Bones." What is the story behind the nickname?

Typically a Chinese or Vietnamese staff meal is pretty basic. Usually there's always a vegetable, there's usually a broth, some sort of soup, a little meat stir-fried with the vegetables. Those are always the three components: protein, vegetable, and soup. And also starch, usually rice. But one day a Caucasian woman on staff just lost it; she said all we eat is "rice and bones" and nothing else. It's pretty cultural. Some people would go crazy if there was too much cheese and pasta.

How do you make sure that everybody walks away from the family meal happy?

I think it's really about treating them like your family. And to treat them like family you have to be on top of everything: financially, psychologically, spiritually.

For home cooks interested in Vietnamese cuisine, what are some ingredients they shouldn't be without?

Definitely fish sauce, shrimp paste, a lot of dried squid—they really add a lot of flavor and more depth to your stock.

What are some of your favorite family meals served here?

Me, I always love a steamed product like steamed pork. Or salted fish and rice.

Do you have a staff meal philosophy?

I think about doing everything at its best. I made some hamburgers the other day, and the staff went crazy for them. I go out of my way to research how to get the meat ground. For the bread I track down these guys that make it seeded, with a little softness to it. We're going to serve it with perfect lettuce and tomato. It's the little things. It just makes it taste so much better.

Why is staff meal important here?

It really brings people together. And I don't think we do enough of that in our lives.

PORK NECK SOUP with DATES and BARLEY

Though born and raised in Vietnam, the Phans are ethnically Chinese, a fact that helps to explain this soup's departure from a more traditional Vietnamese pho. Instead of rice noodles, Mama uses pearled barley, a whole grain that imparts a mild nuttiness to the broth but requires overnight soaking (noodles or rice can be substituted as a shortcut). Charles says this soup—or a close variation—is available to his staff "virtually all day, every day."

As for the general formula for staff meal soup, Charles Phan says it really only requires two things: something sweet (usually turnips or Chinese honey dates) and a cheap cut of meat to make the stock. The Slanted Door uses pork neck in this recipe, but it is a cut that can be hard to find. Pork spareribs work just as well—and are a lot meatier—but you will have to ask your butcher to cut up the rack with the band saw to get properly sized pieces. While it may read as a simple recipe, the end result is all about the broth and the bones, both of which are deeply satisfying to eat.

Serves 4 to 6

½ CUP (100 GRAMS) PEARLED BARLEY

2½ POUNDS (1.1 KILOGRAMS) PORK NECK OR SPARE RIBS, BONES LEFT INTACT, CHOPPED INTO 1-INCH (2.5 CENTIMETER) PIECES

2 QUARTS (1.9 LITERS) CHICKEN STOCK

¼ CUP (24 GRAMS) DRIED PITTED CHINESE HONEY DATES, MINCED (SEE NOTES)

4 CARROTS, HALVED LENGTHWISE AND CUT INTO 2-INCH-LONG (5 CENTIMETER) PIECES

¼ OUNCE (7 GRAMS) DEHYDRATED BOK CHOY, COARSELY CHOPPED (SEE NOTES)

2 TEASPOONS (10 MILLILITERS) FISH SAUCE, PLUS MORE FOR SERVING

2 TEASPOONS (10 MILLILITERS) SOY SAUCE, PLUS MORE FOR SERVING

FOR SERVING

1 BUNCH EACH OF CILANTRO, MINT, AND THAI BASIL

LIME WEDGES

SRIRACHA OR YOUR FAVORITE HOT SAUCE

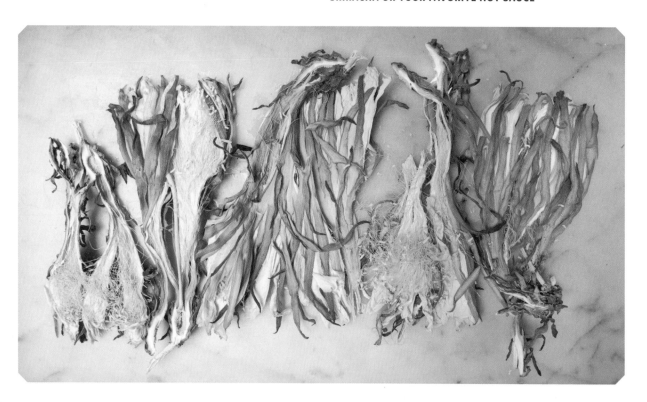

In a small bowl, cover the barley with 2 cups (480 milliliters) cool water and soak at room temperature overnight, or until the grains have softened and plumped slightly.

Drain the barley, and in a colander, rinse under cold running water until the water runs clear. Set aside to drain.

In a large pot, bring 3 quarts (3 liters) water to a boil. Add the pork and return to a boil. A foamy scum will rise to the top; skim and discard. Immediately drain the pork and rinse under cold running water until chilled, about 2 minutes.

Clean the pot of any scum and return the pork to the pot. Add the stock and 1 quart (946 milliliters) water. Over high heat, bring to a boil while skimming away fat and impurities that rise to the surface. Immediately reduce the heat to medium-low and add the barley and the dates. Simmer gently for 1 hour, skimming fat and scum as you go, then add the carrots and bok choy and simmer until the carrots are tender, about 20 minutes. Season the soup with the fish sauce and soy sauce to taste.

To serve, prepare a communal plate with the fresh herbs and lime wedges, and set out on the table along with bottles of sriracha, fish sauce, and soy sauce. Collectively, these ingredients will act as a condiment bar so each person can flavor their soup to their liking. Also set out small bowls of soy sauce so everyone can dip their bones before pulling the meat away with their teeth. Serve the soup hot with extra bowls to collect the sparerib bones.

Notes

Chinese honey dates, also referred to as jujubes, are olive-sized, bright red stone fruits native to Asia. Dried, they taste like a dried apple crossed with a date and can be found in Asian markets alongside the dehydrated mushrooms and seaweed. Middle Eastern dried brown dates can be substituted, but since they are moister than their Chinese counterparts, add them to the pot at the same time as the carrots.

Dehydrated bok choy (also sold as dehydrated cole) is powerfully concentrated in flavor. A little bit goes a long way in making the soup broth slightly tangy, almost mustardy, so use sparingly. Depending on the brand, store-bought dehydrated bok choy may still be sandy. A 30-minute soak in warm water will help rid grit. A few handfuls of coarsely chopped fresh bok choy can be substituted for a less intense flavor.

STIR-FRIED BOK CHOY
and SHIITAKE MUSHROOMS

The Slanted Door uses gigantic woks over supersized gas burners to execute all their stir-fries. Cranking out over 100,000 BTUs (an average home stove emits about one-tenth of that amount), the flames lick up the sides of the wok like a dragon blasting a knight's shield. We asked for Charles Phan's recommended stovetop procedure for cooks who do not have access to professional wok stoves. He said that the trick is to cook all of the ingredients in small batches, "waiting until the oil is hot each time, then finishing the whole thing with a sauce and wine." He admits it won't lead to an identical result, but it is a time-tested technique: "In China they've been doing it like that for a long time, since their stoves are smaller than ours here."

Serves 4 to 6

1 POUND (454 GRAMS) BOK CHOY

1 TABLESPOON (15 MILLILITERS) CANOLA OIL

2 GARLIC CLOVES, THINLY SLICED

15 FRESH SHIITAKE MUSHROOMS (ABOUT 5 OUNCES/140 GRAMS), STEMS REMOVED, THINLY SLICED

2 TABLESPOONS (30 MILLILITERS) RICE WINE

2 TABLESPOONS (30 MILLILITERS) FISH SAUCE

COOKED JASMINE RICE, TO SERVE

Separate the bok choy head into stalks. Cut off the large, leafy green tips and coarsely chop the white stalks. Dunk the pieces in a sink full of cool water, and agitate to remove dirt and debris. Drain, place in a colander, rinse again under fresh running water, then dry completely.

Prepare a small bowl with 2 tablespoons (30 milliliters) water and place next to the stove. Heat a wok over high heat for about 2 minutes. Drizzle in the oil and heat a few seconds until smoking. Add the garlic, swirling the pan for a second or two, then immediately add the bok choy and mushrooms. Move the vegetables in the pan for about 1 minute using a long-handled wooden spoon. Add the rice wine and continue stir-frying for 30 seconds, until the alcohol has burned off. Add the fish sauce and cook until the white parts of the bok choy are cooked through, about 2 minutes. If the bottom of the wok begins to burn at any point, douse it with a teaspoon or two of water. Remove from the heat and serve immediately over the fluffed jasmine rice.

Note

While a large sauté pan can be used for this stir-fry, a wok will do the job in half the time and with much better results. The key to its success is its high, sloping sides that double the surface area and allow food to easily be shuffled, or stir-fried, to hot spots around the pan. This technique encourages rapid evaporation of moisture, thus allowing foods to be cooked quickly without getting soggy. Most Asian grocers sell large woks for less than $15, and they are worth the minimal investment. A flat-bottomed wok is the preferred type for a home kitchen, as it allows you to use it on a standard gas or electric burner. Do yourself a favor and buy a matching domed lid and a steamer basket to fit inside. Both will come in handy for the Steamed Chicken with Lily Buds on page 253.

STEAMED CHICKEN with LILY BUDS

Something mysterious happens in this recipe when you close the lid. After steaming in a flavorful marinade, the bone-in pieces of poultry emerge coated in a thick, richly savory sauce that is delicious spooned over jasmine rice. We think it has everything to do with the addition of dried lily buds, an edible species of the cultivated day lily. In this dish they add a delicate floral acidity and are quite similar in texture to an al dente noodle. Look to buy the buds in a vacuum-sealed package in the dried goods section of your Asian market. Tightly wrap extra buds in their packaging and store them in your freezer to extend their shelf life.

Serves 4

ONE (3-POUND/1.4 KILOGRAM) CHINESE YELLOW FEATHER CHICKEN (SUBSTITUTE ORGANIC FREE-RANGE)

¼ CUP (59 MILLILITERS) CANOLA OIL

¼ CUP (59 MILLILITERS) RICE WINE

¼ CUP (59 MILLILITERS) SOY SAUCE

¼ CUP (59 MILLILITERS) LUM KEE VEGETARIAN MUSHROOM STIR-FRY SAUCE

2 TABLESPOONS (16 GRAMS) CORNSTARCH

2 TEASPOONS (8 GRAMS) GRANULATED SUGAR

2 TEASPOONS (12 GRAMS) KOSHER SALT

ONE (3-INCH/8 CENTIMETER) PIECE FRESH GINGER, PEELED, SLICED INTO ¼-INCH (6 MILLIMETER) COINS AND LIGHTLY CRUSHED

3 GARLIC CLOVES, LIGHTLY CRUSHED

1 CUP (50 GRAMS) DRIED LILY BUDS (SEE RECIPE HEADER)

1 CUP (80 GRAMS) FRESH WOOD EAR MUSHROOMS, COARSELY CHOPPED (SEE NOTE)

½ CUP (35 GRAMS) COARSELY CHOPPED CILANTRO

COOKED JASMINE RICE, FOR SERVING

Cut up the chicken (including the neck and back) into 2- to 3-inch (5 to 8 centimeter) bone-in pieces. If you do not have a meat cleaver at home, your butcher would be happy to do this for you.

In a large bowl, whisk together the oil, rice wine, soy sauce, mushroom sauce, sugar, cornstarch, and salt. Add the chicken, ginger, and garlic, and toss to coat well. Cover and refrigerate for 1 hour.

Cover the lily buds with warm water and set aside to soak for 30 minutes, then drain them and pat dry.

Arrange a steamer on your stovetop. We used a wok fitted with a steamer insert—metal or bamboo both work—topped with a domed lid. Fill the wok with 2 inches (5 centimeters) of water and bring to a boil.

Next, place the chicken and its marinade in a flat plate or tray (something that is small enough to sit atop the steamer insert; a nonperforated pie plate could work).

Sprinkle the lily buds and mushrooms on top of the chicken, set the tray on the steamer insert, and cover the wok. Steam until the chicken is cooked through, 25 to 30 minutes, and the sauce is bubbling and thick. Check the wok's water level every 8 to 10 minutes and add more, if necessary.

To serve, sprinkle the chicken with the cilantro. Serve over steamed jasmine rice to soak up the flavorful marinade that has now turned into a thick sauce.

NOTE

If you cannot find fresh wood ear mushrooms (also known as tree ear or black fungus) at a nearby Asian grocer, you can substitute rehydrated dried wood ear mushrooms or fresh oyster mushrooms.

ST. JOHN

LONDON, ENGLAND

CARAWAY SEED CAKE AND A
GLASS OF MADEIRA

CRÈME FRAÎCHE CUCUMBER
AND CABBAGE SALAD WITH
NIGELLA SEEDS

CURRIED RICE WITH CHICKPEAS

ergus Henderson's own staff meal instructions are simple: eat quickly, enjoy thoroughly. The haste is a by-product of his hard-earned good fortune. As the chef and co-owner of an expanding empire of London restaurants—all spawning from the original St. John opened in 2004—time for his own meal comes in fits and starts, often alone, and only when and if his schedule allows. "I am usually having elevenses just before the afternoon staff meal is served," says Fergus, explaining the old British habit of a late-morning meal to tide you over until lunch. So while staff meals are sometimes an exercise in camaraderie for Fergus, solitude is a frequent side dish. He blames today's missed connection on "slightly different timetables" and pulls up a stool next to St. John's busy bakery. A table set for one.

As the tide of flour and sugar rises around him, Fergus sits calmly, cordially answering the staff's questions about the evening's menu. Within walking distance of London's historic Smithfield Meat Market, St. John is known for indulging guests with a staggering variety of offal—lamb sweetbreads, ox heart, and marrow all make an appearance tonight—but when we probe for one ingredient no home kitchen should be without, Fergus surprises us: "I suppose good bread, which is as essential as a knife and fork." And just like that, his staff meal arrives piping hot from the oven: a caraway-studded seed cake heady with the aroma of sweet

licorice. As always, it is paired with a small glass of Madeira. Fergus admires the combination and has taken to referring to the miraculous effects of the dense, golden cake and its accompanying sweet spirit as "steadying." To underscore the sentiment, he takes a quick sip of Madeira, his cheeks popping out like crab apples, a complement to the pink–collared shirt underneath his slightly fraying linen jacket.

Fergus's lunch is the opposite of staff meals as previously defined by this book—large, noisy, communal affairs—but somehow creates a definition of its own. His bread and wine tell the story of a small, solitary meal as the antidote for a hectic, overscheduled life, one that includes two restaurants, one hotel, a pair of game-changing cookbooks on nose-to-tail eating, and an active family of four, including his redheaded wife, Margot

Henderson, herself a London caterer of note. There is little doubt that Fergus is a busy man, but he takes it in stride, using thin slivers of tranquility (and cake) to refresh himself. Many chefs and cooks can relate. There are certainly days when eating a meal alone—standing at the prep sink or sitting on a produce crate at the back door—is the only way to turn a frenetic day into a productive service.

"Like an army should never go into battle on an empty stomach, you want your chefs and waiters to go into service not with grumbling tummies," says Fergus, "but ready like sentinels of joy." Today's meal is set to do just that, though not quite as one would expect. While we assumed some manner of offal would find its way to the table, today's staff meal is 100 percent vegetarian: heaping platters of creamy cabbage salad and curried rice with chickpeas. It comes together quickly and effortlessly in the restaurant's upstairs dining room, the crowd of British and expat cooks pouring each other glasses of sparkling water and pulling off hunks of freshly baked bread hot from the bakery.

Cake and Madeira for one aside, rest assured that Fergus is no lone wolf, far from it. While somewhat quixotic in manner with his Coke-bottle glasses and knack for riddle-like sound bites, he is the first to raise a glass in the name of celebration and teamwork. So before he dashes out the door, he makes a quick appearance at the meal to wish the crew well before a busy service. We have just

enough time to ask how the staff meal philosophy of St. John is reflected in the meal playing out before him, as well as the one he enjoyed alone. He raises his finger in the air before responding with a wink: "Always enjoy your lunch." And with that he slips away into the crowd, steadied and ready to greet the day.

A Conversation with Owner and Chef FERGUS HENDERSON

We were surprised to find a vegetarian family meal on the table. Is this the norm?

Life is full of surprises and we try to vary staff meals, which keeps everyone on their toes. Interestingly, it's the fry-up for breakfast on Monday that everyone loves.

Have you ever cooked the staff meal yourself? If so, what did you make?

Shamefully, not for a very long time. I can't even remember what I cooked.

What's one food scrap that you will never throw away?

Not big on throwing away, but we love drippings, lard, and duck fat. You can't have enough up your sleeve.

If you weren't a chef, what career path do you think you would you have landed on?

An architect.

Have you ever invited any special guests to share in the staff meal?

It's not really a meal to invite someone to share; there is a sense of the team preparing mentally and physically for service. Any guests may feel left out.

Do you ever turn to cookbooks for your staff meal inspiration?

Inspiration for staff meals comes from many places but no particular cookbook.

What do you do with staff meal leftovers?

Usually there is very little left over.

What's one cooking tool/piece of equipment that you use in your restaurant that no home cook should be without?

A waiter's friend [wine knife], as chefs do the darnedest things to get into a bottle of wine. Both the dish and the chef require wine.

What should every staff meal include?

Care and love. Never try and feed them slops.

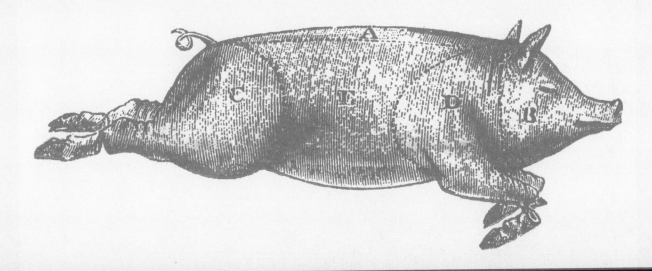

CARAWAY SEED CAKE and A GLASS OF MADEIRA

As anyone who has tried this pairing will tell you, in its simplicity exists the extraordinary. The cake, adapted from Fergus Henderson's cookbook *Beyond Nose to Tail*, is golden yellow—buttery like a good pound cake but lighter in texture owing to the extra flour and leavening—and flecked throughout with caraway seeds that sing an anise high note. As for the wine, it is thick on the tongue, full of plums and Portuguese honey. The two should lock horns for sweetest in show but somehow the effect, as Fergus says, is altogether "steadying."

Cream-line milk is used in the original recipe, which contains a much higher proportion of fat than its supermarket counterpart, whole milk. We have substituted a combination of whole milk and heavy cream to make up for the deficit. If you do have access to unhomogenized or "cream on top" milk, feel free to use it for both the milk and cream measurements.

Yields one (9 x 5-inch/23 x 13 centimeter) loaf pan

9 OUNCES (2¼ STICKS/260 GRAMS) UNSALTED BUTTER, AT ROOM TEMPERATURE, PLUS MORE FOR GREASING

1⅓ CUPS (260 GRAMS) SUPERFINE SUGAR (SEE NOTE)

1½ TEASPOONS (3 GRAMS) CARAWAY SEEDS

5 LARGE EGGS, ROOM TEMPERATURE

2⅔ CUPS (350 GRAMS) ALL-PURPOSE FLOUR

3 TEASPOONS (15 GRAMS) BAKING POWDER

¼ TEASPOON (2 GRAMS) KOSHER SALT

½ CUP (118 MILLILITERS) WHOLE MILK

⅓ CUP (79 MILLILITERS) HEAVY CREAM

MADEIRA, A GENEROUSLY POURED GLASS PER PERSON

Preheat the oven to 350°F (177°C). Butter the loaf pan and line on all sides with parchment paper allowing at least 2 inches of excess to stick up past the pan's lip. This will give the rising cake some stability so it doesn't spill over during baking.

In the bowl of a mixer fitted with a paddle, add the butter, sugar, and caraway. Beat at medium speed, scraping down the sides occasionally, until smooth and fluffy, about 6 minutes. Continue to beat while adding the eggs one at time. Sift in the flour, baking powder, and salt in one go, and beat on low speed until incorporated. Combine the milk and cream; add in a slow, steady stream to achieve a batter that is very thick.

Spread the batter evenly into the prepared pan. Bake until golden brown and a toothpick or fork inserted in the center comes out clean, about 1 hour plus 10 to 15 minutes.

Cool for 20 minutes, then remove from the pan and gently detach the parchment paper. Slice carefully using a serrated knife. Serve in the only way proper: with a glass of Madeira on the side.

The cake will keep in a covered container at room temperature for a day or two or in the refrigerator for up to a week. (We think it actually tastes better the next day.) The cake can also be wrapped tightly in plastic wrap and frozen for up to 1 month.

Note

In Britain, superfine sugar (also known as castor sugar) is simply granulated sugar finely ground, which allows it to dissolve more quickly. If you cannot find superfine sugar at your supermarket, simply blend granulated sugar in your blender on high speed for a minute or two for an approximate substitute.

CRÈME FRAÎCHE, CUCUMBER, and CABBAGE SALAD with NIGELLA SEEDS

Coleslaw may come to mind here, but this salad is barely slicked with its creamy dressing as opposed to drowning in it. Bound with crème fraîche, it is a gratifying side dish with an optional elegant twist of our own devising, nigella seeds. Also known as Nigella sativa, charnushka, or onion seeds, they are black kernels about the size of mustard seeds tasting of onion, black pepper, and marjoram. They can be found at gourmet markets and help turn a humble cabbage salad into something to adore. After all, the French call their loved ones *mon petit chou*—"my little cabbage."

Serves 4

¾ CUP (178 MILLILITERS) CRÈME FRAÎCHE (SEE NOTE)

1 TEASPOON (5 MILLILITERS) STONE GROUND MUSTARD

1 TABLESPOON (15 MILLILITERS) FRESHLY SQUEEZED LEMON JUICE,
    PLUS MORE AS NEEDED

½ CUP (118 MILLILITERS) CANOLA OIL

1 LARGE CUCUMBER, HALVED LENGTHWISE AND THINLY SLICED INTO
    HALF-MOONS

1 SMALL HEAD GREEN CABBAGE, QUARTERED, CORED, AND THINLY
    SLICED

½ CUP (35 GRAMS) COARSELY CHOPPED FLAT-LEAF PARSLEY

1 TABLESPOON (12 GRAMS) WHOLE NIGELLA SEEDS (OPTIONAL)

KOSHER SALT AND FRESHLY GROUND BLACK PEPPER TO TASTE

In a blender, combine the crème fraîche, mustard, and lemon juice and purée while adding oil in a slow, steady stream until emulsified. Pour into a large bowl and add the cucumber, cabbage, and parsley. Stir until everything is well coated. Season with nigella seeds, salt, pepper, and additional lemon juice, if desired. Refrigerate until chilled, then serve.

Note

Crème fraîche is the French sister of American sour cream, though higher in butterfat, slightly less sour, and much thicker. It can be found in most high-end supermarkets, but whole milk sour cream, Greek-style yogurt, or labneh (see Note, page 224) can all be substituted. Extra crème fraîche is useful to have around the kitchen to add a tangy depth to cream-based soups or an acidic finish to a pan sauce; unlike heavy cream, it will not curdle if heated too quickly.

CURRIED RICE with CHICKPEAS

In 1846, curry's place in the hearts and minds of the British people was forever fixed when William Makepeace Thackeray wrote "Poem to Curry," with its sweeping conclusion, "Tis, when done/A dish for Emperors to feed upon." So as it turns out, St. John's vegetarian curry is British to the core, although some Brits do lament its kudzu-like way of overtaking fish and chips as the national dish. It starts with a quick sauté of onion, celery, and garlic in butter, along with a heaping spoonful of curry powder. Chickpeas are used here for a vegetarian source of protein, but any large legume will do, including fava beans or giant white butterbeans.

Serves 4

1 TABLESPOON (14 GRAMS) UNSALTED BUTTER

1 SMALL WHITE ONION, FINELY CHOPPED

1 CELERY RIB, THINLY SLICED

2 GARLIC CLOVES, MINCED

1 TABLESPOON (6 GRAMS) CURRY POWDER

1 CUP (185 GRAMS) BASMATI RICE

½ CUP (120 GRAMS) DRAINED CANNED CHICKPEAS

¼ CUP (40 GRAMS) GOLDEN RAISINS (OPTIONAL)

¼ CUP (25 GRAMS) TOASTED, SLIVERED ALMONDS (OPTIONAL)

1¾ CUPS (425 MILLILITERS) VEGETABLE STOCK

2 TABLESPOONS (5 GRAMS) COARSELY CHOPPED CHERVIL

KOSHER SALT AND FRESHLY GROUND BLACK PEPPER TO TASTE

LEMON WEDGES, FOR SERVING

In a saucepan over medium-high heat, melt the butter. When the frothing subsides, sauté the onion, celery, and garlic until the onion is translucent, about 6 minutes. Add the curry powder, stirring to release its aroma, about 1 minute. Add the rice, chickpeas, and stock as well as the optional raisins and almonds; bring to a boil. Cover and reduce the heat to medium-low to maintain a gentle simmer. Cook until the rice is tender and all the liquid is absorbed, 15 to 20 minutes.

Remove from the heat, stir in the chervil, season with salt and pepper, and set aside, covered, for 5 minutes.

Fluff with a fork, then heap onto platters bordered with lemon wedges. Encourage guests to add a squeeze or two to the whole affair.

UBUNTU

NAPA, CALIFORNIA

CHICKPEA CLUSTERS WITH
AVOCADO

MUSTARD GREEN MALFATTI

WHEY AND BRINE BRAISED
PORK SHOULDER

WINTER CITRUS HORCHATA

As a restaurant specializing in vegetarian meals—ones that defy the tofu and spelt stereotypes—Ubuntu Executive Chef Aaron London and owner Sandy Lawrence take their produce seriously. So seriously, in fact, that before the restaurant opened in 2007, Sandy transformed her two-acre backyard a few miles from Napa's sleepy Main Street into a fully functional, four-season, biodynamic micro-farm. Neatly plotted and meticulously cared for by head gardener Rose Robertson, the plot can supply up to 95 percent of the restaurant's summer season produce, including Scarlet Damsel turnips, Lolla Rossa lettuce, and Bull's Blood beets. So perhaps nothing more accurately illustrates Ubuntu's devotion to its harvest than the high-tech collaboration between chef and gardener. Installed in Aaron's iPhone is a custom app allowing Rose to update him and his team, minute-by-minute, of every vegetable's status, like an edible Twitter feed.

Yet in spite of this commitment to vegetarian fare, Ubuntu admits to a funny little quirk: during our visit none—not one—of the cooks in the Ubuntu kitchen is vegetarian. While they all love and respect fruits, tubers, sprouts, and greens, what they crave most for their own meal is meat. Aaron is the first to point out that while he has a mad passion for vegetables (his latest Halloween costumes have been inspired by the garden), he also holds on to a stubborn carnivorous streak, as does the rest of his team. To illustrate the point, he shows us a pork

shoulder being cooked sous vide (a low-temperature cooking technique that uses a precisely calibrated water bath to slowly poach vacuum-sealed food) in a liquid of goat's milk whey, naturally fermented olive brine, and charred onions. Then Aaron adds his trademarked surfer-style stamp of approval: "It's hella good."

Ubuntu's restaurant menu is as surreal as the family meal, just more refined. Vibrant, multitextured, and deeply satisfying, the dishes dare customers to reassess what was once considered hippie cuisine. There is, however, a flower-child feel-good vibe of culinary curiosity pulsing through the entire kitchen staff, and we get the sense this may be the root of Ubuntu's critical success. (Among other accolades, the restaurant was awarded a Michelin star in 2011.) Not only does it yield clever dishes that remain substantive without the meat, their constant "What if?" mentality also ensures that every last leaf, root, or stem of the garden's harvest is put to good use. They reduce blackberry leaves to colorful and flavorful ash, infuse oil with fig leaves, wild-ferment just about anything from radishes to beets (per instructions by their fermentation guru Sandor Ellix Katz), and replant onion tops to grow calcots, a kind of supersized, super-pungent scallion.

All of these value-added techniques end up trickling down into the staff meal. A spicy kimchi tops their signature Tokyo hot dogs, a scattering of cucumber peel ash adds a smokiness to mashed potatoes. Even Aaron's favorite staff meal, Pirate's Porridge, is a belly-busting catchall for the

garden scraps and kitchen leftovers. A mountain of a meal, it cleverly hides recipes within recipes that all fit together effortlessly, like edible nesting dolls.

As the exact time for staff meal approaches, 4:45 p.m. on the nose, Aaron sinks a large, cream-colored disk into the fryer, explaining that it is made of leftover gnocchi dough, light as air thanks to special techniques he learned in Bologna. A few minutes later it emerges golden-brown and crispy. Aaron tops it plainly with tomato sauce and grated yellow cheese. We're puzzled. It's not big enough to feed the entire staff, nor anywhere near the creativity level of the other staff meal dishes. When we inquire about it, Aaron explains he makes one every day: "It's for a cook who complained before a staff meal a while back: 'Can't we just have something normal?'" This offering is Aaron's laissez-faire surfer-style way of underscoring that Ubuntu is not about normal, especially not at the staff meal. It's creative, surprising, and unapologetically distinctive. And when you can accept that, it's also hella good.

Is there anything you always serve at family meal?

We make gnocchi every day, so the gnocchi that are a day old, we just fry them up and serve them to the staff. They're awesome like that.

Gnocchi can be as delicate as lead balls if you don't make them correctly. Is there a technique the home cook should know to help keep them light and airy?

I've made gnocchi every day here for the past year and a half. So here's what we do: when we add the flour into the potato, we chop through it [with two pastry bench scrapers, as if drumming the table]. A lot of people would form a well and mix the flour in. Chopping through it helps keep it light. It's the same idea if you were at a bank, you put your money down and it goes through that slot; you are essentially pushing the flour in so the flour isn't worked at all yet, but it's in there. Then I can knead it gently at the very end so it comes together. It was like a revelation when I learned this technique in Bologna.

Besides what you call your "bible," Wild Fermentation by Sandor Ellix Katz, what are some other cookbooks that you reference for the family meal and beyond?

Well, the cookbook that I love is *Essential Cuisine* by Michel Bras.

Is there a certain family meal dish that you like to eat every day?

Pirate's Porridge. That's something that I eat every day, on the weekends at least twice a day. It's something that makes me super happy about this restaurant, that you can basically walk through the kitchen with a bowl and grab a spoonful of everything, and throw it in so it's like nine recipes in one. Then I hide in the walk-in and eat it and it's hella good.

Who contributes to the meal? Do you take turns? Or have a set schedule?

We basically all take turns. I've worked at a bunch of restaurants where everybody has certain days of the week; where it's fish station this day and meat the next, but here we just kinda balance it out. So maybe I'll have a super good idea for a Thursday, so I'll call up the kitchen and say: "Hey guys, I gotta do staff meal today. Can you do Friday instead?" We just pass it around like that.

Do you have a staff meal golden rule?

Oh, absolutely. I'd say in my opinion nothing is more important than sitting down at exactly the right time. At 4:45

p.m. Exactly. Like, I freak out about that. It creates a camaraderie, for sure, but also kinda creates clear rules and a clear timeline. The time coming into service is a super important time. Every minute between 4:45 and 5:30 matters more than the minutes in the middle of the afternoon because it's the point of no return.

What do you think a really good staff meal adds to the day?

Tons. For one, it's a super-important morale thing for everyone to eat dinner together. Two, if people are in the weeds and they keep putting off eating because there's one more thing to get done, then they'll end up going into service missing staff meal. It's happened to me before, and it sucks.

So what happens if you are in the weeds and you do end up missing the staff meal altogether?

It's a horrible way to work. When I was an extern [restaurant cooking apprentice], I put off staff meal over and over again and finally they found me in the locker room, like, passed out. They had to rush me to the hospital. It was during an externship about nine years ago; I was eighteen. I hadn't eaten in two weeks because I was so in the weeds. I ended up in the hospital for three days. So, yeah, staff meal is really important.

CHICKPEA CLUSTERS with AVOCADO

To get their crew full and fueled until closing, the Ubuntu cooks invented a one-bowl trencherman's delight they call Pirate's Porridge. The base consists of stone-ground grits made with whey, heavy cream, cheese, and a touch of fennel seed, then topped with a hearty bean stew made with the restaurant's smoked tomato water. The beans are hidden beneath a thick layer of butter-soaked mashed potatoes infused with ground cucumber skin ash to add a light smokiness. Stacking carbs on carbs, the potatoes are layered with more grits onto which torn burrata cheese is showered. Finally these fried chickpea fritters find their way to the bowl, topped off with a generous dollop of crushed avocado. Alone and as an appetizer, they are an inventive alternative to chips and guacamole.

Makes 12 large clusters

AVOCADO

1 SHALLOT, FINELY CHOPPED

2 TABLESPOONS (30 MILLILITERS) FRESHLY SQUEEZED LEMON JUICE

1 TABLESPOON (15 MILLILITERS) OLIVE OIL

KOSHER SALT AND FRESHLY GROUND BLACK PEPPER TO TASTE

2 RIPE AVOCADOS, PITTED

CHICKPEA CLUSTERS

1½ QUARTS (1.4 LITERS) SAFFLOWER OIL

1 CUP (128 GRAMS) CORNSTARCH

⅔ CUP (83 GRAMS) ALL-PURPOSE FLOUR

½ CUP (118 MILLILITERS) LAGER BEER

3 CUPS (500 GRAMS) COOKED CHICKPEAS, DRAINED AND PATTED DRY

GRATED ZEST AND JUICE OF 1 LEMON

1 TEASPOON (1 GRAM) MINCED ROSEMARY

KOSHER SALT TO TASTE

For the avocado: Place the shallot, lemon juice, and olive oil in a large bowl and season with salt and pepper. Dice the avocados directly into the bowl, then lightly crush with a fork until a chunky paste forms, about 2 minutes. Adjust the seasoning, cover the surface with plastic wrap, and set aside in the refrigerator.

For the chickpea clusters: In a heavy-bottomed pot, heat the oil to 375°F (191°C).

Sift the cornstarch and flour into a bowl; whisk in the beer and ⅓ cup (79 milliliters) water to create a thin batter, about 30 seconds. Toss the chickpeas in the batter; it will be very soupy.

Scoop out ¼ cup (59 milliliters) of chickpeas and batter and gently pour into the oil to create one cluster. Add as many scoops as your pot can handle without crowding. Fry the clusters until lightly golden brown, 3 to 4 minutes. Remove from the oil using a slotted spoon, shaking off excess oil, and drain on paper towels.

Season both sides of each cluster with lemon juice, zest, rosemary, and salt. Serve immediately with a generous spoonful of crushed avocado on top or on the side for dipping.

WHEY and BRINE–BRAISED PORK SHOULDER

If Ubuntu did serve meat to paying customers, this is exactly the type of dish they would be coming back for. The wacky consortium of ingredients—charred onions, whey, live fermented brine—help transform run-of-the-mill pork shoulder into something seductively tender and vaguely Germanic. Sauerbraten is our closest touchstone. Plus, it is an excellent use of the restaurant's whey, a ricotta-making by-product (see DIY Ricotta, page 000) that seems a waste to just throw down the drain.

Ubuntu cooks the shoulder using the sous vide method to create an unparalleled tenderness, but the oven-braising method below was given to us by Executive Chef Aaron London as a good home alternative.

Serves 6 to 8

3 MEDIUM YELLOW ONIONS, HALVED

1 HEAD GARLIC, HALVED

3 ARBOL CHILES

3 TABLESPOONS (45 MILLILITERS) CANOLA OIL

4 POUNDS (1.8 KILOGRAMS) BONED PORK SHOULDER (OR ABOUT 5 POUNDS (2.3 KILOGRAMS), BONE-IN)

KOSHER SALT TO TASTE

1 CUP (237 MILLILITERS) WHITE WINE

1 CUP (237 MILLILITERS) LIVE-FERMENTED OLIVE BRINE (SEE NOTE)

2 CUPS (473 MILLILITERS) WHOLE MILK

2 CUPS (473 MILLILITERS) GOAT'S OR COW'S MILK WHEY (SEE DIY RICOTTA, PAGE 142)

Note

Ubuntu makes their own wild fermented olives, but they can be hard to find in stores. Use naturally fermented pickle juice as a substitute. Bubbies brand pickles are naturally fermented and available nationwide.

Heat a large cast-iron skillet over high heat. Without oil, place the onions and garlic halves cut-side down onto the skillet, cooking until charred black, 4 to 5 minutes. Add the chiles and toast until fragrant and the skin turns light brown, about 1 minute. Remove from the heat and set aside.

Preheat the oven to 325°F (163°C). Heat the oil in a large Dutch oven over high heat until nearly smoking. Salt the pork shoulder, then sear on all sides until crispy brown, about 2 minutes per side. Remove the pork from the pot and set aside. Pour out the fat and discard. Place the Dutch oven back over the heat, and add the white wine, scraping the bottom with a wooden spoon to release the flavorful brown bits still clinging. Reduce the wine for about 1 minute, or until the alcohol has completely burned off, then add the pork along with the brine, milk, and whey (the liquid should reach about three-quarters of the way up the shoulder; if it is less, add more milk or whey). Add the onions, garlic, and chiles and bring the liquid to a fast simmer. Cover the pot with parchment paper, then a lid. Place the pot in the oven for about 3 to 4 hours, or until the meat is very tender (a knife when poked into the center of the shoulder should encounter little resistance).

Remove the pork, tenting lightly with foil. Remove the chiles and garlic from the braising liquid, then using an immersion blender, purée the onions with the liquid to create a smooth sauce. (You could also use a regular blender with caution.) The sauce should be the consistency of thin gravy; if you prefer it to be thicker, reduce over high heat for several minutes but beware: it can become salty. Extra sauce can be stored in the freezer for up to 3 months, then thawed and used as a braising liquid (add a little water if it is too thick) for a meat of your choosing. We had tremendous success with chicken thighs.

Slice the meat as best you can (it will want to break into pieces), arrange on a platter, and cover the meat generously with the sauce. Serve immediately with extra sauce on the side.

MUSTARD GREEN MALFATTI

One cook calls these dumplings "gnocchi's ugly cousin," and he's not far off. Translating to "poorly made," malfatti are in fact incredibly light, cork-sized dumplings made of fresh ricotta and breadcrumbs, often flavored with spinach, though Ubuntu uses the more pithy mustard greens from their garden. It is the technique that earned them their nickname. They require just a rough hack into an approximate shape before being cooked in simmering water. Unlike gnocchi, there is no need to shape each one with the back of a fork; it would be poor form to have malfatti be so perfect.

Serves 6

3 TABLESPOONS (45 MILLILITERS) OLIVE OIL

2 LARGE BUNCHES MUSTARD GREENS, DESTEMMED AND ROUGHLY CHOPPED

2¼ CUPS (560 GRAMS) FRESH RICOTTA CHEESE (PAGE 142)

1½ CUPS (180 GRAMS) FINE BREADCRUMBS, TOASTED

¾ CUP (58 GRAMS) TIGHTLY PACKED FINELY GRATED PARMIGIANO-REGGIANO

3 LARGE EGGS, BEATEN

1 TEASPOON (6 GRAMS) FINE SEA SALT, PLUS MORE TO TASTE

ALL-PURPOSE FLOUR AS NEEDED, FOR ROLLING

1 QUART (946 MILLIMETERS) WARM TOMATO SAUCE (PAGE 140), FOR SERVING

In a large pot, heat the oil over high heat until shimmering. Add the greens, cooking until wilted, 2 to 3 minutes. Add ½ cup (118 milliliters) water and a pinch of salt, then reduce heat, cover, and simmer for 20 minutes, or until the greens are meltingly tender. Remove from heat. When cool enough to handle, wrap in a clean kitchen towel and wring tightly to remove all excess moisture. Using a food processor (or diligent knife work), finely chop. Set aside.

In a large bowl, combine the greens, ricotta, breadcrumbs, grated cheese, eggs, and salt. Stir to combine completely, about 2 minutes. Rest the dough, covered, in the refrigerator for 15 minutes.

Divide the dough into eight equal pieces. On a lightly floured surface, roll each piece into 1-inch-wide (2.5 centimeter) logs, dusting with flour as you work, about 12 inches (30.5 centimeters) long. Once the logs are all rolled, rest them in the refrigerator uncovered for 15 minutes.

Bring a large pot of salted water to a quick simmer (not vigorously boiling, as it could break the dumplings apart). Roughly chop each log into 1-inch (2.5 centimeter) pillow-like dumplings. Working in batches if necessary, drop the dumplings into the simmering water. Gently lift out with a slotted spoon once they have risen to the top and floated for 30 to 40 seconds, about 3 minutes total cooking time. Place them in a serving bowl, lightly dress with warmed tomato sauce, and serve immediately.

WINTER CITRUS HORCHATA

A traditional agua fresca, or "water refreshment," horchata is a rice-based beverage spiked with cinnamon and served icy cold throughout Mexico. Traditional horchata is made with rice and almonds soaked overnight. However, Ubuntu uses whole milk in place of the nuts to mimic the richness in a fraction of the time. They also put a California spin on the drink by infusing it with a variety of citrus zests, many of which grow in the restaurant's nearby garden, including bergamot orange (a cross in taste between a lemon and a grapefruit) and Rangpur limes. If these more exotic fruits prove too hard to find, feel free to substitute whatever citrus is available including pomelos and tangerines.

Yields 1½ quarts (1.4 liters)

1 CUP (185 GRAMS) LONG-GRAIN WHITE RICE

ZEST OF 1 ORANGE

ZEST OF 1 MEYER LEMON

ZEST OF 1 BERGAMOT ORANGE

ZEST OF 1 LIME

ZEST OF ½ GRAPEFRUIT

2 SMALL CINNAMON STICKS

½ CUP (100 GRAMS) GRANULATED SUGAR

1 TEASPOON CHOPPED PRESERVED LEMON OR LIME OR
 ¼ TEASPOON (2 GRAMS) OF KOSHER SALT

3 CUPS (710 MILLILITERS) WHOLE MILK

¼ TEASPOON (.5 GRAM) GROUND CINNAMON

In a large bowl, combine the rice, citrus peels, and cinnamon sticks along with 3 cups (710 milliliters) of boiling water. Soak for 3 hours at room temperature to soften the rice and infuse the flavors. Combine the rice mixture, sugar, and preserved lime (if using) or salt in a blender, and blend on high until smooth, about 1 minute. Strain through a fine-mesh sieve into a pitcher. Stir in the milk and ground cinnamon. Chill in the refrigerator and serve over ice.

Extra horchata stores well in the refrigerator for several days. It tastes equally good (if not better) hot, and can also be used as an imaginative coffee creamer in the morning.

UCHI

AUSTIN, TEXAS

PRAWN HEADS WITH MASAGO MAYO

ONIGIRI WITH FISH CARAMEL
(STUFFED RICE BALLS)

CHICKEN SASHIMI WITH PONZU

SABA AND FURIKAKE RICE

PEANUT BUTTER AND CURRY COOKIES

everal years ago, in the middle of a blistering Texas autumn, Uchi's line cook Gabriel Martinez was having a rough day. He had just broken up with his girlfriend and was rushing back to Austin from Dallas to get to work on time. "I had to go roundtrip within six hours," he says. "I was tired, and I was just trying to make it to the restaurant." Finally, off the windswept desert highway, he stopped to pick up his knives at his house; it happened to be going up in flames. "I was stressing," he says—a sweeping understatement—but when the fire was under control, he made it back to Uchi just in time for their 3 p.m. staff meal. "I got here and Daniella [Leyva] had made rice and albondigas [Mexican meatballs]," he recalls. Despite his overwhelming sense of dread, he sat down to eat. "It was everything that I needed to help turn the day around," he says, "and it was just because I sat down in my chair."

Uchi, which translates to "home" in Japanese, is full of this type of inspiring family meal story: some part lore, some part legend, yet all central to the team's personal journeys as cooks and chefs. There is no need to dig for these anecdotes; they are as ripe for the plucking as the riotous cherry blossoms that adorn the restaurant's walls. We listen to the cook (and part-time model) Christian Camacho, who explains how intimidated he was about making a simple meal for the talented crew. After months on the job he finally bucked up, ordered a bunch of oxtails, braised them for hours, and made a decent variation of osso buco. "I enjoyed it so much," says Christian. "I felt the warm feeling of community, the sense that we are people who enjoy one another's company."

Later in the day, Uchi's pastry chef and director of operations, Philip Speer, retells his tale of a backstage brush with the Wu-Tang Clan. Starstruck, he invited the musicians to the restaurant for dinner. The following day Philip was floored when they actually showed up ... for the staff meal. Not wanting to turn them away, he invited them to stay. The verdict: they loved it. Even Uchi's newest line cook, John Gross, has a staff meal tale to tell. After arranging three whole fish in the restaurant's outdoor tandoor oven—whose temperature reaches near 900°F/480°C—he returned a mere three minutes later to find them fully blackened. "Not the kind of blackened you want," he adds, "pretty much on fire." He continues to take some ribbing about this one.

But it is exactly these types of mistakes, these types of semisweet moments of panic mixed with elation, that Kaz Edwards, Uchi's sous chef, finds so honorable about family meal. "I think one of the biggest misconceptions with kids coming out of culinary school these days is that they automatically think they're going to go into a restaurant and be able to experiment," says Kaz, a cowboy of a cook, wiry, tough, and earnest to the core. "They're not. They're line cooks." Kaz views family meal as a rare creative outlet, an opportunity to pull his staff off the preprogrammed line so they can actually "think about food."

Shortly before the staff gathers around the restaurant's wooden tables, we speak to one last cook on the line, Daniel Tsay, sporting chunky Elvis Costello glasses. With a knife that could shave hair off your arm, he is slicing thin strips of steamed chicken "sashimi" for the family meal. He explains that his first cooking job was at Uchi, but feeling the itch of youthful wanderlust, he went out and about in the world to cook at other places only to find his way back to where he started. When we ask why he returned here to Austin, to the warm-clay aesthetic of Uchi, he stops his slicing. "So many of us do. It really is like coming home."

A Conversation with KAZ EDWARDS
Sous Chef

What is the biggest practical benefit of cooking a staff meal?

It is a training tool for learning how to cook for a large number of people. To learn to make enough to serve thirty, not just four to six at a time.

The Uchi family meal has such a great reputation; do you ever have people off the street ask to join?

On occasion. We've had customers come in and make jokes that they don't know we're closed for lunch, then say, "Hey, can we sit down for that? It looks good." We sometimes let them stay.

Do you feel there are any far-reaching benefits when you take the time to create a nice staff meal?

A general attitude amongst everyone in charge is that we're not just producing cooks; we're producing cooks that are going to be chefs. A lot of restaurants have a "get in, get out, and go home" attitude. We want these guys to be able to cook, create, and lead. Staff meal is a large contributing factor in that.

Today's staff meal is packed with Japanese dishes. Is this the norm?

We try to influence these guys to do a more Japanese/Asian-style family meal, but it often is not. And that's a good thing. We want them to learn different techniques and different styles of food because that's what we're all about.

What do you typically serve here to keep your staff happy and working hard?

We serve at least three courses at the 3 p.m. family meal and make a post-service family meal as well, mainly for the dishwashers who stay here extra long. We allow our cooks to express the things they know. Like the chicken served today. It's simply steamed and served with ponzu and onion, but people want to eat it all the time. It's good for you. It gives you energy for the day.

You've been here at Uchi for more than six years, starting out as a stage and working your way up through the ranks. What is one staff meal that really sticks out in your mind?

For New Year's Eve one year, one of our seafood purveyors was like "Hey, I've got this lobster." It was the biggest thing anyone had ever seen. It was really old, not something we could serve on the menu, but we figured it was New Year's, so why not buy this huge massive lobster for family meal?

How does one serve "huge massive" lobster to their staff on New Year's Eve?

We fried the whole thing, half-cracked out of its shell, in a light cornstarch batter, super crispy. It was amazing.

What is one unbreakable rule that all Uchi cooks must follow when creating the staff meal?

Plan ahead. Definitely. For example, when we've done ribs we'll marinate and dry-rub them, then smoke them the day before. Or a few of the younger guys will come in off the clock to make hamburgers because they want to do a great job on it. We want them to put in this effort because if they don't, then it just gets routine.

And what happens when staff meal does get routine?

When it becomes routine, no one learns anything from it. And then the whole thing becomes pointless.

PRAWN HEADS with MASAGO MAYO

Popular on bar menus in Japan, fried prawn heads are like the pretzels of Asia: crispy, salty, and they go great with beer. The entire head can be eaten, whole, in a bite or two, since the brief deep-frying process transforms their otherwise inedible shells into something both delicately crunchy and easily eaten with chopsticks, the only staff meal utensil available at Uchi. The dipping sauce is made with Japanese Kewpie mayonnaise mixed with masago (smelt roe) and momiji oroshi (Japanese daikon and chili paste), items that will all be found in any Japanese specialty store.

Serves 4

MASAGO MAYO

1 CUP (237 MILLILITERS) KEWPIE MAYONNAISE

2 SCALLIONS (WHITE PART ONLY), THINLY SLICED

2 TABLESPOONS (28 GRAMS) MASAGO (SMELT ROE, SEE RECIPE HEADER)

1 TEASPOON (5 MILLILITERS) TOASTED SESAME OIL

1 TABLESPOON (15 GRAMS) MOMIJI OROSHI (JAPANESE DAIKON AND CHILI PASTE) OR OTHER HOT SAUCE (SEE RECIPE HEADER)

KOSHER SALT TO TASTE

PRAWN HEADS

12 LARGE PRAWN HEADS

2 QUARTS (1.9 LITERS) SAFFLOWER OIL

¼ CUP (26 GRAMS) CORNSTARCH

1 TEASPOON (3 GRAMS) SHICHIMI TOGARASHI (SEE NOTE, PAGE 69)

KOSHER SALT TO TASTE

SOY SAUCE FOR SERVING

For the masago mayo: In a food processor, combine the mayonnaise and scallions and purée until smooth, about 1 minute. Transfer to a large, stainless-steel bowl, and stir in the roe, oil, and chili paste until the mixture is orange-red in color. Season with salt and set aside. Yields about 1 cup (237 milliliters). Mayonnaise can be made ahead and refrigerated in a covered container for up to 3 days.

For the prawn heads: Rinse the heads under cold running water, removing any orange or white viscera inside. Snip off the sharp spike running along the nose using kitchen scissors. Dry thoroughly on paper towels.

In a large heavy-bottomed pot, heat the oil to 375°F (191°C).

Dredge the heads in the cornstarch, shaking off excess. Deep-fry them in batches until golden and crispy, about 3 minutes. Remove from the oil with a slotted spoon, and drain on paper towels.

Toss the fried heads in a bowl with the togarashi and salt. Serve piping hot with soy sauce and masago mayonnaise on the side for dipping.

NOTE

Uchi also fries whole madai (snapper) heads. Your fishmonger will be happy to sell these to you on the cheap; just be sure to call a day ahead so he or she can set them aside for you. To fry a whole fish head, rinse under cold running water, making sure to pull out any slimy dark red organs from skeletal crevices. Soak the heads in cold water for 30 minutes, changing the water when it becomes cloudy. Drain, dry thoroughly with paper towels both inside and out, and proceed to prep, fry, and serve the heads as you would the prawns. Just make sure to turn the heads midway through cooking, and allow a total frying time of 6 to 10 minutes, depending on the size. Fish heads are full of tiny, succulent morsels of meat (including the coveted cheeks, so be sure to explore all the nooks and crannies just as you would a crab. Dip the resulting nuggets into the masago mayo.

ONIGIRI with FISH CARAMEL (Stuffed Rice Balls)

These tangerine-sized fried rice balls are clearly the pride of the Uchi family meal table. We can understand why; they are perhaps one of the cleverest—and most beautiful—uses of leftovers we've seen. At Uchi, any number of cooked meats and fish fill the center of the ball, from pieces of fatty braised pork belly (see recipe, page 125), to extra mackerel from the Saba and Furikake Rice (page 284). Here we made use of the prawn bodies—the heads of which were fried in the recipe on page 278.

Yields 6 large onigiri

FISH CARAMEL

3 CUPS (600 GRAMS) GRANULATED SUGAR

2 TABLESPOONS (30 MILLILITERS) CANOLA OIL

½ SMALL YELLOW ONION, COARSELY CHOPPED

1 SHALLOT, COARSELY CHOPPED

7 GARLIC CLOVES, HALVED LENGTHWISE

1 TEASPOON (3 GRAMS) FRESHLY GRATED GINGER

1 TEASPOON (2 GRAMS) FINELY CHOPPED THAI CHILES

ONE (5-INCH/11 CENTIMETER) STALK LEMONGRASS, THINLY SLICED

½ CUP (35 GRAMS) COARSELY CHOPPED CILANTRO LEAVES, LIGHTLY PACKED

½ CUP (16 GRAMS) COARSELY CHOPPED MINT LEAVES, LIGHTLY PACKED

½ CUP (35 GRAMS) COARSELY CHOPPED BASIL LEAVES, LIGHTLY PACKED

½ CUP (118 MILLILITERS) FISH SAUCE

RICE BALLS

2 TABLESPOONS (30 MILLILITERS) CANOLA OIL

4 OUNCES (113 GRAMS) SHELLED LARGE PRAWNS OR SHRIMP

KOSHER SALT AND FRESHLY GROUND BLACK PEPPER TO TASTE

2 CUPS (400 GRAMS) SHORT-GRAIN SUSHI RICE

4 SCALLIONS, THINLY SLICED (BOTH GREEN AND WHITE PARTS)

1 CUP (8 GRAMS) LIGHTLY PACKED BONITO FLAKES

½ CUP (49 GRAMS) FURIKAKE (SEE NOTE, PAGE 284)

2 TEASPOONS (10 MILLILITERS) TAMARI OR SOY SAUCE

2 QUARTS (1.9 LITERS) SAFFLOWER OIL

"GIVE A MAN A FISH, AND YOU CAN FEED HIM FOR A DAY. BUT TEACH A MAN TO FISH, AND YOU CAN FEED HIM FOR A LIFETIME."

For the fish caramel: Combine the sugar and 3 cups (710 milliliters) water in a small pot. Over high heat, stir to dissolve the sugar completely; set aside.

In a large pot, heat the canola oil over high heat. When hot, add the onion and shallot, lower the heat to medium, and cook until caramelized, about 16 minutes. Add the garlic, ginger, and chile and cook until the garlic is tender, about 2 minutes. Stir in the lemongrass, cilantro, mint, and basil. Deglaze with half the fish sauce, scraping up any brown bits clinging to the bottom of the pan. Stir in 1 quart (946 milliliters) of the sugar syrup and increase the heat to high. Boil to reduce the liquid by half, about 25 minutes.

Add the remaining fish sauce and cook over medium heat, stirring constantly, until the liquid is reduced to about 1½ cups (355 milliliters) and the consistency and color of dark molasses, about 10 minutes. Strain the caramel through a fine-mesh sieve, pushing on the solids to extract maximum flavor. Set aside to cool completely. If the caramel becomes too thick after cooling, whisk in a little water or fish sauce to thin it out. Yields 1½ cups (355 milliliters). Extra fish caramel can be jarred and stored in the refrigerator for several days.

For the rice balls: Heat the canola oil in a sauté pan over high heat. Season the prawns with salt and pepper and cook until bright red, curled tightly, and opaque throughout, 3 to 4 minutes. Remove the prawns from the pan and chop into small pieces. Set aside.

In a colander, rinse the rice under cold running water until the water runs clear. Shake out extra water and transfer the rice to a pot along with 2 cups (473 milliliters) water. Bring to a boil, then lower the heat, cover, and simmer gently for 20 minutes, or until the water has been absorbed. Remove from the heat and set aside at room temperature, covered, for 10 minutes. Transfer the rice to a stainless-steel bowl and briskly stir in 2 tablespoons (30 milliliters) water with a wooden spoon, working the grains until they become very sticky, about 3 minutes. (This step allows the rice balls to keep their shape.)

Add the scallions, bonito, furikake, and tamari and mix until incorporated. Season with salt and pepper.

Lightly wet your hands with water, and then scoop up a large handful of the rice, about ⅔ cup (145 grams), flattening it into a disk about the size of your palm. Place roughly 1 tablespoon (20 grams) of the chopped prawns in the center of the disk. Wet your hands again, if necessary, and gently shape the rice around the filling to form a ball. Compress the ball in your hands as tightly as you can; this will help the rice stay tight and compacted. Set aside for frying and repeat with the remaining rice and prawns. The uncooked balls can be kept in the refrigerator, covered, for up to a day.

In a large heavy-bottomed pot, heat the safflower oil to 350°F (177°C). Carefully place two or three balls into the oil and fry until dark golden-brown and crispy, 2 to 3 minutes, turning midway through frying. Remove from the oil with a slotted spoon, salt and drain on paper towels. Fry the remaining balls in as many batches as necessary, making sure the temperature of the oil returns to 350°F (177°C) before subsequent batches.

Drizzle the top of each ball with warm fish caramel and serve hot with extra warmed fish caramel on the side. Uchi garnishes each ball with feathery bonito flakes.

Do what you love and love what you do.

CHICKEN SASHIMI with PONZU

According to cook Daniel Tsay, this recipe embodies all that the Uchi kitchen stands for: It's uncomplicated. It's clean. And it tastes amazing. "There's really not much to it," he insists, "just steamed chicken and really simple flavors." Indeed, this dish is really just paper-thin slices of thigh meat, a restaurant off-cut, served atop shaved and rinsed onions. It is the citrus-scented ponzu sauce for dipping, however, that reflects Uchi's refined sushi-bar experience. This recipe could also easily work for chicken breasts; just be sure to decrease the cooking time slightly to avoid drying out the delicate white meat.

Serves 4

PONZU SAUCE

½ CUP (118 MILLILITERS) WHITE VINEGAR
½ CUP (118 MILLILITERS) SOY SAUCE
2 TEASPOONS (10 MILLILITERS) YUZU JUICE (OR SUBSTITUTE LIME JUICE)

WASHED ONIONS

1 MEDIUM YELLOW ONION, VERY THINLY SLICED

STEAMED CHICKEN

2 POUNDS (907 GRAMS) BONELESS CHICKEN THIGHS, SKIN ON
1 TABLESPOON (18 GRAMS) KOSHER SALT, PLUS MORE TO TASTE
1/4 CUP (59 MILLILITERS) SAKÉ
1 TABLESPOON (6 GRAMS) SHICHIMI TOGARASHI (SEE NOTE, PAGE 69)
ARUGULA OR WATERCRESS FOR SERVING (OPTIONAL)

For the ponzu sauce: Combine all the ingredients with ½ cup (118 milliliters) water. Mix well and set aside. Yields about 1½ cups (355 milliliters). (Extra ponzu can be stored in a covered container in the refrigerator for several weeks.)

For the onions: Uchi uses a mandoline to shave the onions paper-thin, but otherwise a sharp knife and patience should yield onion slices no larger than ⅛ inch (3 millimeters) thick. Put the onions in a large bowl and cover with very cold water. Swish around as if you were washing lettuce leaves, then drain the now-cloudy water. Repeat this process at least four times, or until the water runs clear and the onions taste and smell noticeably less pungent. Dry thoroughly using a salad spinner and refrigerate.

For the chicken: Arrange a steamer on your stovetop. We used a wok fitted with a steamer insert—metal or bamboo both work—topped with a domed lid. Fill the wok with 2 inches (5 centimeters) water and bring to a boil.

Next, season the chicken and place in a flat plate or tray (something that is small enough to sit atop the steamer insert; a nonperforated pie plate could work). Pour the saké over the thighs, set the tray on the steamer insert, and cover the wok. Steam until the chicken is cooked through, 15 to 20 minutes, or until the juices run clear and the thighs register 165°F (74°C). Check the wok's water level every 8 to 10 minutes and add more if necessary.

Transfer the thighs to the freezer for about 5 minutes to cool them quickly, but do not let them freeze.

Using your sharpest knife, thinly slice the thighs on the bias to create sashimi-like sheets, as thin as smoked salmon slices. Season the sliced chicken with the togarashi and salt. Arrange the slices on top of the onions and serve with small cups of ponzu sauce for dipping. We arranged the onions and the chicken slices on small piles of arugula, then lightly dressed everything with the ponzu to create individual salads for our guests.

SABA and FURIKAKE RICE

Where the fish tail begins to taper is where the Uchi staff meal begins. So after the fillets of the long, slender, silver-gray saba (or mackerel) have all been butchered into neat square portions for Uchi's restaurant menu, the stubby tail-ends (slightly more skin and sinew than flesh) are stacked and saved. Uchi takes these odd triangular pieces and cooks them over high heat so that when coarsely chopped and combined with a flavor-packed rice, thanks to the furikake spice blend (see Note), they become a collective protein to feed the staff. At home, feel free to replace the mackerel with any leftover cooked fish you may have had earlier in the week.

Serves 6

2 CUPS (400 GRAMS) SHORT-GRAIN SUSHI RICE

2 TABLESPOONS (30 MILLILITERS) CANOLA OIL

8 OUNCES (227 GRAMS) SKIN-ON MACKEREL FILLETS

KOSHER SALT AND FRESHLY GROUND BLACK PEPPER TO TASTE

1 CUP (8 GRAMS) LIGHTLY PACKED BONITO (JAPANESE DRIED TUNA FLAKES)

½ CUP (49 GRAMS) FURIKAKE (SEE NOTE)

½ CUP (38 GRAMS) CRISPY SHALLOTS (PAGE 122)

4 SCALLIONS, THINLY SLICED (BOTH GREEN AND WHITE PARTS)

1 TABLESPOON (9 GRAMS) TOASTED SESAME SEEDS

1 TABLESPOON (15 MILLILITERS) TAMARI, PLUS MORE FOR SERVING

1 TABLESPOON (9 GRAMS) FRESHLY GRATED GINGER

2 TEASPOONS (10 MILLILITERS) TOASTED SESAME OIL

In a colander, rinse the rice under cold running water until the water runs clear. Shake to remove excess water, then transfer to a pot and add 2 cups (473 milliliters) water. Bring to a boil then lower heat, cover, and simmer gently (stirring occasionally to prevent sticking on the bottom) for 20 minutes or until the water has been absorbed. Take the pot off the heat, and set aside at room temperature, covered, for an additional 10 minutes. Fluff with a fork.

Heat the canola oil in a large nonstick pan over high heat. Season both sides of the fish with salt and pepper and place skin-side down in the pan. Sear for 3 to 4 minutes, or until the skin becomes brown and crispy. Flip the fish and cook for another 3 to 4 minutes (longer if the piece is especially thick), until the flesh is firm and opaque throughout. Remove from the pan and chop coarsely into bite-sized pieces. (Uchi leaves the skin on.)

Mix the rice with the fish, bonito flakes, furikake, garlic, scallions, sesame seeds, tamari, ginger, and sesame oil. Serve immediately.

Note

Furikake is a Japanese spice blend used to flavor rice, often taking the place of salt on the Japanese table. A colorful combination of sesame seeds, dried bonito (tuna) flakes, and seaweed, furikake can be found in the Asian section at some grocery stores as well as in Japanese specialty stores and online

PEANUT BUTTER and CURRY COOKIES

Reminiscing about a friendly in-house "Iron Chef" competition between Uchi staff members, executive pastry chef Philip Speer yells across the kitchen to line cook Clinton Kendall. "Remember Paul's cookie?"—referring to Uchi's former chef and Top Chef winner Paul Qui—"He had no idea how to make one." Clinton replies point-blank, "Yeah, he really f'ed it up."

In Paul's defense, Philip deems Paul's cookie an interesting one, explaining it was more of a "kitchen sink" variety, cornflakes and potato thrown in for good measure. Not surprisingly, when Paul left Uchi to open his own endeavor—a popular food truck in Austin's burgeoning street food scene called East Side King, serving late night eats inspired by Uchi's staff meals—he called upon Philip to create a sweet to sell. This peanut butter and curry creation was the result. Pastry cook Monica Glenn was responsible for baking them during our visit, declaring them "cookies with a little twist." The peanut butter hits you up front but the warmth of the curry slowly spreads as you chew.

A handful of roasted chopped peanuts, toasted coconut, white chocolate chunks, or semisweet chocolate chips hand-mixed into the batter right after the flour is incorporated all make excellent additions to this basic recipe.

Preheat the oven to 375°F (191°C). Line two sheet trays with parchment paper.

In a mixer fitted with a paddle attachment, cream the butter and sugars on high speed until smooth and noticeably aerated, about 3 minutes, scraping the sides of the bowl with a spatula as necessary. Add the peanut butter and garam masala and mix on high speed until incorporated. Add the egg and mix to combine. Scrape down the bowl; add the baking soda and half the flour, and mix briefly until incorporated. Add the remaining flour and mix briefly again until fully incorporated. On the sheet trays, evenly space ¼-cup (55 gram) balls of dough (a small ice-cream scoop works well for this step), pressing each ball lightly with the palm of your hand to create a thick, flattened disk. Bake for 15 minutes on the middle rack (turning the tray halfway through), or until the edges of the cookies are light brown. Remove from the oven and let cool on the sheet tray to set, about 10 minutes, before serving.

Yields 15 large cookies

8 OUNCES (2 STICKS/226 GRAMS) UNSALTED BUTTER, SOFTENED

½ CUP (115 GRAMS) PACKED LIGHT BROWN SUGAR

½ CUP (100 GRAMS) GRANULATED SUGAR

¾ CUP (178 MILLILITERS) SMOOTH PEANUT BUTTER

2 TABLESPOONS (16 GRAMS) GARAM MASALA (SEE NOTE)

1 LARGE EGG

1 TEASPOON (4 GRAMS) BAKING SODA

2 CUPS (250 GRAMS) ALL-PURPOSE FLOUR

Note

Uchi uses savory Thai red curry paste, but we prefer to use Urban Accents Kashmir Garam Masala Spice, a powdered blend that that does not include garlic, shallot, or onion.

VILLA9TROIS

MONTREUIL, FRANCE

ANCHOVY CREAM WITH ROMAINE

FRENCH FARMHOUSE CHICKEN
AND POTATO BAKE

STRAWBERRY VACHERIN

When we ask chef and cookbook author Stéphane Reynaud whom he would invite, alive or departed, to his staff meal today, we receive something rare in the world of sound bite-wielding culinary icons: a lingering silence. But like most cooks, he can simultaneously be deep in thought while in perpetual motion. So as our question hangs in the air, Stéphane tips over a bowl of shelled hazelnuts and crushes them soundlessly with his fleshy fists. It is all a bit menacing. With the sturdy build and buzz-cut head of a rugby winger, Stéphane looks every bit the unassailable French chef. In actuality, he is about as sweet as cooks come, preferring a quiet, considerate existence at his restaurant, Villa9Trois, in the Paris suburb of Montreuil. Lost in his quiet work, Stéphane studs the nut pieces into flat mats of foie gras and lays a pink strip of suckling pig loin down the center. We start to wonder if he has forgotten the question, as he rolls the torchones tight. Finally, Stéphane's face lights up: "It would be my grandfather."

Hours later the staff gathers outside to eat. It is easy to understand why Stéphane would choose his grandfather to experience this meal. It is both a proud and touching moment. There is the straightforward integrity of the food: wild fennel snipped from along the garden path, creamy anchovy-spiked salad, and a soft farmer's cheese that has been melted and mixed with roasted potatoes. Then there is the setting. A sun-dappled patio filled with white umbrellas and comfortable wicker furniture, quiet except for the rustle of ancient chestnut trees and the soft panting of Vida, Stéphane's gigantic black-and-maize Leonberger. Most important are the staff members themselves, a genial, hard-working bunch who have earned the respect of both Stéphane and each other after decades of working together both at Villa9Trois and in Paris, where many of them started their careers alongside the chef. They and their loyal customers love it here, the rural antidote for any urban poison lingering in their systems.

But Stéphane has his own reasoning for the invite. "I'd invite him because he did not want me to be a cook." In fact, he wanted his grandson to become a businessman, which sounds a lot like "bus man" in Stéphane's thick French accent. "He would always say, 'When you're a businessman, you just work six hours a day,'" says Stéphane, grinning at a mental image of being dressed in fancy suit and tie. We ask if his grandfather was still alive when Stéphane became a business owner in the early 1990s, opening his now-closed first restaurant in Paris's 14th arrondissement. "No, he died before the restaurant opened. He should be here." Most of all, Stéphane insists that his grandfather François Barbe would appreciate spending time with the staff.

Monsieur Barbe was the venerated butcher of Saint-Agrève, a small village in the Ardèche region of France where Stéphane grew up and where his family still lives, a fact that has him navigating the

600-kilometer drive due south each month. So it makes sense that a butcher's grandson's first cookbook—the stunning *Pork and Sons*, published in 2007—would have an air of karmic wisdom. "I learned from him how to choose your animal," Stéphane says. "To choose a good animal, you have to choose good people." So like his grandfather before him, Stéphane develops relationships with the stewards of his trade; one of his closest friends is his milk producer, who manages a small herd of 100 cattle.

The affection extends to the animals as well. Stéphane has often been quoted as declaring pork his good friend, and that while he likes the meat, he loves the living, breathing animals themselves. The chickens for today's staff meal illustrate this point: locally raised, free range, he tells us they are well beyond what the French government would consider organic. "Organic in France is now business foods, not spirit foods," insists Stéphane. Not wanting to waste a morsel, he requests that the roasted chicken carcasses be set aside. He'll gnaw on them, all crisp skin and browned fat, for his own dinner.

Earlier in the morning, well before the staff meal, Stéphane offers everyone a taste of a green leaf he calls "pig's ear." A sea-dwelling plant that spends high tide submersed in salt water, it has an oyster-like brininess. The staff talks about using it as garnish for several seafood dishes. Suddenly, and without warning, the high-pitch squeal of a frantic pig tramples the quiet chatter. Eyes dart, but the squealing stops with a flip. It is Stéphane's ringtone, recorded during a recent pig slaughter. It is at first unsettling, like a soured joke that requires a laugh, but by day's end—after the meal and the conversations—there is more than just shock value behind the squeal. When Stéphane was seven years old, his grandfather was responsible for the seminal event of his childhood: his very first pig slaughter. The ring is just a constant reminder that he is a butcher's grandson at heart. And while he may not have taken all of his grandfather's career advice, he still listened closely to every word.

A Conversation with STÉPHANE REYNAUD

Chef and Owner

Does simultaneously running a restaurant and writing cookbooks contradict or complement one another?

I love to do my books inside the restaurant. It would be impossible to just have a restaurant, or just write books. Sometimes it's very busy, but it's nice to have people come into the restaurant. I also fix all my recipes in the restaurant, so when I do a new book, they are served for staff meals.

As a cookbook author with an international audience, do you find people coming to the restaurant because they are fans of your books?

Yes. The big gift of the book is to meet a lot of people. It's unbelievable. It's opened doors all over the world. I will tell you something funny. After *Pork and Sons*, I received an e-mail from a girl in Australia filled with very friendly things, and at the end she said, "P.S., I'm a vegetarian."

Does Villa9Trois serve a staff meal every day?

Yes, but sometimes it's just what's in the fridge. Because otherwise we would have to throw it away.

What is your staff meal philosophy?

I always have a lot of food. Sometimes you are in a hurry, and when you are in a hurry, you do something very quick. But we always have the staff meal before the lunch and before the dinner service.

And does your dog, Vida the Leonberger, get a staff meal, too?

In lamb season she gets the bones.

Are there any favorite staff meals? Ones that are requested?

Cheese and eggs. We love that. We'll do a French hamburger with onions and fries. Now that it is spring, we'll start to make fresh vegetables with pasta.

Your staff is so relaxed. How do you motivate your team without stressing them out?

When I start to yell, it is very rare. If I do, it's because I have to. When we are in service, it is very quiet. If there is a problem, it is okay. At the end of the service, we talk. I'm a quiet man. And I do a better job with a quiet ambience. It's my character.

And that vibe goes into the food?

That is true.

As an author, do cookbooks figure heavily into the planning of the staff meal?

In France they say that someone who buys a cookbook makes only three recipes from it. So I like cookbooks where you have a story. Like *A Day at elBulli;* you learn something about the life of the restaurant.

What is your advice for cooks coming into the culinary profession?

Twenty-five years ago people in the kitchen had to work fifteen hours a day, six days a week. So one of our big problems is that nobody wants to do this job anymore. With all these TV shows everyone wants to become a cook. They think that it's a TV job. It's nice to show that the job of cook has a good image, but they forget that you have to work a lot.

ANCHOVY CREAM with ROMAINE

This creamy dressing lets its anchovy flag fly, which for those who love them, is a refreshing change in an anchovy-adverse world. So if you are a fan of these tiny salty fish, it becomes a very versatile dressing. We had success tossing extra anchovy cream with roasted spring radishes hot from the oven. It also tastes fantastic drizzled over grilled asparagus and charred lemon slices. And don't shy away from adding the green apple in with the romaine. It may seem like the odd man out but brings a balanced sweetness, and just a little bit of tartness, to the finished dish.

Serves 4 to 6

¾ CUP (173 GRAMS) CRÈME FRAÎCHE OR SOUR CREAM

8 DRAINED OIL-PACKED ANCHOVIES

3 TABLESPOONS (45 MILLILITERS) OLIVE OIL

3 TABLESPOONS (45 MILLILITERS) WHOLE MILK

2 TEASPOONS (10 MILLILITERS) FRESHLY SQUEEZED LEMON JUICE, PLUS MORE TO TASTE

FRESHLY GROUND BLACK PEPPER TO TASTE

3½ OUNCE (100 GRAM) HUNK OF PARMESAN CHEESE

1 GRANNY SMITH APPLE

1 LARGE HEAD ROMAINE LETTUCE, COARSELY CHOPPED

In a blender, purée the crème fraîche, anchovies, olive oil, milk, and lemon juice until smooth. The consistency should be pourable but thick (use extra milk to thin it out, if necessary). Season with extra lemon juice and pepper to taste; salt will probably not be necessary owing to the anchovies. Set aside in the refrigerator. Yields about 1 cup (237 milliliters).

Using a vegetable peeler, peel thin shavings from the hunk of Parmesan cheese to yield about 1 cup (237 milliliters). Peel, core, and quarter the apple, then slice into thin strips.

In a large bowl, combine the cheese, apple, and romaine; toss with about half of the anchovy cream. Everything should be coated in a thin layer of dressing.

Serve immediately with extra dressing for drizzling. Do not delay; this salad wilts quickly.

FRENCH FARMHOUSE CHICKEN and POTATO BAKE

This is one of those "Why didn't I think of that?" dishes. It embodies everything lovely about French farmhouse cooking, minimal fuss using fresh ingredients for maximum impact, plus there's scant cleanup since it's all done in the same pan. The real revelation is that the chicken is stuffed with an herb-packed soft French farmer's cheese. (We used cream cheese instead, but goat's cheese or Boursin would work too.) As the chicken bakes, the cheese inside the bird melts into a fragrant and oozing sauce. After being scooped from the cavity, it dresses both the potatoes as well as the chicken. Stéphane believes that roasts like this one are the perfect staff meal but are also useful for home entertaining. Prepared well in advance and served directly from oven to table, they leave ample time for the cook to enjoy the guests, and a cocktail too.

continues on next page

Serves 4 to 6

6 MEDIUM YUKON GOLD POTATOES (ABOUT 2½ POUNDS/1 KILO-GRAM), UNPEELED, CUT INTO LARGE CUBES

2 MEDIUM YELLOW ONIONS, COARSELY CHOPPED

2 ROSEMARY SPRIGS

2 BAY LEAVES

2 TABLESPOONS (30 MILLILITERS) OLIVE OIL, PLUS MORE FOR DRIZZLING

KOSHER SALT AND FRESHLY GROUND BLACK PEPPER TO TASTE

2 CUPS (400 GRAMS) CREAM CHEESE, AT ROOM TEMPERATURE

3 TABLESPOONS (15 GRAMS) FINELY CHOPPED BASIL

3 TABLESPOONS (15 GRAMS) FINELY CHOPPED CILANTRO

3 TABLESPOONS (15 GRAMS) FINELY CHOPPED CHIVES

3 TABLESPOONS (15 GRAMS) FINELY CHOPPED WILD FENNEL (SEE NOTE)

FRESHLY SQUEEZED LEMON JUICE TO TASTE

1 LARGE (4½-POUND/2 KILOGRAM) WHOLE CHICKEN

Preheat the oven to 450°F (232°C). Place the potatoes and onions in a roasting pan large enough for the chicken. Add the rosemary, bay leaves, and olive oil, season with salt and pepper, and toss well to coat.

In a small bowl, stir together the cheese, basil, cilantro, chives, and fennel. Season with salt, pepper, and a squeeze of lemon juice.

Season the chicken inside and out with salt and pepper. Stuff the bird's cavity with the cheese mixture, then tie the two legs together with kitchen twine or twist tie. Bend the wings underneath the bird, and place the chicken breast-side-up on top of the potatoes and onions. Drizzle everything, including the chicken breasts, with olive oil.

Roast for 25 minutes. Lower the heat to 350°F (177°C) and continue to roast for about 45 minutes to 90 minutes depending on the size of your bird, or until the skin is dark brown and crispy, the juices run clear at the joint when it is punctured with a thermometer, and the internal temperature reaches 165°F (74°C).

Remove the chicken from the oven, transfer to a cutting board, and snip off the twine. With a sharp, heavy knife or heavy-duty kitchen scissors, cut the chicken down the center of the breastbone, splitting it to reveal its molten cheese interior. Measure out about ½ cup (118 milliliters) of the melted cheese and mix it directly in the roasting pan with the potatoes and onions, making sure to incorporate the drippings. Scoop out any remaining melted cheese into a bowl and season with salt, pepper, and lemon juice; keep warm.

Cut the chicken into 8 pieces and serve with the potatoes, onions, and extra melted cheese for slathering over the chicken.

Note

Wild fennel is related to cultivated fennel but lacks its white edible bulb. It can be approximated by using the soft, feathery fronds left intact on untrimmed storebought fennel. Any thin stalks left behind can be steeped in boiling water for about an hour, then chilled to make a refreshing iced fennel tea.

STRAWBERRY VACHERIN

This is an adaptation from Stéphane Reynaud's cookbook *365 Good Reasons to Sit Down to Eat*. As he explains it, this creamy, cold dessert is a mythical love story you can consume. It tells the ancient Norman tale of the god of Chantilly cream, Léon Vachecrot (from the French word *vacherin* or "dairyman"), and his marriage to the pretty, meringue-topped Marie. The three-day forest feast to celebrate the union would surely have included these pretty layered concoctions—a loose interpretation of the traditional vacherin where whipped cream and fresh fruit are stacked between plate-sized meringues. For the winter months, a dollop of lemon curd in place of the sorbet would suit the season quite nicely.

Purée half of the strawberries with the lemon juice, granulated sugar, and liqueur to create a smooth and pourable sauce. Break the meringues into bite-sized pieces. Whisk the cream and confectioners' sugar to stiff peaks. In four tall glasses wide enough for spoons to easily dig into, create alternating layers with the remaining strawberry slices, strawberry sauce, meringue pieces, and whipped cream. Finish with a scoop of sorbet in the center; serve immediately.

Serves 4

2 POUNDS (907 GRAMS) RIPE STRAWBERRIES, STEMMED, HALVED, AND THINLY SLICED

JUICE OF 1 LEMON

2 TABLESPOONS (25 GRAMS) GRANULATED SUGAR

2 TABLESPOONS (30 MILLILITERS) ST-GERMAIN LIQUEUR

8 SMALL MERINGUE SHELLS

1¼ CUPS (296 MILLILITERS) HEAVY WHIPPING CREAM

¼ CUP (35 GRAMS) CONFECTIONERS' SUGAR

1 PINT (473 MILLILITERS) STRAWBERRY SORBET

WD~50

NEW YORK, NEW YORK

CASHEW AND FENNEL SALAD WITH
HONEY MUSTARD VINAIGRETTE

GRILLED HANGER STEAK WITH
CLASSIC BÉARNAISE SAUCE

PEAS 'N' BACON 'N' ONIONS

COFFEE PROFITEROLES WITH
CHOCOLATE GLAZE

THIS KITCHEN IS SEASONED WITH LOVE

The twice-daily staff meals at wd~50—Manhattan's Lower East Side temple to experimental American cuisine—always include a dessert. Sometimes two. By decree of chef and owner Wylie Dufresne, not a single day goes by without something sweet to end the meal—"We have a good staff meal all the time," he says adamantly. Matter-of-fact and with an acerbic wit, Dufresne is easy to spot given his signature look: a blend of Berkeley academic, British real ale enthusiast, and '70s rock star. So perhaps channeling the trio, he makes a confident aside that sticks with us: "I would be surprised if anyone out there said they don't eat well."

No one does. Especially when it comes to dessert. Every staff member can special-order one on his or her birthday, which has led to a host of sweet wonders: Oversized fried funnel cakes the width of an end table. A towering croquembouche cloaked in a gossamer sugar web. Cobbler made with local peaches from Union Square farmers' market. Or gargantuan coffee profiteroles, like the ones being served today, the size of toadstools, slicked with dark chocolate and dotted with whipped cream. But as Malcolm Livingston II, wd~50's recently appointed pastry chef, knows, making a dessert every day requires a few tricks. "Things that set quickly, maybe using gelatin or an ice bath, are easier to make on a daily basis." His best example? A quick chocolate pudding. "Really simple but really tasty."

"Dessert is not for satiation. It is purely for pleasure," says pastry chef Alex Stupak, who has since left wd~50 to oversee his own Mexican restaurant Empellón in New York City's West Village. Handsome and manicured with a tendency toward judge-like stoicism, Alex explains that dessert at the family meal sends a definite message to the staff: we care about you here. "In that sense, it is also a very indirect way of taking care of customers," he says, confident that the concern put into the staff trickles down to the restaurant's guests. When asked if he will be making a staff meal at his own restaurant, which opened just a few months later, Stupak breaks into a wide, rare grin, "No doubt! Absolutely."

While serving sweets to your staff is clearly the exception to the industry rule—no other restaurant in the book serves a dessert every day—it is not terribly surprising, coming from a kitchen known as much for its bad-boy pastry department as its witty, avant-garde cuisine. (The original rock star/pastry chef, Sam Mason, is an alumnus, as is Momofuku Milk Bar's Christina Tossi.) What

is surprising is that from their sizable wall of chemical compounds—including containers labeled with transglutaminase, maltodextrin, and methylcellulose—not one is used. Neither for the staff meal dessert nor the staff meal itself. These celebrated parlor tricks certainly have their place. After all, diners are paying top dollar to find their shrimp turned into noodles, their buttermilk into gel, their popcorn into soup. But for the staff meal, it is always back to basics. Chef de Cuisine Jon Bignelli believes that doing this daily exercise in the opposite feels good: "It's why cooks kinda get into cooking in the first place." Plus, he says, "Old-school food is still loaded with technique."

With béarnaise, pastry cream, and profiteroles all on the menu, today's meal is clearly all about the culinary classics. It has also been enjoyed before. When chef Michel Bras—the three-star Michelin chef from Laguiole, France covered on page 188—took over the wd~50 kitchen for one night in September 2009, New Yorkers were in a tizzy trying to score a seat alongside culinary luminaries like restaurateurs Jean-Georges Vongerichten and Tom Colicchio. With a meticulously plated nine-course vegetarian tasting menu on the horizon, the wd~50 cooks decided to create the polar opposite for the staff meal: heaping platters of casual French bistro fare. "I'm not sure if he was too excited about it," confesses line cook Ben Freemole, "because he mostly eats vegetables." However, the staff enjoyed it enough to request an encore on the night of our visit.

As Ben grills the massive marinated hanger steaks, we press him on other guests invited to the staff meal table. He admits they are not always as illustrious as Michel Bras, but are equally appreciated. "When repairmen come in, we offer them staff meal, a glass of wine. It's just a very convivial atmosphere." When asked whom he would bring along for his personal plus one, he pauses for a beat, tapping his pointer finger on which the tiny tattoo of a mustache is stenciled. "I'd definitely invite this girl I'm trying to date," an invite as sweet as a wd~50 dessert.

Has wd~50 always served a staff meal?

Wylie: We eat like this all the time. Staff meal has always been very important here.

Why?

Wylie: I don't think everybody here is the best of friends, but for the most part I think they're friendly. So if you can't make good food for your friends, how can you make good food for strangers?

Jon: Plus, it's one of the few perks other than alcohol!

We in fact have heard far and wide about how great the staff meals are here. What is the formula to your success?

Jon: We try to do something special every day, and try to utilize what we have. For example, we make a lavash bread for service—it's like a cracker crossed with flatbread—and for years we were throwing away a lot of scraps. Then Malcolm, the pastry sous chef [now executive pastry chef] who usually makes staff meals, figured out a way to stretch it like pizza dough. Now every other Sunday we have pizza.

Along those lines, is there something that your staff eats that your customers couldn't even pay for if they wanted to?

Jon: Duck confit. We get in whole ducks and we only use the breast. We use it in duck tacos, pulled duck sandwiches, duck chow fun, General Tso's duck, duck stew, duck cassoulet. We've done everything. Actually, everyone's a little sick of duck confit. Stages work here for like a week and they're like, "Oh wow, duck confit for staff meal!" and we're like, "f'ing duck confit for staff meal again."

Can you name two cookbooks that you turn to for family meal inspiration?

Jon: *Thai Food* by David Thompson. *The Flavor Bible* by Karen Page and Andrew Dornenburg—they break down in hundreds of tables how ingredients' flavors relate to one another.

As a restaurant that continues to push the evolution of modern cuisine, has there been any sort of evolution in your family meal tradition?

Wylie: Yes, it's changed a lot. Since Jon's been in charge of staff meal, there's been much more ethnicity.

Jon: It's thanks to everyone. I started a tradition last year where during the last week of a long-term stage's stay, I ask them to make something traditional to their culture. Recently these two guys from Singapore made chicken rice, a traditional Singaporean street food dinner. It was awesome.

What was your most memorable staff meal?

Wylie: Every Thanksgiving. We do a big spread, a huge feast.

Jon: For me it was the staff meal that I made for Wylie's fortieth birthday. Pork ribs, fried chicken, deviled eggs, baked beans, collard greens, coleslaw, and mac 'n' cheese. The pastry department made cookies, cake, and profiteroles.

wd~50 is one of the world's most creative, forward-thinking restaurants. Does staff meal help in any way to keep you on the cutting edge?

Jon: I give cooks homework assignments for staff meal. I tell them that I just had Singapore chow fun at Great N.Y. Noodletown two days ago, and I want them to go home and learn how to make it for staff meal this week. So it's an exercise. It gets them thinking about food so they then contribute to the menu at wd~50, which is expected of all the cooks here. So yeah, staff meal is just really cool. In some ways I don't think this place could exist without it.

CASHEW and FENNEL SALAD
with HONEY MUSTARD VINAIGRETTE

Guests will never be served a salad at wd~50. Ever. Chef and owner Wylie Dufresne is not a fan of leafy greens. No reason really . . . he just doesn't like them. The end. Salads such as this one do appear at the staff meal, but Wylie prefers to graze from quart containers full of raw vegetables cut specially for him. While this may sound like a diva moment, we learned that every staff member's dietary requests are honored. Meals are made for both the vegetarians and fish-but-no-meat-eating pescetarians. Portions are also set aside for individuals who cannot eat garlic, onions, dairy, pork, and red meat: all separate requests. "This is the first place I've been that does the custom thing for the staff," says line cook Roxanne Spruance. She makes the second staff meal most nights. It's mainly served to the dishwashers who stay late and is often much spicier than the after-noon meal since spice-averse Wylie is no longer on site. "Catering to individual needs might be a pain in the ass sometimes," she admits, "but it definitely makes people feel like they're cared for."

Combine the shallot, honey, mustard, and vinegar in a blender and purée on high speed until combined. Add the oil in a slow, steady stream while continuing to blend, until the dressing is thick and creamy, about 30 seconds. Season with salt and pepper. Yields about 1½ cups (360 milliliters). Extra dressing can be refrigerated in a covered container for up to a week.

Toss the arugula, fennel, and cashews with enough dressing to make everything glisten, and serve immediately.

Serves 6

1 SHALLOT, MINCED

2 TABLESPOONS (30 MILLILITERS) HONEY

1 TABLESPOON (15 MILLILITERS) DIJON MUSTARD

½ CUP (118 MILLILITERS) CHAMPAGNE VINEGAR

1 CUP (237 MILLILITERS) GRAPE SEED OIL

KOSHER SALT AND FRESHLY GROUND BLACK PEPPER TO TASTE

6 CUPS (120 GRAMS) ARUGULA

½ LARGE FENNEL BULB, THINLY SHAVED

¼ CUP (35 GRAMS) CASHEWS, ROASTED AND COARSELY CHOPPED

GRILLED HANGER STEAK
with CLASSIC BÉARNAISE SAUCE

Chef de cuisine Jon Bignelli is pretty specific about his grilling technique for this archetypal French bistro dish. "First, bring the meat to room temperature. Second, if you don't have a super-hot grill, sear the meat on both sides in a cast-iron pan, and then finish it in a hot oven. And third, always shoot under in terms of doneness because you can always finish it up. We don't have the technology yet to reduce cooking." Although don't fret if while on the grilling highway you accidentally miss the medium-rare exit; an extra dollop of buttery béarnaise hides a multitude of sins. This dish was served with wedges of triple-cooked potatoes (see Note) similar in nature to McCrady's Beef Fat Fries (page 180). They become the most perfect instrument for spooning up any sauce pooling on the plate.

Serves 6

STEAK

2 HANGER STEAKS (ALSO SOLD AS HANGING TENDER), ABOUT 1½ POUNDS/680 GRAMS EACH

2 CUPS (473 MILLILITERS) RED WINE

6 GARLIC CLOVES, CRUSHED

10 THYME SPRIGS

2 TEASPOONS (6 GRAMS) BLACK PEPPERCORNS

1 BAY LEAF

2 TABLESPOONS (30 MILLILITERS) CANOLA OIL

BÉARNAISE SAUCE

3 SHALLOTS, MINCED

¼ CUP (59 MILLILITERS) CHAMPAGNE VINEGAR

2 TABLESPOONS (30 MILLILITERS) WHITE WINE

2 TARRAGON SPRIGS, TIED TOGETHER WITH STRING

1 CUP (255 GRAMS) EGG YOLKS (FROM ABOUT 14 LARGE EGGS)

1 TEASPOON (5 MILLILITERS) FRESHLY SQUEEZED LEMON JUICE, PLUS MORE AS NEEDED

8 OUNCES (2 STICKS/225 GRAMS) COLD UNSALTED BUTTER, CUT INTO 1-INCH (2.5 CENTIMETER) CUBES

1 TABLESPOON (4 GRAMS) MINCED TARRAGON LEAVES

BEEF FAT FRIES (PAGE 000), **FOR SERVING (SEE NOTE)**

KOSHER SALT TO TASTE

For the steak: Remove any excess fat and silver skin—the slightly opaque tissue shrink-wrapped onto the meat—from the steaks with an exceedingly sharp knife. Place the steaks in a resealable container and add the wine, garlic, thyme, peppercorns, and bay leaf, making sure both steaks are completely covered in liquid. Refrigerate overnight or up to 24 hours.

About 1 hour before serving, remove the steaks from the marinade, pat dry with paper towels, and allow to come to room temperature. Heat a grill to high. If you don't have a grill, heat a large cast-iron pan over high heat and preheat the oven to 400°F (204°C).

For the béarnaise sauce: While the steaks are coming to room temperature, combine the shallots, vinegar, wine, and tarragon in a small pot and bring to a boil. Reduce the heat to low and barely simmer until the shallots are meltingly tender and all the liquid evaporated, about 45 minutes. Cool to room temperature. Remove and discard the tarragon.

In a double boiler over gently simmering water, combine the egg yolks and lemon juice and whisk vigilantly until the mixture thickens to the consistency of thick pancake batter, about 5 minutes. Heed the wd~50 warning and "be careful not to scramble the yolks" by keeping the liquid moving and the bowl above the water in the double boiler, not sitting right in it.

When the egg mixture has thickened, add the cold butter a few cubes at a time,

whisking until the butter is melted and completely incorporated before adding the next few cubes. After the butter is incorporated, add the shallot mixture, minced tarragon, and salt to taste. If serving immediately, you may want to brighten the sauce by adding a little extra lemon juice. If this sauce is going to sit for more than 30 minutes before being served, the acid in the reduction will intensify over time, so hold off on adding more lemon. Keep the sauce in a warm but not hot spot on the stove. (A sanitized insulated coffee carafe is the perfect storage container to reserve the finished sauce, keeping it warm for about an hour.) Béarnaise will break when reheated, so use it as soon as possible.

Season the steaks with salt and pepper, then brush all sides of the meat with the canola oil. Grill over medium-high heat to medium-rare, 6 to 8 minutes on each side. To cook the steaks without a grill, sear the steaks on both sides in the cast-iron skillet over high heat until a dark brown crust has formed, about 3 minutes per side. Place the skillet in the oven until the steaks are cooked to medium-rare, about 12 minutes.

Rest the steaks for 10 minutes, then slice against the grain of the flesh into ½-inch (13 millimeter) strips. Serve with the béarnaise sauce on the side.

Note

Like culinary exchange students, chefs from all over the world travel to the wd~50 kitchen to work for a few days, weeks, or longer. In an attempt to impress or simply to practice techniques that they've learned along the way, a visiting cook will re-create a dish from their kitchen's repertoire. And just like that, a foreign recipe has been quickly and quietly spliced into another kitchen's genetic code. The thrice-cooked potatoes served alongside the hangar steak are a perfect example of this cross-pollination. Kyle Connaughton first created them in the culinary lab of Heston Blumenthal's Fat Duck restaurant in Bray, England (see page 128). No one quite remembers who first brought them to wd~50, but they have been re-created many times since. In fact, they are almost identical to the Beef Fat Fries served at McCrady's (page 180), a testament to how a great recipe can travel far. The cooking technique for the wd~50 version remains the same as the McCrady's recipe but instead of slicing the potatoes into fries, cut them into chunky wedges. Keep in mind that their larger size may lead to a longer boil time to get them to tender. And no need to hunt down beef fat: wd~50 fries their potatoes in safflower oil.

PEAS 'n' BACON 'n' ONIONS

Chef de cuisine Jon Bignelli explains that he uses frozen peas as opposed to fresh because the flash-freezing process preserves their sweetness: "Plus, they really take no time at all." Unfortunately, the same thing cannot be said of peeling pearl onions. To help loosen the stubborn skins before peeling, trim off the root end with a sharp paring knife, then give them a brief dip in boiling water—about 15 seconds—after which a light squeeze should help the skin slip right off.

Serves 6

3 SLICES THICK-CUT SMOKED BACON, COARSELY CHOPPED

16 WHITE PEARL ONIONS, PEELED

1 QUART (576 GRAMS) FROZEN PEAS

KOSHER SALT AND FRESHLY GROUND BLACK PEPPER TO TASTE

¼ CUP (6 GRAMS) COARSELY CHOPPED CHIVES

In a heavy-bottomed pot, cook the bacon over medium-high heat until crispy, 6 to 8 minutes. Without draining the fat, add the onions and cook until softened and slightly browned, about 12 minutes. Add the peas and cook until warmed through, 4 to 6 minutes. Season with salt and pepper, sprinkle with chives, and serve immediately.

This recipe is long and exacting but stay the course and you will be rewarded. wd~50's precision approach to pastry leads to a magnificent—and more importantly, reliable—end result every time. To add a decorative touch to the filled pastry, pastry chef Malcolm Livingston II pipes dots of stiffly whipped cream onto the outside for a "fairy mushroom" effect. Regardless of the finishing flourish, be sure to serve these massive pillows of coffee and cream with extra chocolate glaze on the side for dipping.

Yields 12 very large profiteroles

PÂTE À CHOUX

4 OUNCES (1 STICK /112 GRAMS) UNSALTED BUTTER

½ TEASPOON (1 GRAM) GROUND CINNAMON

¼ TEASPOON (2 GRAMS) FINE SEA SALT

1 CUP (125 GRAMS) ALL-PURPOSE FLOUR

½ TEASPOON (2 GRAMS) BAKING POWDER

5 LARGE EGGS

PASTRY CREAM

6 TABLESPOONS (84 GRAMS) UNSALTED BUTTER

¾ CUP (96 GRAMS) CORNSTARCH

1 QUART (946 MILLILITERS) WHOLE MILK

¼ CUP PLUS 2 TABLESPOONS (30 GRAMS) COARSELY GROUND DARK-ROASTED COFFEE

6 LARGE EGGS

1 CUP (200 GRAMS) GRANULATED SUGAR

¾ TEASPOON (4 GRAMS) FINE SEA SALT

1 CUP (230 GRAMS) SOUR CREAM

1 TEASPOON (4 GRAMS) POWDERED GELATIN

CHOCOLATE GLAZE

6 OUNCES (175 GRAMS) DARK CHOCOLATE, PREFERABLY VALHRONA 72% ARAGUANI

2 TABLESPOONS (35 GRAMS) COCOA BUTTER (SEE NOTE)

continues on next page

For the pâte à choux: Put a small metal bowl in the freezer. In a saucepan, melt the butter over medium-high heat until frothy. Once the froth subsides, continue to cook, stirring constantly, until the butter solids at the bottom of the pan turn a rich brown and give off a nutty smell, about 4 minutes. Remove the pan from the heat, pour the browned butter into the now slightly chilled bowl, and swirl the liquid to stop the browning process. If you accidentally went too far and the solids are more black than brown but the liquid is still golden, carefully decant the liquid and discard the solids.

In a separate pot, combine the browned butter, 1 cup (250 milliliters) water, the cinnamon, and salt and bring to a boil. Add the flour and stir to incorporate it into a fist-sized ball of slightly tacky dough. Lower to medium-high heat, and stir the ball vigorously with a wooden spoon, flattening and mashing it around the pot, until a thick skin forms on the bottom and sides of the pot, about 6 minutes. The dough will be noticeably less wet.

Transfer the dough to the bowl of an electric mixer fitted with a paddle attachment. Add the baking powder and beat for 1 minute. Add the eggs one at a time, incorporating each one completely and scraping the edges of the bowl before adding the next. The final result should be smooth, glossy, and stiff enough to hold a peak but runny enough to be piped. Depending on the size of your eggs, you may not need to add them all to achieve this consistency.

Transfer the mixture to a piping bag fitted with a ½-inch (13 millimeter) plain tip. In a pinch, fill a large resealable plastic freezer bag and, using scissors, snip a ½-inch (13 millimeter) opening off one of the corners. The staff at wd~50 uses 3-inch (8 centimeter) silicone demisphere trays to mold their piped pâte à choux. If you don't have one of these in your cupboard—few outside the pastry world do—on a half sheet tray lined with parchment paper, draw twelve 3-inch (8 centimeter) circles using a pencil and a ring mold (a large mason jar lid will also work). Make sure they are equally spaced at least ½ inch (13 millimeters) apart, as profiteroles expand greatly while baking. Flip the parchment paper upside down. The circles should still be visible. Using them as your guide, hover the tip of the pastry bag in the center of one of the circles and begin to pipe, letting the pressure of piping push the dough to within ¼ inch (6 millimeters) of the perimeter of the circle, creating a flat disk about ½ inch (13 millimeters) high. Pull up the pastry bag and tamp down with a wet thumb the small peak of dough left in the middle.

Place the sheet tray in the freezer for at least 30 minutes or until completely frozen. If baking the following day, remove the tray after 30 minutes, cover lightly with plastic wrap, and return to the freezer.

continues on next page

For the pastry cream: Brown the butter according to the directions for the pâte à choux, cool, and set aside.

In a small bowl, combine ½ cup (125 milliliters) water with the cornstarch, whisking with a fork to form a slurry.

Prepare an ice bath. Over medium heat, bring the milk and ground coffee to a boil. Reduce the heat to low and simmer for 5 minutes to infuse the milk with the coffee, stirring occasionally. Remove from the heat and strain through a fine-mesh sieve, reserving the milk and discarding the grounds. Rinse the pot of any grounds.

In a large bowl, whisk the sugar into the eggs until frothy, about 1 minute. Whisk in ½ cup (125 milliliters) of the hot milk to temper the eggs. Continuing adding and incorporating hot milk ½ cup (125 milliliters) at a time while whisking vigorously, until combined. Whisk in the cornstarch slurry, then transfer the mixture back to the pot. Bring to a boil over medium-high heat, whisking vigorously, and continue to cook until the mixture is very thick (a wooden spoon could almost stand up in it) and devoid of any uncooked starchy taste, 4 to 6 minutes. (It may become lumpy when the cornstarch activates as the mixture comes to a boil, but keep whisking vigorously and it should smooth out. If it doesn't, strain the finished cream through a fine-mesh sieve after cooking.) Once thickened, remove the pot from the heat and add the brown butter, sour cream, and gelatin, whisking to combine. Place the entire pot in the ice bath and whisk until cooled to room temperature.

Place plastic wrap directly onto the pastry cream to prevent it from developing a skin, and refrigerate until chilled, about 30 minutes.

To finish: Preheat the oven to 375°F (191°C). Remove the profiteroles from the freezer, discard the plastic wrap, and place directly in the oven. Bake the profiteroles until dark golden brown (they should feel very light and hollow when you pick them up), about 40 minutes, rotating the tray midway through baking. Turn off the oven and allow to dry inside for another 10 minutes. (If using molds, defrost the frozen profiteroles, remove from the molds, arrange on a sheet tray lined with parchment paper, and bake for 30 minutes before turning off the oven to let them dry for another 10 minutes.) Remove from the oven, transfer gently to a cooling rack, and cool to room temperature.

Transfer the pastry cream to a piping bag fitted with a ½-inch (13 millimeter) plain tip. Lop off the top of a profiterole using a serrated knife (about one-third of the way down), pull out any doughy "guts," and generously pipe in the pastry cream. Replace the top of the shell. Repeat with the remaining profiteroles and pastry cream.

For the chocolate glaze: Melt the chocolate and cocoa butter in the top of a double boiler, about 3 minutes. Drizzle the chocolate glaze decoratively over each profiterole.

Alternatively, wd~50 gently pokes a small-tipped pastry bag filled with cream into the side of a profiterole and pipes in the pastry cream to fill the hollow center. The tops of these filled profiteroles can be dipped into the warm chocolate glaze. If you are hosting just a few guests, only fill as many shells as you think you will need—they will become soggy if the pastry cream sits inside overnight.

Note

In professional pastry kitchens, food-grade cocoa butter—the fat extracted from the cocoa bean during the chocolate-making process—is used to thin dark chocolate to allow for a more delicate, shiny coating. Edible cocoa butter can be ordered online and is sometimes found in health food stores, but an equal measure of canola or coconut oil can be substituted.

RECIPE INDEX

MAIN DISHES

DESSERTS

CONDIMENTS, SAUCES, AND STAPLES

FAMILY OF PHOTOGRAPHERS

TIMOTHY AGUERO

(The Herbfarm)

SEATTLE, WASHINGTON

Timothy is a New Yorker by birth, a Pacific Northwesterner by choice, and a hockey player at heart.

aguerophoto.com

NEIL JOHN BERGER

(The Bristol)

CHICAGO, ILLINOIS

Neil would have pushed harder to become a chef after high school but as a third-generation photographer, his destiny was simply unavoidable.

strongholdphoto.com

KYLE DELAHUNT

(Piccolo)

MINNEAPOLIS, MINNESOTA

At a tender age, Kyle's father gave him some sound advice: "Shoot a roll a day." He still does.

PETER FRANK EDWARDS

(McCrady's & Uchi)

CHARLESTON, SOUTH CAROLINA

A former fishmonger and restaurant sous chef, Peter splits his time between Charleston and a small cabin on the coast of Maine.

pfephoto.com

JENN FARRINGTON

(The Slanted Door)

PORTLAND, OREGON

After photographing a definitive guide to tequila and a handbook for West Coast bartending, Jenn can mix one mighty fine cocktail.

jennfarrington.com

OWEN FRANKEN

(Villa9Trois & Michel et Sébastien Bras)

PARIS, FRANCE

Owen Franken studied physics before traveling the world to document revolutions and politicians, including his brother, Senator Al Franken. He moved to Paris in 1988 and stayed for the oysters.

owenfranken.com

KEN GOODMAN

(Craigie on Main & Au Pied de Cochon)

NYACK, NEW YORK

Prior to toting a camera full-time, Ken spent two decades as a professional chef. He now gets his pork fix as a proud member of the award–winning barbecue competition team, IQUE.

kengoodmanphotography.com

CHRIS GRANGER

(City Grocery)

NEW ORLEANS, LOUISIANA

A New Orleans native and *Times-Picayune* photographer, Chris is no stranger to the Casamento's oyster loaf. Dressed, of course.

chrisgranger.com

ROBIN JOLIN

(Ubuntu)

OAKLAND, CALIFORNIA

Robin, an avid gardener, was smitten with the Ubuntu farm. She returned again to admire the veggies and glean a few growing tips.

robinjolin.com

JASON LOWE

(The Fat Duck, St. John, Mugaritz & Arzak)

LONDON, ENGLAND

Along with being a continent-hopping photographer, Jason is also a cafe owner in his home town of London. He makes sure his staff at Towpath is well-fed.

jasonlowe.eu

MATTHEW NOEL

(Cochon)

NEW ORLEANS, LOUISIANA

Matthew recently ate deep-fried chicken feet for the first time at local haunt, Cochon. They are his new favorite appetizer.

findingflavors.com

MARC PISCOTTY

(Frasca)

DENVER, COLORADO

When not winning Pulitzer Prizes for photography, Marc can be found snowboarding in the backcountry. He believes it's where his best ideas live.

marcpiscotty.com

EVAN SUNG

(Annisa, Morimoto & wd~50)

BROOKLYN, NEW YORK

Spanning the worlds of high fashion and food, Evan is as charmed by gentleman Italian tailors as he is inspired by cooks who take the time to feed each other well.

evansung.com

KRISTIN TEIG

(Grace & Oleana)

BOSTON, MASSACHUSETTS

While studying painting in Italy, Kristin explored food, photography, and most importantly, family meals. After her Boston restaurant visits, she left with a new definition for the term.

kristinteig.com

JANIS TURK

(Cochon)

SEGUIN, TEXAS

Equal parts Texan and New Orleanian, Janis can talk Austin food trucks as fluently as she can Sazeracs. She is also equal parts photographer and writer, penning helpful travel guides for the Southwest.

janisturk.com

ERIC WOLFINGER

(Ad Hoc)

SAN FRANCISCO, CALIFORNIA

A former cook and a baker, the contribution Eric may best be remembered for—at least among the Tartine staff—are his epic family meals. That he also shot their award-nominated cookbook makes perfect karmic sense.

ericwolfinger.com

VIGFÚS BIRGISSON

(Dill)

REYKJAVIK, ICELAND

A native Icelander, Vigfús spends most of his time capturing the wild landscapes of his homeland. He's well aware that a shot of Brennivín can go a very long way on a very cold night.

glowimages.com

INDEX

Come In, We're Closed